The Making of Modern Korea

This fully updated second edition of *The Making of Modern Korea* provides a thorough, balanced and engaging history of Korea from 1910 to the present day. The text is unique in placing emphasis on Korea's regional and geographical context, through which Buzo analyses the influence of bigger and more powerful states on the peninsula of Korea.

Key features of the book include:

- comprehensive coverage of Korean history;
- up-to-date analysis of important contemporary developments, including North Korea's controversial missile and nuclear tests;
- comparative focus on North and South Korea;
- Korea examined within its regional context;
- a detailed chronology and suggestions for further reading.

The Making of Modern Korea is a valuable one-volume resource for students of modern Korean history, international politics and Asian Studies.

Adrian Buzo lectures in Korean at Macquarie University, Sydney, Australia.

Asia's Transformations
Edited by Mark Selden
Binghamton and Cornell Universities, USA

The books in this series explore the political, social, economic and cultural consequences of Asia's transformations in the twentieth and twenty-first centuries. The series emphasizes the tumultuous interplay of local, national, regional and global forces as Asia bids to become the hub of the world economy. While focusing on the contemporary, it also looks back to analyse the antecedents of Asia's contested rise.

This series comprises several strands:

Asia's Transformations aims to address the needs of students and teachers, and the titles will be published in hardback and paperback. Titles include:

State and Society in Twenty-first Century China
Edited by Peter Hays Gries and Stanley Rosen

Japan's Quiet Transformation
Social change and civil society in the twenty-first century
Jeff Kingston

Confronting the Bush Doctrine
Critical views from the Asia-Pacific
Edited by Mel Gurtov and Peter Van Ness

China in War and Revolution, 1895–1949
Peter Zarrow

The Future of US–Korean Relations
The imbalance of power
Edited by John Feffer

Working in China
Ethnographies of labor and workplace transformations
Edited by Ching Kwan Lee

Korean Society, second edition
Civil society, democracy and the state
Edited by Charles K. Armstrong

Singapore
The state and the culture of excess
Souchou Yao

Pan-Asianism in Modern Japanese History
Colonialism, regionalism and borders
Edited by Sven Saaler and J. Victor Koschmann

The Making of Modern Korea, second edition
Adrian Buzo

Asia's Great Cities

Each volume aims to capture the heartbeat of the contemporary city from multiple perspectives emblematic of the authors own deep familiarity with the distinctive faces of the city, its history, society, culture, politics and economics, and its evolving position in national, regional and global frameworks. While most volumes emphasize urban developments since the Second World War, some pay close attention to the legacy of the longue durée in shaping the contemporary. Thematic and comparative volumes address such themes as urbanization, economic and financial linkages, architecture and space, wealth and power, gendered relationships, planning and anarchy, and ethnographies in national and regional perspective. Titles include:

Bangkok
Place, practice and representation
Marc Askew

Beijing in the Modern World
David Strand and Madeline Yue Dong

Shanghai
Global city
Jeff Wasserstrom

Hong Kong
Global city
Stephen Chiu and Tai-Lok Lui

Representing Calcutta
Modernity, nationalism and the colonial uncanny
Swati Chattopadhyay

Singapore
Wealth, power and the culture of control
Carl A. Trocki

Asia.com is a series which focuses on the ways in which new information and communication technologies are influencing politics, society and culture in Asia. Titles include:

Japanese Cybercultures
Edited by Mark McLelland and
* Nanette Gottlieb*

Asia.com
Asia encounters the Internet
Edited by K. C. Ho, Randolph Kluver and
* Kenneth C. C. Yang*

The Internet in Indonesia's New
** Democracy**
David T. Hill and Krishna Sen

Chinese Cyberspaces
Technological changes and political effects
Edited by Jens Damm and Simona Thomas

Literature and Society is a series that seeks to demonstrate the ways in which Asian literature is influenced by the politics, society and culture in which it is produced. Titles include:

The Body in Postwar Japanese Fiction
Edited by Douglas N. Slaymaker

Chinese Women Writers and the
** Feminist Imagination, 1905–1948**
Haiping Yan

Routledge Studies in Asia's Transformations is a forum for innovative new research intended for a high-level specialist readership, and the titles will be available in hardback only. Titles include:

1. **The American Occupation of Japan**
   and Okinawa*
   Literature and memory
   Michael Molasky

2. **Koreans in Japan***
   Critical voices from the margin
   Edited by Sonia Ryang

3. **Internationalizing the Pacific**
   The United States, Japan and the
     Institute of Pacific Relations in war
     and peace, 1919–1945
   Tomoko Akami

4. **Imperialism in South East Asia**
   'A fleeting, passing phase'
   Nicholas Tarling

5. **Chinese Media, Global Contexts**
   Edited by Chin-Chuan Lee

6. **Remaking Citizenship in Hong Kong**
   Community, nation and the global city
   Edited by Agnes S. Ku and Ngai Pun

7. **Japanese Industrial Governance**
   Protectionism and the licensing state
   Yul Sohn

8. **Developmental Dilemmas**
   Land reform and institutional change
     in China
   Edited by Peter Ho

9. **Genders, Transgenders and**
   Sexualities in Japan
   Edited by Mark McLelland and
   Romit Dasgupta

10. **Fertility, Family Planning and**
    Population Policy in China
    Edited by Dudley L. Poston, Che-Fu
    Lee, Chiung-Fang Chang, Sherry L.
    McKibben and Carol S. Walther

11. **Japanese Diasporas**
    Unsung pasts, conflicting presents and
      uncertain futures
    Edited by Nobuko Adachi

Critical Asian Scholarship is a series intended to showcase the most important individual contributions to scholarship in Asian Studies. Each of the volumes presents a leading Asian scholar addressing themes that are central to his or her most significant and lasting contribution to Asian studies. The series is committed to the rich variety of research and writing on Asia, and is not restricted to any particular discipline, theoretical approach or geographical expertise.

The Making of Modern Korea

Second edition

Adrian Buzo

Routledge
Taylor & Francis Group

LONDON AND NEW YORK

First published 2007
by Routledge
2 Park Square, Milton Park, Abingdon, Oxon OX14 5RN

Simultaneously published in the USA and Canada
by Routledge
270 Madison Ave, New York, NY 10016

Routledge is an imprint of the Taylor & Francis Group, an informa business

© 2007 Adrian Buzo

Typeset in Times New Roman
by Keystroke, 28 High Street, Tettenhall, Wolverhampton
Printed and bound in Great Britain
by MPG Books Ltd, Bodmin, Cornwall

British Library Cataloguing in Publication Data
A catalogue record for this book is available from the British Library

Library of Congress Cataloging in Publication Data
Buzo, Adrian.
    The making of modern Korea / Adrian Buzo. – 2nd ed.
        p. cm. – (Asia's transformations)
    "First published 2007 by Routledge . . . Abingdon Oxon . . . "
    "Simultaneously published in the USA and Canada by Routledge."
    Includes bibliographical references and index.
    ISBN 978–0–415–41482–1 (hardback : alk. paper) –
    ISBN 978–0–415–41483–8 (pbk. : alk. paper) 1. Korea–History–20th century.
    2. Korea–History–Japanese occupation, 1910–1945. 3. Korea (South)–History.
    4. Korea (North)–History. I. Title.
    DS916.B89 2007
    951.904–dc22   2007012393

ISBN10: 0–415–41482–2 (hbk)
ISBN10: 0–415–41483–0 (pbk)
ISBN10: 0–203–96461–6 (ebk)

ISBN13: 978–0–415–41482–1 (hbk)
ISBN13: 978–0–415–41483–8 (pbk)
ISBN13: 978–0–203–96461–3 (ebk)

To my family, to countless former students, and to the many people in both Koreas and among the diaspora who inspired this work

Contents

Preface

This book is aimed at both students and general readers who seek a broad, serviceable account of modern Korean history. Its central focus is, of course, the Korean people and the way they have shaped outcomes in both North and South Korea, while it also places events in the wider context of regional and international affairs. This wider context is important, for one cannot understand the impact of Japanese colonialism on Korea merely as a function of Japanese actions and Korean response, for Japanese colonial policy was determined by a much broader set of circumstances, which require due consideration. Similarly, events in the immediate postwar period are all but incomprehensible without an understanding of the Cold War context and its consequences within Korea. Nor can one understand the phenomenon of Kim Il Sung and the state he built without an understanding of the international political forces which shaped the DPRK. Similarly, the particular set of economic policies adopted by the Republic of Korea during the 1960s were not simply the product of independent political actors within Korea, but were also shaped by their past colonial experiences, and by international economic forces.

Where to draw the line between traditional Korea and modern Korea? Many works draw it in 1876, when Choson Korea signed the Treaty of Kanghwa with Japan, its first 'modern' treaty and a prelude to the opening of the country's ports to foreign commerce. This date is rich in symbolism, and many changes followed; but, while significant sections of Choson society began to undergo modernisation, a traditionalist, dynastic élite remained in charge. On the other hand, in 1910, when the Choson dynasty fell, for the first time a thoroughgoing modernising élite – Japanese, with a measure of Korean collaboration – supplanted the existing political and economic élite, and Korea underwent profound change. By 1945 no possibility existed of reconstituting the Korean state on the basis of indigenous political tradition, or of consciously incorporating elements of the old in the new. In the South the Japanese model remained the paradigm, and in the North the Stalinist model swiftly became the paradigm. It therefore seems appropriate to me to take 1910 as the point at which the modern history of Korea begins.

In certain respects my chapter divisions differ from those of other general histories. After 1931 the complexion of Japanese domestic politics and foreign policy changed considerably, and as military aggression on the Asian mainland intensified this produced important changes in Japan's Korea policy. I am not the first to see a considerable difference between the 1920s and the 1930s in terms of Japanese policy and the Korean response, but I have tried to give further emphasis by division into separate chapters. Likewise, it seems to me that by 1948 the die was essentially cast for the escalation of the intra-Korean conflict. It therefore seems more logical to consolidate the period 1948–53 around the single theme of war preparation and execution.

Dealing with two such contrasting states presents obvious problems. Many readers are conditioned to expect comparisons, but these two states and societies are different in so many fundamental ways that they should be seen in their own light, not in the reflected light of their antagonistic neighbour. I have therefore kept comparisons to a minimum, unless they illuminate some larger point. On the matter of striking a balance in the space devoted to the two Koreas, because we know immeasurably more about political, economic and social life in the South compared with the North, the South is treated in greater detail.

This work is organised chronologically, for time provides the essential yard-stick for measuring the sequences, degrees and patterns of historical change. However, such an account often takes note only of the channel markers, while beneath the surface currents of history eddy in more profound, though often only dimly perceived, ways. Thus, alongside the chronological record of events, some knowledge of the forces which have shaped modern Korean society provides an indispensable guide to the unfolding of events in the various Korean régimes since 1945. A treatment of such dimensions both lies largely outside the scope of this volume and yet must also permeate it. This volume therefore offers an introduction to modern Korea for the student and non-specialist.

Modern Korean historiography remains highly politicised and passionate. The history of modern Korea, whether written by traditionalists, nationalists, chauvinists, revisionists or Marxists, remains contentious, tendentious, and as confused and complex as the Korean response to modernity itself. The meaning individuals extract from their reading of modern Korean history depends upon the patterns they choose to weave from events, but the search for some overarching significance, some manifest destiny is bound to be illusory. A general history cannot usefully include discussion of alternative opinions, judgements and speculations, and so the reader is left to assume that many events, issues and personalities are by nature controversial; that evidence is often ambiguous, intentions and outcomes unclear; and that omniscient theories and explanations can only imprison history within ideological or philosophical systems.

A final note on Korean names: for names of people, places, titles and terminology, I have followed the McCune–Reischauer (M–R) system of romanisation with the following modifications.

- For technical reasons I have omitted the diacritic marks.
- I have romanised DPRK personal names, place names and ideological terminology (e.g. 'Juche') according to DPRK practice.
- In the case of ROK public figures I have used the spellings carried in Yonhap News Agency's *Korea Annual* since this is how such people are most widely known.

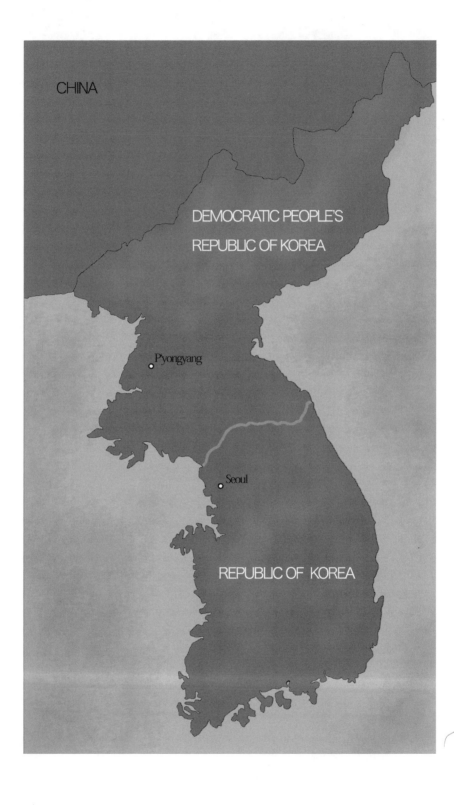

Introduction

Compared with China and Japan, modernity entered Korea relatively late. Whereas for China defeat in the Opium War in 1842 began a sustained process of Western penetration, and for Japan the Perry mission in 1853 likewise announced the beginning of Western challenge, Korea did not sign its first modern treaty until 1876. The Treaty of Kanghwa with Japan in 1876 provided the basis for the subsequent opening of Korean ports to Japanese and Western ships. In the years that followed, Korea was never a major focus of Western imperialism, and in fact the Western powers were largely quiescent in the steady growth of Japanese diplomatic and military power on the peninsula. This resulted in the Japanese annexation of Korea in 1910, from which it emerged after the Japanese defeat in the Pacific War in 1945 as a would-be independent nation, under interim US and Soviet occupation. This occupation and the resultant Korean War (1950–53) established a lasting division into two hostile Korean states which after sixty years shows no sign of ending soon. Such turbulent political change has been accompanied by economic, social and cultural transformation. Western missionaries and businessmen, Japanese colonisers, Soviet political and military cadres, US soldiers and, of course, legions of Koreans returning home after foreign study have all acted as spearheads in the modernisation process, during which Korean leaders and would-be reformers have laboured amid, and often against, the defining currents of political, economic and intellectual life in the twentieth century – capitalism, Marxism–Leninism, colonialism, nationalism, hot and cold war, the rise and collapse of global communism, and Asia–Pacific economic dynamism.

Even as such people have sought to impose their visions on Korea, Korean cultural values have continued to shape outlooks and outcomes, and in essence continue to reform the reformers. Like many other modernising societies, Korea presents a patchwork of continuity and change. Those who emphasise continuity in either Korea tend to see the shape of organisational and social behaviour as still closely bound to such traditional Neo-Confucian norms as hierarchy, status, personal loyalty, rigorous social etiquette, and social stratification in terms of gender, age, education and family prestige. To such people the composition of the élites has changed, but the values of hierarchy, personalism and localism still constitute a deeply internalised system of basic values that guides social and political behaviour. On the other hand, those who emphasise change tend to concentrate on political, economic and social transformation. They see Koreans as having broken free of the shackles of the status-ridden 'feudal' past to create open, meritocratic mass societies where tradition is given little meaningful role to play, other than to evoke feelings of nationalism and collective cultural identity.

Such issues of change and continuity are inherently controversial. Some argue that 'traditional society' and 'modern society' constitute little more than convenient mental images used to depict unfamiliar societies and cultures. Thus, while describing Korean society during the Choson dynasty (1392–1910) as 'traditional' affords the illusion that we are somehow describing a stable, timeless entity of little relevance to modern Korea, closer investigation reveals that the Choson dynasty was underpinned by a dynamic, ever-changing society. Of course, the opposite view can be just as illusory, for ignoring that some basic characteristics of modern Korean society derive from attributes of geography or ecology which have undergone minimal change over long periods of time can only diminish our understanding of the context within which modern Korean governments and political forces have operated. Such features are central to an understanding of modern Korea, and so they preface this book.

Geography is a useful starting-point, for in the two Koreas one immediately senses the powerful contradictory forces of isolation from and engagement with the world. Isolation derives from the distinct peninsular geography, created by three seas and a northern wilderness – 'almost an island', in the words of one observer – while internally isolation is reinforced by a distinct and remarkably uniform pattern of steep hills and narrow, fertile valleys. The modern air traveller is usually struck by the rugged uniformity of this landscape; though the hills are steep, they are rarely high, and yet they seem to tower over the intervening narrow, fertile valley floors.

In its entirety, the Korean Peninsula forms a sloping table-top, tilting south. The highest mountains are in the far north, and the land gradually subsides until it disappears into the East China Sea in a maze of islands. This north–south tilt is supplemented by an east–west tilt, whereby the east-coast mountains gradually subside into the plains of the west coast, whose rich farmlands and major riverine estuaries have provided the setting for most of the major cities and dynasties of Korea: the Koguryo capitals of Hwando on the Yalu and Pyongyang on the T'aedong, the Paekche capital of Puyo on the Kum, the Koryo capital of Kaegyong near the Imjin, and the Choson capital of Hansong (Seoul) on the Han. While the Korean landscape does not offer up a great diversity of mountains, plains, deserts, great rivers and forests, closer inspection of its rugged uniformity reveals further distinct geographical boundaries, which in turn have reinforced distinct regional characteristics. Most prominent among these are the mountain ranges of far northern Korea, which divide the more populous Pyongan provinces in the north-west from the remote, sparsely populated north-east Hamgyong provinces. These mountains feed into the ridge-line of the T'aebaek mountain range, which runs almost the entire length of the eastern coast, providing the source of the many rivers which wind across the peninsula into the Western Sea. The T'aebaek range in turn becomes the Sobaek range, which dominates the southern part of the Korean peninsula, dividing the Cholla provinces in the west from the Kyongsang provinces in the east, and providing a physical basis for a well-developed sense of regional identity.

Forces of isolation are counterbalanced by forces encouraging engagement with Korea's neighbours. The most obvious of these is Korea's lesser size and strength *vis-à-vis* China and Japan, for throughout its history Korea has faced geo-political challenges that no state could ignore. Thus, while pre-modern Korea is habitually referred to as the 'Hermit Kingdom', this expression – itself a nineteenth-century Western invention – can be grossly misleading, for in the thousand years or so of recorded Korean history prior to the inception of the Choson dynasty the various Korean kingdoms and dynasties maintained complex and comprehensive relations with their neighbours. For example, during the period of the cosmopolitan Chinese Tang dynasty (618–907) significant numbers of Korean scholars, traders, Buddhist priests and laymen travelled to and from China, while significant Korean communities flourished in Chinese coastal cities. Despite complicated and often dangerous geopolitical circumstances, the Koryo dynasty (918–1392) also maintained diverse, active relations with the Sung rulers (960–1279) and the Mongol Yuan dynasty (1279–1368), as well as with the more evanescent Khitan Liao and Jurchen Chin dynasties.

Beginning early in the Ming period (1368–1644), China became increasingly inward-looking as it began to turn its back on its cosmopolitan past, and on its tradition of maritime trade and exploration in particular. Beginning in the early seventeenth century, Japan too rigorously excluded foreigners and foreign influence from its realm. Choson could not of course ignore such developments, especially as they affected its tributary relationship with Ming and then Qing China (1644–1911). There was no incentive to revive the rich and diverse pattern of foreign relations that had characterised the earlier Silla and Koryo courts, and yet Choson was not conspicuously more isolationist than either China or Japan at this time. The modern world stresses interdependence and is therefore unsympathetic to isolationism. Nevertheless, Choson isolationism was originally a calculated, not a reflexive, policy and was based on a rational assessment of the merits of domestic economic self-sufficiency and diplomatic self-sufficiency within the Chinese world order.

Human settlement in Korea has a long history. About fifteen thousand years ago, the various peoples who began their wanderings through North Asia as the last Ice Age retreated began to reach Korea from various directions. From the south, sea-borne communities reached the southern parts of Japan and then Korea, and in time formed a distinct culture along the southern coast of the peninsula whose cultural influence, including some of the earliest pottery types, gradually spread northward. From the west, Chinese influence spread across the Yellow Sea and around the rim of the Liaodong peninsula to north west Korea. From the far northern steppes further admixtures came from southward migrations, which brought with them characteristic early Korean cultural traits such as shamanic religious beliefs and animal totemism. They may also have determined the linguistic map of Korea, for the modern Korean language itself has characteristics

Lary

that are also shared by Manchu, Mongolian and Turkish, suggesting a strong pre-
historic tie with Central Asia.

Modern-day Koreans continue to debate the direction and proportion of these
migrations, but the location of Korea lent itself to diverse influences and patterns
of migration, and this defeats attempts to designate a single or dominant ancestral
source. What is clear, however, is that, over an extended period of time, common
climate, food supply, trade and intermarriage developed a sense of common identity
among the diverse peoples of the Korean Peninsula. As an identifiable culture
whose distinct features were evident to neighbours and visitors alike, Koreans
have lived on the Korean Peninsula for a very long time. Significant evidence for
distinctiveness lies not only in their fragmentary mythology, but also in the nature
of their language, food, clothing and housing, and in basic properties of religious
belief, music and aesthetics.

Early human settlement developed in the estuaries of the western and southern
coasts and gradually spread inland. The peninsula contained innumerable small
valleys of sufficient fertility to support a viable village-based agricultural economy,
and in time the rugged terrain acted as a strong factor of uniformity, binding
together what was originally a diverse population in common experience and
response. The terrain, the lack of navigable rivers, and the high degree of food
self-sufficiency inhibited any large-scale movements of people, and so before 1900
few Koreans saw horizons beyond their immediate neighbourhood. The village
and its surrounding area therefore constituted a basic economic and social unit.
This common place of origin gave people a powerful sense of shared identity,
and in turn provided the foundation for a sense of common political cause
and alliance.

Sense of place was further reinforced by the nature of village society, where
typically a single clan lineage predominated, and where marriages were contracted
outside the clan but within the broader district. Geomantic practices (*p'ungsu*) also
reinforced a sense of the spiritual significance of land forms in the immediate
surroundings, and further emphasised the ties that bound a local community to
its land. Popular legends and more serious scholarly works alike associated famous
(and infamous) men with the geomantic properties of their place of origin, and
the reputation of people from a given district could be affected by the actions of a
local individual. Koreans see themselves as a single race, or *minjok*, and use the
concepts of nationality, culture and ethnicity interchangeably, but it was these
innumerable 'little Koreas' which constituted significant political, as well as
social, communities, and which made the sense of being a Korean real to the
individual far more than the abstract concept of the Korean 'state' or 'nation'.
In a very important sense, then, Korean polity and culture is the sum of its
individual communities, spreading outward like innumerable intersecting ripples
on a pond to form the common historical entity we call Korea. An understanding
of modern Korea presumes some understanding of this complex multi-faceted
heritage, for it remains ever present, pushing modern Korean society in directions
that are distinct from those of its neighbours and distinct from those of its
chosen models.

Choson society was founded on a strict social hierarchy based on access to the official examination system, or *kwago*. The gentry class of scholar-officials known as *yangban* (literally 'two [career] streams', indicating that they had passed either the central civil or military examination) comprised perhaps 5–10 per cent of the population, and dominated the political, economic and intellectual life of Choson through their tight control of access to the official government posts, which were exclusively for successful examinees. The commoners, mainly farmers, merchants and artisans, comprised some 70–80 per cent of the population, while a further 10 per cent of the population comprised an outcaste group, defined by occupations such as meat and animal-skin processing, professional entertaining, and Buddhist devotion.

Commoners were disqualified from formal political participation by their non-participation in the education system, and from this flowed a distinct attitude to authority that was marked by an acceptance of place in a hierarchical society and of exclusion from political participation, but was also balanced by an ethically sanctioned awareness of the reciprocal rights and obligations of ruler and ruled. Élite and commoner – and by extension ruler and ruled – shared the same clan-based agricultural village heartland with its complex set of communal institutions and behavioural traits, and in the religious and cultural life of the Korean village there were copious examples of easy overlap between the two traditions. They therefore do not appear in competition with each other but, rather, coexisted in complementary and interactive mode. Where such implied reciprocity failed, the law of the popular riot was often invoked. But riots, revolts and rebellions do not figure prominently in the history of the Choson dynasty, and where they do occur they are often associated with severe conditions such as drought, famine and disease, rather than with simmering class-based hatred.

Another significant feature of Choson society was the rich circulation of ideas, independent of state ideological control. The local élites undertook voluntary and autonomous activities, such as building and maintaining public works, maintaining public security, and the securing of education, welfare and community betterment through fund-raising and public levying. Less organised, but crucial to intellectual life, were the literary activities of scholars, especially those of reform advocates, which took place within the commodious confines of the vast Neo-Confucian canon. Popular forms of artistic expression such as dramatic recitative *p'ansori* and the masked dance *t'alch'um* mirrored social issues and problems, while village poetry competitions, market days, and family, clan and communal festival days all afforded venues and occasions where people, conversation, and thus ideas, concepts and opinions circulated beyond the realm of the state and formed a species of 'public opinion'. Where circumstances permitted, this 'public opinion' could assume an evanescent political significance, usually in the form of remonstrance, petitioning to authority or, as a last resort, riot and insurrection. The net effect was that nineteenth-century Koreans – whether male or female, élite or non-élite – thought, spoke and acted in ways that were quite different from those of their fifteenth-century ancestors. Religious and ritual life, intellectual and social horizons, gender relations, family relations, inheritance, agricultural practices, diet, language, literacy and artistic traditions all evolved substantially. The fact that such changes took place within a traditional agricultural society with a small population of course makes them all the more notable.

Strong social-status barriers were also reinforced by the relative lack of important urban communities or centres of commerce which might otherwise have acted as social leaven. During the Choson dynasty, Seoul was the only city on the Korean peninsula comparable in size to the major cities of China and Japan, and the scale of commerce in the country was not remotely comparable to either neighbour. Local economies were vibrant, but were restricted in the possibilities for development by a largely self-sufficient pattern of agriculture and an ideologically derived hostility to commerce on the part of the local élites. Since the élite tended to shun commerce, economic activity also tended to be bound by the norms of commoners, and was carried out with a strong and unspoken assumption that goods existed in finite quantities and were to be distributed in accordance with the needs of family, kin and community mutual obligation. Acquisition of wealth for purposes beyond these was seen as an activity that could only result in loss and disadvantage to other members of the community. This meant that economic transactions with outsiders were not bound by strong, reciprocal ethical norms, and could therefore be quite predatory in nature. In the absence of such agents of mobility, it is not surprising to find a strong degree of consistency in the composition of these élites over extended periods of time. The longevity of the Choson dynasty, the relative absence of internal unrest and, in the modern era, the ability of many local élites to maintain their authority amid the challenges of imperialism, foreign invasion and modernisation are all testimony to the social stability achieved under the traditional political system.

Many centuries of literate culture, proximity to China and the resultant adoption of Chinese norms at the political centre encouraged centralising administrative tendencies. In a normative sense, Korean monarchs exercised wide powers as vassals of the Chinese emperor, but the substance of their power was largely limited to moral suasion and to symbolising and upholding the political, intellectual and cultural prestige of the state. Otherwise, royal authority was constrained by a number of factors, including the external legitimisation of Korean dynastic rule by the Chinese imperial court, lack of royal control over the bureaucracy, lack of control over the civil and military examination system which functioned as the bureaucracy's instrument of recruitment, the operation of institutions such as the Censorate, the Royal Secretariat and the Royal Lectures, the monarch's inability to exercise decisive control over land ownership and use, and the normative restraints of Neo-Confucian thought which abhorred excessive concentration of royal power.

Caricatures of dynastic despotism proliferate in the non-specialist literature, and are often adduced to suggest historical roots for Korean political authoritarianism in its various modern guises. Such views notwithstanding, the view of tightly constrained traditional royal authority is persuasive and helps explain why, with the exception of actual dynasty founders and early shapers, we associate few noteworthy achievements with specific Choson monarchs. In practice, the nature of the polity gave rise to normative centralisation but little expectation of dynamic political action, except in times of extreme crisis. Royal intellectual activities were derivative, not innovative, and their principal activity lay in the cultivation of self or, more accurately, having their 'self' cultivated for them by royal tutors and remonstrators. They did not involve themselves in the secular well-being of the country except in a ceremonial or symbolic capacity, and rarely left the palace precincts except in huge ritual cavalcades.

In addition to equilibrium between monarch and bureaucracy, the traditional Korean political system also sought equilibrium in the relationship between centre and periphery. The local élite was not subject to overbearing central control, nor was central control weak enough for local tyranny or other forms of private arrogation of state functions such as feudalism to emerge. The constant flow of personnel between the capital and the provinces meant that high culture in Korea remained remarkably uniform and overwhelmingly rural-based. As in China, the central government maintained a presence at the local level through a centrally appointed magistrate who was almost entirely reliant on the co-operation and authority of the local élite clans to carry out his duties, which consisted principally of tax collection, the levying of various imposts, the construction and maintenance of public works, and the preservation of law and order. This system was a major factor in the preservation of a high degree of local identity and political autonomy throughout the Choson period.

Authority issued out of a system of education which evolved in emulation of Chinese practice and which centred on the mastery of the Neo-Confucian canon. Members of the élite were also conscious adherents to a world order based on Chinese cultural hegemony, though from their own viewpoint this did not cause them to lose their distinctive cultural identity as Koreans. Art, philosophy and law were just three fields in which practitioners proceeded from a deep familiarity with Chinese norms and precedents but achieved outcomes that were distinctively Korean. A central institution of this gentry culture was the village-level school, whose curriculum was controlled by the local élite lineages, and which reinforced a sense of local tradition in the intellectual life of the country. In this manner, the political tradition enforced a local allegiance to the political centre that was normative and based on a shared élite culture. From these schools the sons of the local élite clans could proceed to sit for centrally administered examinations, and those who were successful comprised an élite cadre who staffed the central government bureaucracy and exercised guardianship over the dynasty's rich intellectual and spiritual life. In contrast to the emergent Western concept of the separation of Church and State, political and moral authority issued from the same institution and relied on a common framework of ideas. The language of politics was therefore frequently couched in the language of Neo-Confucian morality, and its ends were characteristically described in metaphysical as well as material terms. This flavour informs much of the highly categorical political rhetoric in both Koreas today.

Taken as whole, Korean social etiquette – and, for that matter, Korean aesthetics – draws strongly on the great tradition norms of Neo-Confucianism, but has also acquired considerable individuality through the little tradition norms of the village. This is an atmosphere in which the agricultural heartland, with its pattern of periods of intense physical effort followed by periods of extended idleness, its strong reliance on communal effort, and its highly personalised forms of interaction, deeply influences the norms of social intercourse. There is little call for timetabling, or for the precise scheduling of social events, for people are usually available or else willing to make themselves available for group activities at very short notice. Nor is there much need for the creation of formal channels for the circulation of information, since people use the channels that arise through constant informal contact with each other.

In modern times, whether in Pyongyang or Seoul, these traits can often surface in seemingly trivial matters such as the arrangement of meetings at extremely short notice, or else failure to communicate important information to interested parties. While powerful forces of egalitarianism and secularism have reshaped this ethos in the modern era, characteristic Korean social values such as small-group orientation, spontaneity, gregariousness and rough egalitarianism still owe much to their still-recent agrarian past. These social practices and values help to define a distinct manner in which people continue to conduct public business. Because they impress on a personal level, they often form the basis of an external observer's perception of a distinct political culture in operation. Yet we should be careful to distinguish between such mannerisms and the more abstract, formal features discussed above, for such mannerisms can often exaggerate the way in which the Korean past informs the Korean present. As individuals and as members of political groupings, Koreans make sense of the present through selective re-ordering of the past, and the social, cultural and political turmoil that has afflicted much of the country this century has encouraged widely divergent interpretations of this past. As we turn to a consideration of modern Korean history it is important to bear in mind that competing political ideologies are often buttressed by competing and often mutually hostile historiographical traditions. Again like people everywhere, Koreans sometimes seem to need to convince themselves (and unwary others) of the profound appropriateness of current policies by offering sweeping condemnations of past practices, often coupled with highly selective and tendentious readings of historical events and process. This can often give the impression that past political and social orders were far more unpopular and repressive than the contemporary record might indicate.

Sustained foreign influence has also reshaped the Korean tradition. During the twentieth century all major powers in the East Asian region – China, Japan, Russia and the United States – have fought wars to protect what they saw as their vital interests in Korea. However, while foreign invasions are certainly a prominent part of modern Korean history, the five hundred years prior to the Sino-Japanese War of 1895 are conspicuous for their lack of foreign invasion. Compared to the almost constant warfare in Europe and Eurasia, during this period Choson suffered one brief, albeit highly destructive, invasion from Japan during 1592–98, and two brief Manchu punitive raids in 1627 and 1636. Foreign intrusion in the modern era has been more sustained and destructive: the Sino-Japanese War of 1895 which was fought mainly on Korean soil, the Russo-Japanese War of 1905, the Japanese annexation in 1910 and the thirty-five years of colonial occupation which followed, the US and Soviet occupations during 1945–48, and US and Chinese involvement in the Korean War. Such events have obscured the historical memory of centuries of earlier, calmer times.

The common equation of external influence with foreign invasion tends to obscure the fact that there have always been significant foreign overlays in Korean culture. In particular, proximity to the centre of Chinese civilisation led to a high degree of Chinese political and cultural influence throughout the pre-modern era. This influence rarely entered Korea through outright invasion, but seeped in to mould the taste and outlook of the Choson élite. Over a period of many centuries, the country became imbued – often deeply so – with the values of Chinese philosophy, religion, art, literature and politics, though always, underneath, folkways and the unchanging realities of climate and geography drew Korea along its own individual path. Again, it is difficult to discuss the nature of Chinese influence apart from perceptions that the Choson élite were uncritical consumers of Chinese culture and less 'Korean' for this. Suffice it to say that the Korean–Chinese relationship was a dynamic, complex cultural relationship which cannot always be understood by the imposition of modern political standards of judgement. Choson Koreans were far from undiscriminating in their approach to China, especially during the Manchu Qing dynasty (1644–1911), and continually adopted from China only what they judged to suit their own needs.

Japanese influence has constituted a further, somewhat less welcome overlay in the modern era. After 1868 the Japanese themselves adopted and adapted economic organisation, education, technology and military norms from the West. Many Korean progressive thinkers in the 1880s and 1890s admired the manner in which Japan set about the task of modernisation, and urged similar policies on their own government. However, such admiration fell away as Japan became overtly imperialist. While some Koreans continued to see Japan as a model of successful modernisation, harsh colonial pressure to adopt many of these norms aroused considerable resentment. The trauma of the Japanese occupation has inhibited discussion of Japanese influence on Korean modernisation, but nevertheless the fundamental model of the capitalist developmental state, with its co-operative, collusive relationship between government and business, and the extension of the command–response military style to many areas of civil society, carried a profound influence into postwar Korea, and remains prominent in ROK military, business, education and government organisation.

But while some Koreans tend to stress the negative effects of foreign influence – and in fact this is an integral feature of state ideology in the North – it would be a mistake to present such influence as a basic determinant of postwar Korean politics. It is true that the Soviet Union under Stalin contributed profoundly to the manner in which the DPRK took shape; but institutional borrowings became indigenised, and direct Soviet and Chinese influence became marginalised.

Likewise, in the South, the US has sought to influence the ROK in various ways, but it played no meaningful role in the downfall of Syngman Rhee, the rise of Park Chung-hee and Chun Doo Hwan, or the reversion to democratisation in 1987. Foreign influence has hovered in the background, shaping the broader international environment but only indirectly influencing how Korean leaders interpreted that environment and acted.

The modern vestiges of Korean political tradition remain matters for keen debate. The DPRK has of course dismissed Neo-Confucianism as utterly backward, while in the ROK an uneasy mix of attitudes prevailed. Neo-Confucianism *per se* is often seen as intellectually feeble and obstructive of modernisation, yet somehow selective retention of its mores still provides bearings to a society in the midst of major transformation. For the élite, Neo-Confucianism describes a purpose, style and design for leadership, combining austerity, restraint and rigorous hierarchy, while for the general population it prescribes a strong sense of place within this hierarchy. Thus, on the individual level, such traits as acceptance of hierarchy, communal solidarity and consensus, and respect for rank and authority still prevail in both Korean societies as a deeply internalised cultural value system, reinforced practically from birth in such settings as the home, the school, and throughout all forms of business and social organisation.

In actual practice, however, Neo-Confucianism can only give broad-brush guidance. Rather, what is usually referred to as 'the Korean political tradition' is a tradition of considerable complexity and internal variety, while the pattern of foreign encroachment and the adoption of foreign ideologies by Korean political actors have involved the overlapping and interpenetration of Korean and non-Korean philosophies, conventions, thoughts and practices. These often present themselves to the outsider as a series of overlays, comprising persisting elements of tradition, Neo-Confucian prescriptions and norms, and Western influences. This means that Korean politics, especially in their ROK setting, often defies formal analysis, while election results, cabinet reshuffles, party platforms, debates, confrontations and, of course, media and academic commentary on these events do not always provide an accurate guide to the fundamental issues at stake.

The relationship between past and present in the North is especially problematic. In describing the DPRK, commentators sometimes note the existence of striking similarities between Choson dynasty and DPRK polity and society, notwithstanding the obvious huge differences. Here the difficulty is not so much in detecting such similarities as in analysing them meaningfully. Some features, such as near-deification of a sage-leader, domination by an élite recruited on the basis of family and ideological rectitude, and lack of popular political participation, seem 'traditional', but such features are more or less generically common to traditional societies and have little specific Korean content. Moreover, many features commonly claimed for a specifically Korean political tradition in fact derive from the massive ingestion of Stalinist ideology which, despite its revolutionary rhetoric, contained manifold traditionalist features reworked from the Russian past. The heavy use of kinship metaphors (e.g. 'the Fatherly Leader') to reinforce political authority and hierarchical relationships, and the concept of the genius philosopher-king, capable of providing definitive guidance on a broad range of subjects, including economics, history, philosophy and linguistics, are only two of the more prominent features of DPRK political culture which are absent from Korean political tradition and modern ROK political practice, but are heavily present in the Soviet Union throughout the Stalinist era.

Compared with the North, in the ROK continuity with the past is more salient than attempts at transformation. The normatively strong but functionally weak monarchy has disappeared, and in its developmental stage the ROK evolved an exceptionally strong state, capable of penetrating into selected areas of civil society and influencing the outlook and values of groups and individuals. But, while power remains highly concentrated in the executive organs of government, there are also many forces in ROK politics which have been subversive of centralism, and in fact the current trend is towards ever weaker executive authority. The military-backed authoritarianism of the period 1961–87 appears more and more to be the product of a particular set of circumstances, rather than an essential expression of Korean political tradition.

The dynamic public sphere in Choson retains a powerful vestige in the strong state-contentious society phenomenon in the ROK today. ROK society remained dynamic and challenging through the period of political authoritarianism; and, while only a minority engaged in active anti-government struggle, society as a whole remained far from docile. Economic prosperity has muted many forms of protest, but a strong civil society has provided a strong counterbalance to the claims of a strong state. A major factor in this has been the persisting strength of localism, for the tendency to identify with leaders and other followers with whom one shares a particularistic tie, such as a common blood tie, a common place of origin, or a common education, remains pronounced. It continues to promote a pattern of personalised political loyalties, and mitigates against the striking of durable alliances based on common causes or policies outside one's core associational group. The major political parties remain the rallying-points for their leader, and the fortunes of the party depend in the first instance on his perceived needs and strategies. Personalism, or 'bossism' as it is often called, continues to dominate ROK politics and adds important colourings to ROK democracy. While ROK citizens elect their leaders and legislators, public and legislative policy debate continues to play a marginal role in political life. In turn, the emphasis on obedience to personal authority undermines the legal framework and provides poor defences against such features as nepotism and corruption.

The sense that authority issues from educational achievement remains strong, and the universities, especially Seoul National University, remain prime recruiting grounds for senior government ministers and officials. This practice seems to carry with it a vestige of the Neo-Confucianist view of the scholar as somehow morally superior and, whether or not one actually rises to a position of responsibility and power, graduation from well-known Korean or foreign universities remains a key source of prestige and respect. In addition, Korean public discourse seems to retain many of the features of Neo-Confucian rhetoric, and political leaders and followers alike often tend to frame issues in ethical terms, reinforced with moralistic rhetoric that seems hostile to the practical pursuits of ordinary politics. The ideal of just and wise leadership, driven by pure motives for the good of society, remains embedded in the political culture despite the almost daily contradictions thrown up by actual political behaviour.

These diverse currents and conflicts are refracted to the outside world through international media accounts. Such accounts generally portray the ROK as a major economic success story, despite having shed some of its gloss owing to its 1997 financial crisis. On the other hand, images of the DPRK have been far more fragmentary. They have leaned heavily on the more extreme manifestations of the Kim Jong Il personality cult and, more recently, on the human toll of the North's endemic food shortages. They have established the prevailing image of a reclusive state, unstable and menacing to world peace. Such popular images make for easy media copy, but they usually contrast with the images which arise from conversations with both North and South Koreans about their daily experience. Thus, any description of non-official North Korean attitudes must include residual pride in the past achievements of the DPRK, cynicism about the present, fear of the future, and often sincere bewilderment at the hostility of so much of the outside world. The current generation in the South also tends to cynicism, and while the 'economic miracle' rhetoric remains robust in official circles its academics, intellectuals and activists stress the darker side of the ROK's performance. They increasingly accept the fact of prosperity and plenty, but they point out that important residues of military authoritarianism remain, that corruption and cronyism are rife, that social inequalities continue to grow, that the environment continues to be degraded, that national politics remains dysfunctional and that peaceful reunification seems as far away as ever. Such disparities announce the Korean Peninsula as a land where perceptions and realities rarely match, and emphasise the complex multi-faceted process by which the two Koreas evolved into modern states. This process is our story.

Selected reading

Cho, Hein 1997, 'The Historical Origin of Civil Society in Korea', *Korea Journal*, vol. 37, no. 2, pp. 24–41.

De Bary, William Theodore and Haboush, JaHyun Kim (eds) 1985, *The Rise of Neo-Confucianism in Korea*, New York: Columbia University Press.

Deuchler, Martina 1992, *The Confucian Transformation of Korea: A Study of Society and Ideology*, Harvard, Mass.: Council on East Asian Studies.

Haboush, JaHyun Kim 1988, *A Heritage of Kings: One Man's Monarchy in the Confucian World*, New York: Columbia University Press.

Pratt, Keith 1980, 'Politics and Culture within the Sinic Zone: Chinese Influences on Medieval Korea', *Korea Journal*, vol. 20, no. 6, pp. 15–29.

1 Joined to the empire, 1910–31

As European imperialism in East Asia reached a new peak in the 1890s, Japan's leaders decided that the country's strategic defence perimeter should expand to include Korea. Tokyo therefore began a new phase of involvement and interference in Korean affairs, aimed at the elimination of influence from the only other two powers influential in Korea – China and Russia. Chinese influence effectively ceased following its defeat in the Sino-Japanese War (1894–95), and Russian influence likewise ceased after the Russo-Japanese War (1905).

Korea responded to Japanese expansionism by instituting a drive for modernisation at home, and searching for allies abroad. The domestic drive for modernisation during 1876–1910 was considerable, but it was simply not effective enough to safeguard sovereignty. Korea had begun its modernisation drive half a generation later than Japan, and the roots of modernisation in the political and social fabric of the country remained shallow, so the Korean state remained significantly weaker than its neighbour in all meaningful indices of state power. Moreover, Korea could not counter the power and reach of Japanese diplomacy, and so could not find effective foreign-power backing to withstand the Japanese challenge. As a result, on 29 August 1910 the 518 year-old Choson dynasty ceded the remaining vestiges of its sovereignty to Japan, and Korea became a colony of the Japanese Empire.

The Japanese established an administration at the apex of Korean government which embarked upon a major drive to modernise and integrate Korea into the Japanese Empire. Thus began a thirty-five year period of colonial rule which had profound consequences for the manner in which modern Korea took shape. The new colonial government was intensive but selective in its reach. In some areas of major interest such as the economy and the suppression of Korean nationalism, the Japanese were highly interventionist, whereas in other areas such as social policy they left many aspects of Korean tradition and custom to continue virtually undisturbed. In all fields, however, Japan determined colonial policy in the broader context of its domestic and foreign policies. We therefore begin our account of the Japanese colonial period with a consideration of this context.

Japanese colonial policy reflected the world-view of its rulers. By 1910 some forty-two years had passed since the Meiji Restoration had installed a new, modernising élite at the apex of Japanese politics. Age, illness, assassination and suicide had culled this élite group, known as the *Genro*, or Elder Statesmen, down to a mere handful of men, but they retained a far-reaching and pervasive hold on power, which they characteristically exercised out of sight of the workings of formal political institutions. The process by which fundamental policy decisions were reached remained poorly institutionalised in Meiji Japan, and the state characteristically took its bearings from the deeply held convictions of a small number of ageing men about the nature of the world and Japan's place in it.

These convictions were at once simple and complex. They were simple because they evolved from the shared experience of youthful struggle against the Tokugawa shogunate in the 1860s. They were complex because they refracted many layers of subsequent experience: a profound conviction that Japan was small, weak and vulnerable; a sense of racial and cultural inferiority *vis-à-vis* the imperial powers; compensatory feelings of racial and cultural superiority *vis-à-vis* less-developed neighbouring states; a belief in the values and virtues of militarism; a defensive pride in Japan's achievements since 1868; a belief in the efficacy of colonialism; and a hierarchical view of the international order, buttressed by theories of social Darwinism and its basic doctrine of survival of the fittest.

Initially, Meiji foreign policy had pursued the relatively clear-cut objective of avoiding foreign entanglements while building up domestic economic and military strength. However, as Japan grew stronger, and as the *Genro* grew older, the lack of recognisable policy principles issuing from a consistent intellectual or philosophical base grew more pronounced. Thus, as the economic and military disparity between Japan and its neighbours grew, so did the drive to extend the Japanese defensive perimeter wherever possible. The net effect was a pattern of imperialistic behaviour which fed on success and became increasingly aggressive and reckless. When victory in the Russo-Japanese War (1905) removed Japan's last serious military rival from North-East Asia, vistas of unchecked military and economic expansion on the Asian mainland beckoned to the Japanese military and their civilian supporters. In 1910 the efficacy of imperialism and the conversion of mainland North-East Asia into a Japanese sphere of influence were axioms of Japanese foreign policy.

However, while such foreign policy axioms led to the annexation of Korea, they gave no clue as to how Japan would find the economic means to rule and develop its new possession. Here Japanese weaknesses were more significant than its strengths. Crucially, although the scale of the Meiji transformation was substantial, in 1910 the Japanese economy was still weak in many areas. Heavy concentration of resources on military-related industries had produced a sector capable of supporting the expanding armed forces, but the country still relied on agriculture and forestry for well over half the nation's export income. Moreover, the nation was still heavily in debt from the recent war with Russia. Investment capital on the scale necessary to develop the new colony was not available within Japan, and so the new colony would have to pay its own way as much as possible, as well as contribute wealth to the mother state. This mandated a strong governmental structure in Korea, capable of maintaining public order, mobilising and directing the efficient use of scarce resources, and implementing the basic strategies which had been successful in the early Meiji period – that is, the creation of a stable, self-sustaining land tax revenue base and the development of agriculture as the prime means of wealth generation.

Domestic Japanese politics imposed another set of constraints on colonial policy in Korea, for such policy naturally mirrored the complex oscillations and contradictions of domestic Japanese politics during 1910–45. The repressive policies of the late Meiji–early Taisho period, the relative liberalism and openness of the early and middle 1920s, and the militarism of the 1930s all affected Korea and Koreans in various ways. Initially, the colonial administration ruled harshly, but as government by civilian-led political parties in Japan during in the early 1920s became relatively liberal in the context of time and place these excesses were curbed. Then, as illiberal forces reasserted themselves in the mid-1920s, policy-making lost this element of restraint, and colonial rule became harsh once more. This trend intensified further during the 1930s.

Japanese policies were also subject to broader international and regional developments, where the First World War (1914–18), global economic recovery in the 1920s, the Great Depression, the Bolshevik Revolution (1917), and the rise of Nationalist China all influenced colonial policy in important ways. The First World War delivered substantial wealth to the Japanese economy, alleviated its debt burdens and prompted Japanese investors to look abroad. This in turn caused a significant liberalisation of colonial economic policy. Moreover, while the general global prosperity of the 1920s stimulated the development of Korean agricultural and light industrial production, the drastic decline of commodity prices in the late 1920s affected Korea deeply. The Great Depression further highlighted the vulnerability of the colonial economy and had major economic consequences for Korean agriculture. The Bolshevik Revolution in 1917 also had a deep effect on the rulers of Japan. The spectre of the nation's underclass rising up and seizing power was deeply disturbing to the Japanese élite, and they became convinced of, if not obsessed with, the need for pre-emptive, highly repressive counter-measures against communists and socialists in general. Similarly, Japan's well-developed sense of strategic insecurity reacted strongly to the growth of Nationalist China during the 1920s. Like the Western imperialist powers during the nineteenth century, Japan stood poised uncertainly between fear of the power vacuum created by a weak China and fear of the threat posed by a strong China. Exploitative during the First World War, Japan grew more accommodating during the early 1920s, but as the Nationalist Chinese forces grew in strength the Japanese again resolved to undermine and bring military pressure to bear on China. This had important consequences for Korea, for as Japanese military aggression against China proceeded virtually unchecked in the 1930s, Korea became a forward staging area and an important source of supply for the war effort. As a result, a nascent industrial infrastructure began to take shape in the north east of the peninsula, comprising mining, mineral processing, and iron and steel production.

Although basic economic strategy was clear, social policy in Korea remained ambiguous. Emulating European colonial rhetoric, the Government-General constantly stressed its 'civilising mission' and emphasised the 'backwardness' of its new colonial subjects, but it did not seek radical reform of the existing social structure. Lack of resources was one reason, and the general compatibility of this Neo-Confucian structure with Japanese objectives was another. Therefore, although the Japanese presence grew more intrusive during the 1930s as the mobilisation of Korean resources in support of the Japanese war effort grew more intense, social change in colonial Korea was essentially a by-product, not a main objective, of colonial government. Under Japanese rule, the Korean family and clan systems remained virtually untouched, and society remained organised on strongly authoritarian, patriarchal and generational lines. Moreover, although literacy and education participation rates rose sharply, they remained low in absolute terms, as did the status of women.

The perception of Korea and Koreans held by ordinary Japanese was also an important driver of policy. Various emotions vied in the Japanese mind: the exclusive nature of the Japanese social system, the sense of cultural 'uniqueness', pride in their own modernity, a lingering sense of inferiority in great-power circles, aggression in pursuit of modernisation policies, loss of restraint and inhibition when dealing with a subject people, a sense of racial and cultural superiority towards the Koreans, and an emphasis on Korean 'backwardness'. These elements were in turn reinforced by a jingoistic and authoritarian education system which promoted a number of key Japanese myths, such as the ancient racial and cultural homogeneity of Japan. Despite official professions of benevolence, the average Japanese, whether in Korea or in Japan proper, viewed Korea and Koreans with contempt, and frequently treated individual Koreans harshly.

Many foreign governments shared this perception of Korean 'inferiority' and tacitly accepted the Japanese takeover. They did so primarily because they believed that Korea could not modernise alone, and because they were conditioned to accept and advocate the necessity and the benefits of colonialism. To such people the Japanese annexation of Korea seemed a rational and inevitable outcome. Thus, US President Theodore Roosevelt recommended and endorsed Japanese tutelage, and a string of eminent foreign visitors to colonial Korea were happy to contrast what they perceived to be Korean indolence with Japanese vigour and efficiency. For Japan, such international approbation meant a relatively free hand in Korea, while for Korean nationalists it meant a struggle without ready support from either foreign governments or prominent foreign individuals.

However, to the Japanese the simple proclamation of a civilising mission in the name of modernisation was not sufficient. It was equally important to demonstrate the historical inevitability of Korean annexation. This gave rise to a rather sinister assimilationist ideology which highlighted images of geographical proximity, shared heritage, and 'backwardness' in all spheres of Korean life in support of the argument that Korean culture and civilisation had outlived their time and should therefore be 'rejoined' to Japan as the big brother and superior civilisation. As one senior colonial official described it in 1913, the colonial mission involved 'advancing the intellectual and moral character of the new subjects of the Empire, by reforming all their antiquated and evil customs and manners, in order to assimilate them completely to the original people of the Empire'. This ideology was present at the outset but, like so many other facets of colonial rule, its application followed the contours of domestic Japanese policy. The relatively liberal 1920s supported flexible tactics which allowed the tiny Korean economic and cultural élite to espouse a mild form of Korean cultural nationalism. However, in the illiberal 1930s the Japanese returned to first principles and sought the swift implementation of assimilationist measures, including the prohibition of the teaching of the Korean language and the forced adoption of Japanese names by Koreans.

The consolidation of colonial power

The spearhead of Japanese rule in Korea was the Government-General. This was an authoritarian, centralised government structure, quartered in what was then by far the largest, most elaborate modern building in Seoul, erected with crass symbolism directly in front of the throne-hall of Kyongbok Palace, the major royal palace of the Choson dynasty. At the apex of the administration stood the Governor-General, appointed from the highest reaches of the Imperial Japanese Army active list by the Emperor, and independent of the Japanese Cabinet. Consistent with the government's first priority of pacification, he relied heavily on police powers, and ruled with the powers of a general in a theatre of war. A series of civilian departments functioned as a command staff, but he himself was responsible for all significant decisions relating to personnel, oversight of police and judicial functions, and administration of the economy. This system provided subsequent Korean leaders with a powerful model for authoritarian rule.

The first priorities of the Government-General in 1910 were the disbanding of the remnants of the Choson dynasty political and intellectual élite and the crushing of lingering armed resistance. This élite generally comprised a more passive, compliant section of the intelligentsia, and it offered little resistance. Most of its members accepted generous pension offers from the government and retired or returned to their ancestral clan villages, where they remained economically and socially powerful at the local level in ways that generally supported Japanese objectives. For the less compliant, the potential for resistance in urban areas was nipped in the bud by the suspension of publications, the prohibition of public gatherings, and the disbanding of political organisations. In December 1910 the new Government-General provided a practical display of the new order when it arrested 105 prominent Christians, educationalists and intellectuals on the grounds of conspiracy to assassinate the new Governor-General Terauchi Masatake. Many were eventually acquitted after lengthy and rigorous pre-trial imprisonment.

The crushing of armed resistance in the countryside was more prolonged and violent. This resistance was led by irregular Korean troops known as the *uibyong*, or the Righteous Army. Such forces had grown in strength and sophistication since the demobilisation of the Korean Army in 1907, but were no match for the Imperial Japanese Army. Largely out of foreign view in the remote Korean country-side, the Japanese conducted a series of military campaigns with considerable ferocity, employing scorched earth tactics as well as widespread summary and reprisal executions. It is impossible to calculate the exact civilian and military casualties of the ensuing Japanese campaign, although Korean historians estimate that roughly 20,000 Koreans had died by the time the *uibyong* either faded into the rural population or else went into exile, from where they continued the struggle as the armed wing of the Korean nationalist movement.

In economic policy, the Government-General addressed the needs of colonial economic development in the light of Japan's own economic predicament at the time of the Meiji Restoration. Like late Tokugawa Japan, Korea possessed a largely subsistence-oriented agricultural base in which land use was controlled by a traditional élite which was at best indifferent to, and often hostile towards, commerce. Commercial infrastructure was underdeveloped, the country lacked an adequate land survey, and so the tax-revenue base was uncertain and deeply corrupted. The Japanese therefore saw their first major task as the preparation of an accurate inventory of the land resources as the basis for a rational tax structure modelled on the Meiji government survey of 1873–76. Because of the failure of an earlier attempt by the Choson government during 1898–1904, the country possessed an arbitrary and uncertain land tenure system for which up-to-date and accurate data were lacking. Consequently, during 1912–18 the Government-General carried out a rigorous land survey, classifying holdings according to type, productivity and ownership. As in Meiji Japan, the land itself, rather than the more uncertain annual harvest, became the basis of a land tax system which began to be implemented in 1914. By 1930 this tax was responsible for 45 per cent of annual government revenue. Since many farmers held their land by custom rather than by formal deed, some commentators have interpreted this survey as a means of dispossessing Koreans of their land. However, the Japanese land development companies such as the Oriental Development Company, which acquired major land holdings at this time, concentrated on acquiring ex-royal estate holdings. Comparatively little land passed into Japanese ownership from the ordinary Korean village landowner at this time.

The new land survey reflected the reality of a complex rural society in which social status lines were usually clear but their economic implications were frequently not. Although the Choson élite had discouraged social mobility, centuries of fractional rises and falls in the fortunes of individual families had produced a situation where 'landlords' could not always be distinguished from 'peasants'. Landlords might be wealthy absentee town-dwellers, but more typically they were impoverished village-dwellers of *yangban*, or gentry, status who lived alongside commoners and rented out portions of their small holdings or else hired seasonal labour to till it. Commoner landowners themselves might do likewise, or else supplement the incomes from their own lands with seasonal labour.

Another major priority of government was the overhaul of the country's education system. With the abolition of the traditional civil service examination during the Kabo Reforms of 1894–96, schools with relatively modern curricula mushroomed alongside the traditional Confucian-oriented village school structure. They expanded under both private and government initiatives, and in 1910

Korea possessed a significant school education infrastructure. This presented twin challenges to the Japanese: how to encourage its modernising, assimilating potential and at the same time curb the potential for 'seditious' learning. They opted to close down many of the existing private schools and to pursue the rapid expansion of basic school education with strict centralised control of the curriculum. The new mass education programme aimed at developing elementary education, not higher education. It assumed that Koreans had limited need and perhaps potential for education since the Japanese would run things. It also meant that Korean students went abroad, usually to Japan, for the higher education denied them in Korea. Thus, the numbers of Korean students in Japan increased from 790 in 1909 to 3,171 in 1912, as a new, Japan-oriented Korean educated élite began to form.

Nominally, Koreans were subjects of Japan and possessed equal rights to those of Japanese citizens, but in practice they exercised no meaningful political rights in their own country. In terms of representation, they elected no members to the Japanese Diet, nor to any representative or consultative body within Korea. A token Korean advisory body, the Central Advisory Council, was appointed from 'native Koreans of ability and reputation' – that is, loyal and collaborative elements – in 1910, but the Governor-General did not consult it at all during 1910–19, and only on minor matters thereafter. As a result, an authoritarian and coercive pattern was passed down with little or no Korean input through layers of Japanese bureaucracy to the local level, where the colonial police force, a cohesive, rigorously trained and supervised cadre, implemented policy in areas such as law and order, public health, and minor public works.

The revenue stream from land taxes began to flow in 1914 and was augmented by mineral royalties, as well as by traditional government monopoly sales of rice, ginseng, tobacco, salt and opium. This revenue in turn financed a vigorous programme of public works which extended the railway, road, coastal navigation and port infrastructure. The colonial government also instituted the establishment of a modern monetary and banking system, closely linked with the parent Japanese system. In 1909 the Bank of Korea had already been established as a central bank, and after 1910 the largely autonomous royal household economy was amalgamated with the overall colonial economy. Education, public health, veterinary extension services, reforestation and flood control programmes likewise proceeded rapidly. However, such material improvements made little impact on the great mass of Koreans. The experiences they remembered were of individual and collective contempt and ill-treatment, denial of civil liberties, strict censorship, expropriation, new taxes and fines on wines and tobacco, the forced cultivation of new cash crops, and an avalanche of new regulations covering animal slaughtering, common cemeteries, firewood gathering, and the licensing of traditional medicine (*hanyak*) practitioners. In the words of one Korean quoted in a Japanese report at the time, 'It is better to lead a hard life with real parents than to enjoy a comfortable life with step-parents'. This first decade of Japanese rule was a harsh, dislocating period which left few Koreans untouched.

The March First Movement

On 1 March 1919 the many strands of Korean experience during the first decade or so of Japanese rule briefly flowed together in massive demonstrations against Japanese rule, known collectively as the March First Movement. The movement took shape under the specific impetus of the end of the First World War and the diplomacy of US President Woodrow Wilson. With the causes of this war strongly in mind, in January 1918 Wilson framed his Fourteen Points as a statement of Allied war aims. A number of these points advanced the principle of self-determination for significant national minorities, especially those contained within the borders of enemy Axis powers such as the Austro-Hungarian Empire with its Balkan possessions. However, no European government thought seriously of applying this principle outside a European context, for it would have meant freedom for their colonies. But as Korean students and intellectuals, especially those who were abroad, became aware of the Fourteen Points they saw potential for international intervention to free Korea from Japanese rule.

The defeat of Imperial Germany in 1918 and the opening of the Versailles Peace Conference in January 1919 lent urgency to discussions among various Korean groups on the implications of the principle of self-determination. The diversity of the Korean groups and the rigour of Japanese repression inhibited communication, planning and co-ordination, but during January diverse élite groups such as former Choson government and court officials, newly returned overseas students, and religious leaders in the major Chondoist, Christian and Buddhist denominations gradually became aware of the common threads in their thinking. As they did, they recognised that if the Korean case were to be brought to international attention they would need to dramatise their cause as quickly as possible.

At this point chance intervened with the death of ex-King/Emperor Kojong on 22 January 1919. Kojong, who had ruled from 1864 to 1907, had been the last effective Choson monarch, and although many younger, politically aware Koreans associated Kojong with the calamitous pre-1910 failure to preserve Korean independence, the subsisting former dynastic tradition was still sufficiently alive for others to see in Kojong a potent symbol of Korean political and cultural unity and integrity. Accordingly, the Korean independence movement, which otherwise had no standing leadership or formal organisation, determined that it would make a statement on the day of Kojong's funeral, 1 March, when large crowds were expected to congregate in Seoul to witness the funeral procession. Actual planning fell by default to religious groups, because their churches and associated educational and social bodies offered a significant infrastructure for communication and mobilisation which to that time had largely escaped direct Japanese control. Thus, conservative leadership determined that the demonstration on 1 March would take the form of a petition to the colonial government for the redress of grievances, in the form of a Declaration of Independence.

At two o'clock on the afternoon of 1 March, twenty-nine members of a group of thirty-three prominent religious figures from the Chondo (a native Korean religion), Christian and Buddhist churches, who had previously had little contact with each other, and afterwards would also quickly go their separate ways, met at the Myong'wolgwan restaurant in downtown Seoul to read out the Declaration of Independence which all thirty-three had signed. Meanwhile, a crowd of several thousand people, mainly students, began to gather in nearby Pagoda Park where they anticipated a public reading of this declaration. In fact, the leaders feared the potential for violence at a mass outdoor gathering and opted instead to read it at the restaurant. They were immediately arrested there, and the initiative for further political action therefore passed to the now-leaderless crowd. Initially, demonstrations consisted of relatively peaceful readings of the long, solemn, erudite independence proclamation, followed by cries of 'Manse!' ('Long live [Korea]!'). These demonstrations, often accompanied by strikes and business shutdowns, spread throughout the peninsula, and increased in frequency throughout March, reaching their peak in early April. These demonstrations were more raucous and intimidating than violent, but they gradually wore down always-thin Japanese reserves of self-restraint, and this led to violent counter-measures from police and gendarmes. In Seoul, in Pyongyang, and in countless other towns and villages across Korea hundreds of Koreans died and thousands more were arrested, brutalised or forced into exile before relative calm descended once more in mid-April.

Outside Korea, these events had a radicalising effect on émigré Korean groups. The armed Korean struggle, all but abandoned after the repression of the *uibyong*, re-emerged in southern Manchuria. Former *uibyong* commanders such as Yi Tonghwi and Hong Pomdo reactivated their followers, proclaimed the founding of the Korean Independence Army (*Tongnip-gun*) and moved from their places of self-imposed exile in Siberia to Chiendao near the Manchuria–Korea border. Armed by the Soviet Union, tacitly supported by the Chinese, and with a local Korean population which had expanded from 71,000 to 308,000 during 1907–21, the army held out hope of sustainable military resistance against the Japanese. However, in a brief, intense campaign in late 1920 the Japanese cleared the area of armed Korean nationalists, who were again forced to retreat northward, even further from Korea and Korean communities.

Meanwhile, Korean nationalists in Shanghai followed up the March First Movement by declaring a Korean provisional government on 9 April, and by lobbying sympathetic governments to raise the issue of Korean independence at the Versailles Peace Conference. A Korean envoy from the Shanghai group took up residence in Paris for the purpose of distributing copies of the Declaration to delegates, but to no avail. Japan had aided the Allied cause in East Asia during the war, and was now a powerful state in its own right. By contrast, the Koreans were poor, stateless and powerless; and, while the British, for example, remonstrated briefly with the Japanese over police brutality in Korea, no Western government offered support for Korean independence. The Korean cause quickly left the international agenda, and despite two further decades of tireless lobbying and armed struggle by a variety of Korean nationalist and communist groups it did not attract major power interest again until the complex and chaotic diplomacy of the Second World War (1939–45) again brought Korea to great power attention.

The Japanese response

The March First Movement had significant repercussions in Japan as well. Wartime prosperity in Japan and the victory of the Western democracies in the First World War had infused Japanese politics with a more liberal spirit, which manifested itself in the growing power of popular political parties and demands for extended voting rights. The appointment of Hara Kei, who was both a commoner and a party politician, as prime pinister in 1918 presaged the short-lived flowering of relatively liberal politics in Japan during the 1920s, often referred to as 'Taisho Democracy'. Hara himself did not hold liberal views, but he was a political pragmatist, and he also believed that the broad, informal political power wielded by the remaining members of the *Genro* should be curbed. He expressed open distaste for the military's actions in Korea, as did other influential sections of the bureaucracy such as the Ministry of Foreign Affairs. Some foreign powers, especially the British, also made energetic representations to the Japanese to seek more moderate colonial policies, partly out of humanitarian motives as they surveyed mounting evidence of Japanese atrocities, and partly out of concern that Japanese behaviour in Korea could tar all colonial administrations with the same brush.

Major Japanese business interests also favoured modifications to colonial policy, though for different reasons. Japan's wartime boom had extinguished its sizeable foreign debts and created a sizeable pool of investment capital. The natural destination for capital which could not be efficiently absorbed at home was the colonial empire, and so Japanese businessmen began to lobby for change to the restrictive provisions of the colonial government's company laws. These laws, first enacted in 1911, required Government-General approval for the establishment of new companies and other business operations in Korea. It was directed chiefly at foreign economic interests, and in fact succeeded in driving out almost all non-Japanese commerce, such as mining and tobacco interests, but Japanese companies themselves also suffered in the process.

The outcome of these pressures was acceptance in Tokyo that Japanese colonial policy could not return to pre-March 1919 methods. Accordingly, in August 1919, Japan announced the reorganisation of Japanese rule in Korea under the slogan *Nissen yuwa* ('Harmony between Japan and Korea'). Although Tokyo's assimilationist policies in Korea remained a deep article of faith in Japanese leadership circles, the harsh military face of military-oriented rule under Hasegawa Yoshimichi was replaced by the softer countenance of Admiral Saito Makoto, who announced a number of policy changes, known collectively as the 'Cultural Policy'.

The Cultural Policy had two key objectives. The first was to tighten security to ensure that widespread political demonstrations could never happen again; the second was to placate moderate Korean nationalism. The demonstrations had been seen as an affront to Japan's good intentions and as an international embarrassment. For this reason the Government-General resolved to put an end to pro-independence organisation and activity. In 1920 it designated public order as its highest priority, and quickly established a police presence in every local district in the country. A new cadre of civilian police officers were transferred to Korea from Japan, where political surveillance training and practice were far more sophisticated and rigorous. These moves were effective, for no further major demonstrations occurred under Japanese colonial rule. Ultimately, it became impossible to conduct even minor pro-independence political activity on Korean soil.

Saito's second objective was to placate and co-opt those sections of the Korean population which stood to benefit from more gradualist and moderate colonial policies. The Government-General identified the harsher forms of control over the lives of ordinary Koreans as impediments to recognition of Japan's broader 'benevolent' intentions. Accordingly, the Seoul government adopted a series of measures to eliminate discrimination, abandon some of the more petty forms of government interference in daily Korean life, provide more opportunities for Koreans in education and civil service employment, allow more freedom of expression and assembly, and facilitate Japanese investment in Korea because, as Saito put it, 'The Koreans and the Japanese must be treated alike as members of the same family'. In Japanese eyes, such a gradualist approach would allow the Koreans to assess the benefits of assimilation in a more positive manner. Korea would remain, as Hasegawa still described it, 'Japan's base for development on the continent and the perimeter of defense for the home islands', but Japan would also create a certain space for Korean cultural self-expression, and within that space members of the Korean intelligentsia worked to restore and defend their culture against Japanese pressure.

The economic reform measures taken in the wake of the March First Movement constituted an important spearhead of colonial policy, and also marked the foundation of modern Korean capitalism. As with the Meiji economic system, the chief feature of the new government–business relationship in colonial Korea was the overwhelming dominance of the state. The Government-General established the parameters and priorities for economic development, and through close control of the financial and regulatory structures ensured that economic activity took place in accordance with its policies. The business sector remained heavily dependent upon official contacts and favours, and its formal input into development planning was restricted to membership on an industrial advisory commission, a body which consisted of Korean and Japanese officials and businessmen. Command of capital gave the Government-General control of investment, which it used to maximise returns to Japanese investors.

Most of this new business activity in Korea was carried out by Japanese entrepreneurs using Japanese capital and expertise. By contrast, Korean economic activities suffered from multiple disadvantages in the form of restricted access to capital, poor business networks, and a near-total reliance on Japan for education and training. Nevertheless, a small Korean business community came into existence around the edges of the Japanese business world. Such businessmen were a diverse grouping, but most typically they were entrepreneurs who were capable of transforming the traditional wealth they derived from family land holdings into modern, diversified, family-controlled business activities ranging across agriculture, food processing, finance and light industry. In the agricultural sector, for example, since the Japanese sought to streamline, rather than revolutionise, the rural economy, Koreans played a significant role in front-line processing of agricultural produce; and so, by 1928, Koreans owned and operated 70 per cent of the colony's rice mills. Patterns of familistic organisation, responsiveness to state economic policy, and close ties to Japan became common, and they created a pattern of business activity that strongly influenced the development of Korean capitalism after 1945.

However, the major economic priority continued to be the development of Korean agricultural production. By 1920 the possibilities of increasing agricultural output in Japan by means of improved seeds, fertilisers and better farming methods had narrowed substantially. However, while output was levelling off, population growth and rising per capita income was stimulating a level of domestic demand which the government could not satisfy. Shortages, supply bottlenecks, and corruption led to serious unrest, most notably in the form of the Rice Riots, which broke out in many parts of Japan in August 1918. Accordingly, Japan increased its investment in Korean agriculture. A major campaign to increase rice production began in 1920, and a new agricultural administration network supervised and coordinated the application of substantial new inputs, such as new seed strains, improved irrigation and drainage works, the application of crop rotation principles, and the expanded use of agricultural machinery. Modest though many of these inputs were, their judicious, cumulative application enabled Korean agricultural output to rise steadily during 1920–30. Strong Japanese demand for Korean rice sustained high prices and initiated a period of rapid market growth. Rice exports to Japan increased faster than production, stimulating 'famine export', whereby many Korean producers sold their rice and consumed grain substitutes such as barley, sorghum and millet. Supporting infrastructure also grew, stimulating continuing construction of road, rail and port facilities, rolling stock, storehouses and mills. The cash economy grew as an estimated one-third of agricultural produce was now sold on the market, and coastal villages such as Wonsan, Inch'on, Kunsan, Naju and Mokp'o grew into sizeable townships.

The benefits fell unevenly. Tenant farmers, who comprised a clear majority of the rural population, had little or no access to the credit facilities needed to introduce new technology, and many continued to pay roughly half their crop to landlords as rent. Thus, owner-cultivators became the chief beneficiaries of increased output and higher prices. This affected the sense of balance and continuity that had prevailed in rural Korea in the midst of the momentous changes of the previous half-century; but while tenant farmers became more assertive, and the number of tenancy disputes increased markedly, the general prosperity of the times tended to blunt tenant–landlord antagonism. Both, however, were seriously affected as the rural boom came to an end and the rice price declined by almost two-thirds during 1927–32. More than 70 per cent of farming families paid rent on part or all of their land, generally at a rate of 50 per cent of the crop, and by 1930 many tenants and owner-cultivators were hopelessly in debt at high interest rates, with many of the latter facing imminent bank foreclosure.

Korean society in the 1920s

During the 1920s the forces of modernisation had limited impact in the country-side. The family and clan system with its Neo-Confucian underpinnings claimed primary loyalties, and most people's horizons barely extended beyond the village. While actual living conditions often barely distinguished gentry and commoner, traditions of deferential behaviour, respectful forms of address, and distinctive clothing kept alive the traditional class and status system of the Choson dynasty. The gentry remained the major influence in politics at the local level, and most commoners continued to defer and look towards them as a means of safeguarding and advancing their various interests. Meanwhile, the gentry's material means and tradition of learning often provided a platform from which their children could obtain a modern education and enter colonial employment. They therefore dominated the new social and political groupings that began to appear in the cities and among the Korean élites in the early 1920s. Meanwhile, customary, patriarchal law remained all-powerful – all the more so as the Japanese excepted broad areas of law, including legal competence, kinship and inheritance from the application of their civil law code to Korea. This meant that Japanese laws had little effect on the social and legal position of women, and so the husband's role as family patriarch remained unchallenged and unchallengeable. Property inheritance provisions, by which the eldest son was the prime inheritor, remained more or less unchanged, and women remained bound to their husband's household. Divorce was possible only by mutual agreement or litigation, but a divorced woman was effectively cast out, and could not set up a separate household.

The Cultural Policy also stimulated new developments in Korean cultural life. Once again, Koreans were able to organise to pursue educational, religious, literary, economic, welfare, developmental, regional objectives, and so the number of officially registered organisations mushroomed during 1920–22. This period also witnessed the foundation of a modern Korean vernacular press, the emergence of a modern Korean literature, significant growth in the number of Koreans entering the education system, and the beginnings of organised nationalist, socialist and communist political organisation in Korea. All of this stimulated analysis and debate on the ways in which Koreans interpreted their past history and present predicament. Tiny communities of young intellectuals in Seoul took advantage of increased freedom of movement and assembly openly to pursue writing, debating and publishing activities. These new intellectual, literary and artistic societies marked the beginning of distinctly modern Korean traditions in historiography, literature, drama, music and film, and the interests, tastes and prejudices of this founding generation profoundly influenced subsequent generations.

The easing of censorship enabled the establishment in 1920 of the vernacular daily newspapers *Donga Ilbo* and *Choson Ilbo*, which to this day remain pillars of the modern Korean vernacular press. By 1930 they reached an expanding readership estimated at over 100,000. They published works by many of the leading figures in early modern Korean literature, while their news reports and commentaries became major sources of information for those participating in this new, vigorous period of social organisation. In a society with few institutions capable of transcending small-scale, particularist forms of organisation, the press performed a valuable role in providing a focus for many activists in the nationalist movement whose paths would otherwise rarely have crossed. Censorship was still tight, and ownership generally entrepreneurial and therefore conservative-pragmatic, but the politics of staff writers was generally populist and socialist. The newspapers became a training ground for the early post-1945 South Korean political élite.

The generational factor was as important as government policy in the growth of Korean nationalist consciousness during the 1920s. Koreans who reached school age in the mid-1890s became the first Korean generation to have access to modern education, including education abroad. Science and mathematics, rather than ethics and philosophy, dominated their curriculum, and the products of this first generation of modern education increasingly identified prosperity and well-being with a strong interventionist state directing economic development, not with royal Confucian virtue presiding over a self-regulatory traditional society. Students of this new generation began to graduate and embark upon careers during the 1910s, and although they soon confronted the reality of patriarchal authoritarianism and colonial repression, they entered into their prime in the early 1920s at precisely the time that the authorities were increasingly willing to grant them expanded means of self-expression.

Intellectual influences on Korean students abroad entered and struck roots within Korea. Such students had moved from the strictly controlled Korean environment to experience the more liberal, vibrant, cosmopolitan worlds of major Chinese or Japanese cities and then back again. Those who went to China became exposed to the radical tendencies of the Chinese student movement in the aftermath of the May Fourth Movement of 1919, and found they had much in common with their Chinese counterparts. The majority, however, went to Japan, where they experienced Taisho liberalism, and where many encountered radical politics through their fellow students and academic mentors. Various contradictory elements vied in the minds of this new élite-in-formation, and their attitude towards the colonial government and the Japanese in general was complex. They regarded Tokyo as the intellectual and artistic centre of their universe, which in many ways it was, but respect and admiration for Japan's achievement of the elusive goal of a prosperous modern country able to defend itself against external threat vied with profound resentment and humiliation at the loss of sovereignty and at the second-class status imposed upon them in their own country.

Some young Koreans discovered a Japanese literature which had brilliantly assimilated many currents of European thought and technique. More important, they became systematically exposed to the philosophical foundations of European and Japanese political discourse. Their responses were diverse, but most shared a heightened sense of anti-Japanese nationalism. This caused writers such as Yi Kwangsu, Hyon Chin'gon and Na Tohyang to embark on a search for Korean self-identity in the modern world which was radically different from the search of the previous generation of Korean thinkers. Much of their writing reflected the limited worldly experience of a tiny coterie of young aesthetes in a cultural backwater, as often as not still held in thrall by memories of cosmopolitan Tokyo, their creative vision profoundly undermined by the repressive atmosphere in which they wrote. Nevertheless, in the suffering of their fictional characters they articulated general, even universal, themes of isolation, anomie and self-discovery, and gave voice to a widely felt sense of malaise which otherwise had no specific outlet.

Nowhere were the contradictions of colonial-era Korean intellectuals more clear than in their attitude towards their own cultural past. The anguish of early-modern Korean nationalists over the loss of sovereignty to the Japanese produced a bitter, often vengeful attitude towards the Choson dynasty and its ruling class as the parties chiefly responsible, and so the Korean nationalist and Japanese colonialist historiographic traditions, which both stressed themes of stagnation, lack of originality and non-development, commingled in strange and often ironic ways. At the same time, however, scholars such as Ch'oe Namson revived interest in Korea's more distant past and rescued many important documents and texts from obscurity and possible oblivion. In the process they established modern foundations for the study of Korean history.

The 1920s also witnessed the formation of a tiny working class and the beginnings of Korean radicalism. The first nationwide labour organisation, the Korean Workers Mutual Aid Society, was founded in Seoul in 1921. Their members were chiefly drawn from the cotton textiles, chemicals, metals, machines and machine tools, electricity generation and distribution, sugar refining, cement, beer and alcohol manufacturing plants which grew up as Japanese investment in Korea expanded. Poor, without bargaining power, and without even the tenuous, hard-won measures of political and legal protection won by their Japanese colleagues, Korean workers had few means of bringing influence to bear on the colonial government. In contrast to the limited freedoms granted to the emerging Korean élite, the Government-General, seemingly obsessed by the spectre of Bolshevism, brought a formidable array of security measures and criminal legislation to bear on any and all attempts of labour to organise. This inaugurated a decade of communist and non-communist labour resistance and agitation, which only subsided in the 1930s in the face of sustained repression.

Meanwhile, beyond the activities of the Seoul-based intellectuals, important shifts were beginning to occur in popular consciousness. Underlying the mood of the country was an unarticulated but keen awareness not just of political loss, but also of profound cultural loss resulting from the fracturing of the Neo-Confucian world-view. When the Choson dynasty fell, Koreans lost an entire edifice of faith which had undergirded the life of the country for five hundred years, linking people and their daily thoughts and activities to monarch, to country and, beyond, to the universe. The fact that some had been shaken loose from this order in the final stages of dynastic decline, and the fact that this order has so often been portrayed in modern Korea as thoroughly backward and reprehensible, tends to obscure the fact that well after 1910 the meaning of life for the vast majority of Koreans continued to be sought and found within traditional Neo-Confucian parameters. Neo-Confucianism retained its hold on almost every facet of individual, family and institutional life. At the same time, however, Neo-Confucianism ceased to be an active, monolithic faith. Sense of identity, of purpose in life, and of the significance of daily activities became crowded with unanswerable questions, and neither spiritual leaders nor colonial authority could offer guidance to people disturbed and uprooted by momentous change. For some, Christianity and other new religions filled the spiritual void, and Buddhism also began to experience a modest revival. For others – especially intellectuals and the colonial élite – materialism, existentialism, humanism or simply nihilism became fashionable. This was an age marked by a gathering sense of loss, confusion, and ardent spiritual yearning.

Korean nationalism

Korean nationalism flourished in the years following the March First Movement as the country witnessed a kaleidoscope of nationalist activity. Within Korea these activities encompassed cultural, literary and educational enlightenment movements, patriotic economic activities and propaganda activities, while abroad more direct forms of activism flourished, including armed resistance, guerrilla warfare and terrorism. Within Korea, criticism of colonial rule *per se* was prohibited, but debate on specific issues, such as what might constitute purposeful and ethical participation in the colonial order, was permitted. Moderate nationalist or gradualist groups, encompassing many members of the new élite, emerged and began to direct their energies towards promoting Korean nationalist consciousness and supporting the pragmatic reform of traditional social practices. Such mainstream leaders as Yun Ch'iho, An Ch'angho, and Yi Kwangsu saw the Japanese occupation as symptom, not cause, for it merely underlined their contention that Korea had lost its independence because of material and spiritual backwardness. This showed itself in an inability to engage in sustained, purposeful activities in the public sphere – as shown by the failure of the March First Movement to achieve the goal of independence. In the view of moderate nationalists, until Koreans as a people became more 'advanced', they would not be able to sustain a modern nation. This led to an emphasis on the task of 'awakening' the masses by advocating various forms of self-strengthening and self-modernising.

However, the moderate nationalists found that specific public activities were difficult to mount. This was not just because of Japanese restrictions, but also because this diffuse movement was directed by intellectuals who were both inexperienced in the techniques of direct political action and too young to command an effective following. Their major work therefore concentrated on public debate, publishing, and other intellectual activities, such as efforts to preserve, reform and extend the use of the Korean language, and a campaign to establish a national university with a major focus on the study of Korean history and culture. Economic issues also became a key preoccupation, and awareness of growing inequities of the rural sector led to calls for reforms in agricultural policy. Activists also sought to support Korean-owned businesses through Buy Korean campaigns organised by groups such as the Korean Products Promotion Society, founded in Pyongyang by Cho Mansik in 1922. Such activities reflected a common belief among the Korean élite that Korean society had to reform and modernise itself in the industrialising world, as Japan had done, and as China had not done.

Other nationalists immediately tested the limits of permissible political debate. Radicals and leftists denounced moderate nationalism as illusory, since the nature of Japanese political authority issued from the nature of the underlying forces of capitalism and imperialism. The real enemy, they argued, was an exploitative class system in which the gradualists and collaborationists willingly participated. This assessment was fundamentally different from the moderate nationalist assessment, and provided a conduit for the spread of socialist and communist ideas inside Korea. The iconoclasm of the radical Korean nationalists was thorough and so, just as the moderate nationalists were opening select little windows on the Korean past, the radicals were drawing a new veil over the same past. To them this past was a burden, to be uprooted and recast as the mythology of a future powerful modern state. This tendency encouraged them to seek totalistic ideological solutions to Korea's problems, and in time they mounted a significant challenge to the intellectual leadership of moderate nationalists.

The activities of Koreans abroad constituted another significant division within the Korean nationalist movement. As we have seen, few foreign governments showed interest in the cause of Korean independence. Apart from the support of the Soviet-backed Comintern for Korean communists, Nationalist China provided a haven, though little else, for exiles in Shanghai. It was there that predominantly young Korean nationalists established the Korean Provisional Government (KPG) in April 1920. In an attempt to give their organisation stature, they invited many prominent activists to participate, but in seeking to bind together disparate and mutually antagonistic elements they seriously weakened their organisation. Successive would-be leaders such as Syngman Rhee and Yi Tonghwi came to Shanghai to see what scope the KPG offered for them to advance their own political strategies and interests, but soon departed, never to return. Within two years the KPG was virtually defunct. Later, in the 1930s, it came under the control of Kim Ku and a shadowy group of supporters whose major instrument of struggle was terrorism. Increasingly denounced by leftists and centrists alike, the KPG maintained its precarious existence but did not receive any international recognition, either before or after Korea's liberation in 1945.

The Korean communist movement constituted a second major strand to Korean émigré politics. This movement originally developed as part of the nationalist movement in the period immediately after the Bolshevik revolution, and by 1918 had established itself as part of the broader armed struggle abroad in Korean émigré communities, most notably in Irkutsk and in Shanghai. In 1925, Soviet efforts to establish a Korean Communist Party within Korea began, but ceased after repeated unsuccessful efforts. In 1928, Korean communists were instructed to join the party of the country in which they were operating. This had a profound effect on Korean communism because it meant that the Korean communists' activities abroad were restricted to activities among the local Korean population on behalf of foreign communist parties, most notably the Chinese and Japanese parties. This scattering of the Korean communists not only weakened the movement but also laid the foundations for important factional groupings in Korea, especially in the North, after 1945. Within Korea itself, activists carried on agitation and propaganda work, usually based on urban and industrial localities such as Seoul and, later, Hamhung and Hungnam in the North. However, by 1931, communists within Korea lacked the resources of a central organisation, and could carry out only sporadic low-level activities.

The high point of broad public nationalist debate within Korea was reached by the mid-1920s, and after 1925 most moderate nationalist campaigns lost momentum. Almost simultaneously, the fragile basis for democratic government in Japan came under ever-stronger attack from military and bureaucratic interests. The political parties, intellectual societies, labour unions and other social movements which were the principal mainstays of Taisho democracy were unable to withstand the power of entrenched supra-constitutional influence, and government in Japan grew unrepresentative and decidedly illiberal once more. As Japanese militarism flourished in the late 1920s, it countermanded the trend towards acceptance and support of Chiang Kai-shek and the Nationalists in China. The appointment of General Tanaka Giichi as prime minister in April 1927 marked a significant swing away from civilian control of government and initiated an increasingly aggressive foreign policy. On the mainland the major instrument of Japanese policy became the Kwantung Army, whose job was ostensibly to protect and police Japanese-owned assets such as the South Manchurian Railroad.

However, by 1928 the Kwantung Army had moved beyond the effective control of Tokyo. In a campaign to secure the absorption of Manchuria within the Japanese Empire, it instigated the assassination of Chang Tso-lin, the effective Chinese ruler of Manchuria in June 1928. The resulting uproar in Tokyo eventually forced Tanaka from office in July 1929, but the return of civilian-led government under Hamaguchi Osachi was temporary. Amid widespread unemployment and destitution in the aftermath of the Great Crash of 1929, the Japanese public grew increasingly willing to tolerate decisive, non-parliamentary actions. Intolerance of constitutional government on the part of the military reached a new level in the wake of ratification in November 1930 of the London Naval Treaty, which they viewed as unacceptably restrictive. The subsequent demise of the Hamaguchi government effectively ended civilian control of the Japanese government, while the military takeover of Manchuria after the Manchurian Incident in September 1931 initiated an era of military expansionism which continued until final defeat in the Pacific War (1941–45).

Under the influence of these events, the Government-General itself grew more repressive. During 1920–25 press censorship in Korea had been relatively casual, but the enactment of the Peace Preservation Law in June 1925, perhaps most notorious for its provisions against holding 'dangerous thoughts', also signalled a new cycle of repression. On 10 June 1926 the colonial authorities demonstrated their new-found efficiency by easily thwarting efforts by activists to revive the March First Movement on the day of the funeral of the last Choson emperor, Sunjong. As a result, Korean activists gradually came to understand that Japanese tolerance of moderate Korean nationalism was itself a tactical means of pursuing the fixed strategy of assimilation. Thus, as time went by, the invidious position of cultural nationalists in a colonial state became clearer to all, frustrating moderate participation and vindicating radical intransigence.

This poisonous atmosphere nudged the movement as a whole aside from the practicalities of political organisation into extended and increasingly acrimonious internal debate. Specific activities such as the National University and Buy Korean campaigns became ineffective, and leaders could neither articulate nor act on any persuasive set of alternative nationalist goals. The respective failures of moderates and radicals prompted a change of tactics, and in 1927 they pooled their dwindling support bases and formed a united front organisation, the Singanhoe, which uncomfortably combined moderate leadership and radical organisation activities at the grass-roots level. However, not only did this united front combine two forces in eclipse, it also had to contend with a renewed Japanese campaign to suppress radicalism. By 1929 the involvement of radical elements within Singanhoe in the 1929 Kwangju Student Movement demonstrations underscored a growing distaste for gradualism, and marked the beginning of the end for united-front activities. The subsequent demise of the Singanhoe in 1931 marked the passing of the last significant nationalist political organisation on Korean soil.

The essential failure of the Korean nationalist movement reflected some important traits in Korean society. Nationalists were united in common resistance to the Japanese occupation, against which they contrasted long centuries of autonomous political, social and cultural tradition within distinct physical boundaries. At the same time, however, the high degree of Korean self-regulation and localism, a major force for stability under the old order, became a paradoxical weakness in the modernisation process, which called for mobilisation, not stability. The Korean conception of nation was really a cultural and ethnic collectivity, made real partly by dynastic tradition, but mainly by family, kin, and local district ties. While intellectuals might use the language of modern nationalism, they remained localist and particularist in their conceptual and organisational framework. The nationalist political agenda remained encased in a deep-rooted, intricate social order and, as a result, Koreans were not readily responsive to mobilisation under banners which transcended the comfortable ties of family, class and region. Korean nationalists urged Koreans outward, beyond familism and localism to the nation-in-waiting and beyond, but simultaneously Korean culture urged the nationalists inward, back towards the deeply rooted social and cultural norms in which they had been raised. They quickly began to appreciate and repeat the bitter Chinese nationalist comment on how the Chinese stuck together 'like grains of sand'. In diversity there was weakness, not strength.

Conclusion

Where, then, did Korea stand by 1931? Korea's loss of sovereignty to Japan in 1910 marked the onset of a deep cultural trauma which has profoundly influenced modern Korea. It was not simply because the Japanese were strongly antipathetic conquerors and occupiers – the first invaders to actually conquer and rule Korea since the Mongols almost seven hundred years previously – although this alone was disastrous enough. Nor was it that they were self-appointed modernisers. The essence of this period for Korea was that it had been forced to submit to a régime which aimed clearly and unambiguously at the extinction of Korea as a separate, identifiable, autonomous culture.

Economically, the size of Korea relative to limited Japanese resources had mandated a colony that would have to pay its own way and remain highly self-regulatory. Paying its own way meant attachment to the Japanese economy as a cheap, reliable producer of agricultural and light industrial goods. Accordingly, during 1919–31 agriculture became better organised and more productive, and a significant light industry sector began to emerge. However, Japan did not intend colonial Korea to proceed further down the path of its Meiji model to industrialisation. Therefore, the Government-General pursued quantitative economic growth, but not qualitative economic development, and the colony settled into its economic role as a docile colonial provider of raw materials and foodstuffs to the Japanese Empire.

Politically, modern Korean nationalism began to come of age during this era. The March First Movement was a galvanic event, through which flowed many diverse currents of modern Korean history: armed struggle, radical nationalism and cultural enlightenment. However, the March First Movement and the various organisations which drew inspiration from it achieved few practical political objectives. The Japanese remained in control, mainly because of the subtlety and efficiency of their surveillance methods but also because of the disparate political strategies pursued by the Korean nationalists themselves. Moderate economic and cultural nationalists believed that direct confrontation with the Japanese was a self-defeating tactic, and assessed that there was no real choice other than to work within existing parameters and gain whatever concessions the Japanese were willing to give. Meanwhile, the Korean communist movement and other radical groups believed that the objective of Korean independence could only be achieved through the destruction of the Japanese colonial edifice itself. Dialogue between the proponents of such divergent approaches became increasingly difficult during the 1920s, and the questions of what constituted true patriotism, what constituted collaborationism, and what Koreans should do to regain their independence became increasingly complex, difficult and divisive.

No new Korean leaders arose in the course of these events to replace the thirty-three arrested on 1 March 1919, nor did any clear political organisation arise directly out of the movement. The best-known, most representative of the Korean nationalist leaders remained émigré figures: An Changho in China, Yi Tonghwi in Manchuria, and Syngman Rhee in the United States. This inability to unite and direct large numbers of people towards any practical, attainable objective, and the failure to achieve any sustainable political momentum, must be counted as a sign of failure for a political movement. Yet any realistic assessment of the March First Movement should also take account of the nature of Japan as a ruthless, all-powerful occupier which suffered from none of the ambiguities of purpose and scruple which allowed, for example, a Gandhi to operate in British India.

In more general terms, the early 1920s witnessed the emergence of a new, modern Korean élite. Forms of capitalism became established in Korea through the imported Japanese financial and banking system, and they began to make important inroads on traditional attitudes. The communal assumptions of a traditional society were compromised as the accumulation of surplus wealth became a more common pursuit, and the first stirrings of an acquisitive consumer society emerged in the urban centres of Korea. This in turn provided the germ of the idea of 'progress', the idea that moral and material progress was not only possible but also an increasingly integral part of human society. Such ideas filtered into Korean society via Japan and became commonplaces among the emerging Korean élite, especially among those who worked within the Japanese system. The businessmen among them became the founders of modern Korean capitalism, while the first truly modern generation of Korean intellectuals, with its youth, its harsh view of Korea's pre-modern traditions, its often unconscious absorption of Japanese intellectual norms, and its efforts to free intellectual and creative life from the colonial context through radicalism and socialism were enormously influential on subsequent generations. They set many of the key themes around which modern Korean intellectual debates still revolve to this day.

Beyond the narrow sphere of political and cultural debate, broader social trends are apparent. A population of about 15 million in 1910 rose to 21 million inside Korea by 1931, while a further 1.5 million Koreans lived outside Korea, mainly in Manchuria (*c.* 1.1 million) and Japan (400,000). An increasing proportion of the population lived in the growing urban centres of the peninsula, chiefly in Seoul (1932 population: 374,000), Pusan (148,000), Pyongyang (145,000) and Taegu (103,000), but over 80 per cent of the population still lived in small, clan-dominated rural villages. As in dynastic Korea, there was virtually no governmental presence at the village level, where patriarchal law and customary practices prevailed.

The urban centres themselves underwent rapid transformation. The old walled precincts enclosing a skein of twisting narrow alleyways had already overflowed during the Choson dynasty, but now the walls themselves were quarried for building stone and most of the city gates demolished to make way for new tramways, railways and grid-patterned roads. At the city centre the new economic and administrative life of the colony transformed neighbourhoods with new public and commercial buildings, military and police barracks, schools, marketplaces, factories and workshops. The new homes of the Japanese and Korean colonial élite replaced the old residences of the court officialdom, and newly built Christian churches raised their spires on higher ground. Increasingly shorn of their distinctiveness, Korean cities acquired the look of drab functionalism.

Plentiful and cheap labour, the large guaranteed markets within the yen bloc, the growth of transport infrastructure and the influx of Japanese capital all contributed to urban growth. Such an enumeration of factors underlines the extent to which the Japanese national interest dictated the terms of economic life in Korea, and hence the pattern of urban life. Koreans worked under and alongside a steadily growing Japanese community, whose authority dictated the conditions of working life and whose fashions and outlook moulded the fashions and outlook of the tiny Korean middle class. Events in Manchuria were about to transform Japanese colonial policy in Korea but, in 1931, Korea was still a poor, overwhelmingly rural country on the periphery of the Japanese Empire, from which the Japanese sought little more than military security and cheap primary produce for the metropolitan factories. In this manner, the reach of the powerful, centralised Government-General was selective, while Korean society remained self-regulatory in many important respects. Nevertheless, the machinery was there, and would shortly be used in a more ruthless, thoroughgoing manner.

Selected reading

Conroy, Hilary 1960, *The Japanese Seizure of Korea 1868–1910*, Philadelphia, PA: University of Pennsylvania Press.

Deuchler, Martina 1977, *Confucian Gentlemen and Barbarian Envoys*, Seattle, WA: University of Washington.

Duus, Peter 1995, *The Abacus and the Sword: The Japanese Penetration of Korea 1859–1910*, Berkeley, CA: University of California Press.

Ku, Dae-Yeol 1985, *Korea under Colonialism*, Seoul: Royal Asiatic Society Korea Branch.

Lee, Chong-Sik 1965, *The Politics of Korean Nationalism*, Berkeley, CA: University of California Press.

Li, Mirok 1956, *The Yalu Flows: A Korean Childhood*, East Lansing: MI: Michigan State University Press.

McNamara, Dennis L. 1990, *The Colonial Origins of Korean Enterprise, 1910–1945*, Cambridge: Cambridge University Press.

2 The dark gulf, 1931–45

Korea's role within the Japanese Empire changed drastically during the 1930s. As Japanese ultra-nationalists gained control of the Japanese government and embarked upon major military campaigns in Manchuria and China, Korea became less a colonial outpost and more a vital military rear support base. This transformed the nature of Japanese colonial rule as the colonial government mobilised Korea and Koreans to support this war effort. In 1931 food and agricultural production still dominated the colonial economy, but as Korea's growing infrastructure began to direct manpower and supplies northward to Japan's new frontiers its immense pool of agricultural labour was pressed into service in the new mines and factories which opened up. By 1940 production in mining, heavy and chemical industries such as oils, rubber, fertiliser, drugs and medicine had also become significant. Meanwhile, many Koreans left their homeland, and by 1945 nearly 4 million Korean soldiers and civilians, or roughly 16 per cent of the total population, were working abroad within the Japanese Empire.

Japan's military priorities enforced higher levels of mobilisation and repression in Korea. As we have already seen, colonial rule in Korea had grown more repressive as the 1920s progressed, and this trend accelerated during the 1930s. Even mild expressions of cultural and literary nationalism first became increasingly hazardous and then virtually impossible within Korea as Japan re-emphasised and promoted cultural assimilationism. Measures included forced worship before imperial shrines, the use of Japanese in schools, wide-ranging restrictions on use of the Korean language and script, and finally the forced adoption of Japanese names. By the time of the Pacific War (1941–45), there was every reason to believe that the Japanese would succeed in extinguishing Korea as a separate, identifiable culture, and that any future reconstitution of a Korean state would be rendered impossible. Only the military defeat of Japan in 1945 prevented this.

Not all Koreans were simply mute sufferers at the hands of the Japanese. In various ways, Japanese expansionism also offered material opportunity as many Korean soldiers and civilians, driven by motives as diverse as ambition, venality, idealism, the desire to escape poverty, and simple acceptance of the fact that Japan represented the way of the future, left their villages and joined the nascent industrial workforce in the North. Others looked and travelled eastward to Japan and northward to Manchuria, where they sought their fortune away from the restrictive horizons and lost causes of their homeland. Korean entrepreneurs, some of whom later became driving forces behind the huge industrial conglomerates, or *chaebol*, in South Korea, became increasingly accepted as junior members of the Japanese colonial business world in the 1920s. In the 1930s they used their contacts to develop larger-scale business interests in Manchuria, including agricultural processing and commodity trading, finance, textiles and light industry. Others, including future leaders of the South Korean military élite, took advantage of new opportunities for military careers and trained as Imperial Japanese Army officers in Tokyo and Manchuria.

Meanwhile, other Koreans found their calling in unremitting anti-Japanese struggle, and throughout most of the 1930s participated in nationalist and communist movements, both openly and underground in foreign countries, most notably China and Manchuria. In the short term, they met with little success and had minimal impact on Japanese rule, but in 1945 they returned to positions of leadership in liberated Korea. Many leading figures in postwar South Korea such as Syngman Rhee, Kim Ku and Shin Ik-hui made their reputations in émigré politics, while the future ruling élite of North Korea led by Kim Il Sung arose out of the guerrilla campaigns against the Japanese in Manchuria led by the Chinese Communist Party.

Japanese policy

The roots of Japanese policy on the Asian mainland during the 1930s lay in a growing atmosphere of economic, social and political crisis within Japan. Despite the steady growth of its industrial sector, during the early 1920s the Japanese export economy still relied mainly on agriculture, forestry products and textiles. This base could not fund the imports of the advanced capital equipment, manufactures and technologies which the country needed, and so by the mid-1920s Japan had acquired a serious and growing foreign debt. The burden of this economic decline fell disproportionately on rural communities, small business and labour, and increasingly these sectors grew alienated from existing political and economic institutions, which they saw as functioning primarily as servants of élite interests. Ultra-nationalist rhetoric served as a lightning rod for growing discontent, insisting that Japan should reject such decadent and alien concepts as individualism, liberalism, socialism and materialism, and rally around such 'traditional' Japanese values as frugality, loyalty and obedience to authority, self-sacrifice and proper social order. It stressed the unity and indivisibility of the Japanese people and state, and portrayed prevailing economic policies as opening fissures in Japanese society – between rural and urban communities, between workers and management, between small industry and the *zaibatsu* conglomerates, and between ordinary people and the industrial, political and social élite.

This ideology attracted support from many quarters within government, the military and civil society. Socially, many ultra-nationalist activists came from poor, predominantly rural backgrounds, and they harboured a well-nurtured sense of distrust and dislike of members of the Tokyo élite, whom they saw as 'soft' and lacking a spirit of self-denial and self-sacrifice for the state. Their view of politics and politicians was dismissive, and they remained highly suspicious of industrialists and of capitalism in general. The energy of these industrialists needed to be harnessed, but they also needed to be kept under firm control to ensure that they worked towards 'national' goals, not company goals. As the Great Depression deepened, so the clear-cut solutions of the ultra-nationalists, often backed by political terrorism, weakened support for civilian party politics; and ideologies such as militarism and state socialism, or corporatism which seemed to embody these ideas, became powerful forces in Japanese politics. From 1932 on, civilian political party leaders ceased to sit in the Cabinet, as the first of a series of 'national unity' cabinets took office under heavy army and navy influence. Governments ceased to be accountable to either popular or constitutional pressures, and the Japanese 'defence state' of the 1930s evolved as militarists began to mobilise the entire population for war against a wide range of internal and external enemies in the name of national unity and manifest destiny.

Such an ideology found its natural outlet in chauvinism and aggression. Abroad, Japan detached Manchuria from China in 1931, and further advances into northern China met with little effective resistance from the hard-pressed Nationalist Chinese. In the wake of criticism from the Western powers over its actions in Manchuria, Japan withdrew from the League of Nations in 1933, and so began to operate outside an increasingly shaky and impotent international order. Military activities in northern China gradually increased in scale and intensity until major military operations against China began in July 1937. This initiated an eight-year period in which the Japanese Empire experienced total war mobilisation.

The Korean economy in the 1930s

Colonial policy in Korea reflected the changing priorities in Japan. The replacement of Governor-General Admiral Saito by General Ugaki Kazushige in June 1931 began a new phase in Japanese colonial rule marked by the encouragement of military values throughout society, the provision of economic relief and recovery through state socialism, and the strenuous repression of labour activists, radicals, socialists and Korean nationalists. Ugaki took office at a time when the Great Depression had plunged the Korean rural economy – and hence the economy as a whole – into deep crisis. The collapse of rice prices in Japan in the late 1920s led Japanese businessmen to reduce imports, thus driving prices for Korean rice down. Meanwhile, costs rose as income fell, and so taxation rates, interest rates, and the purchase of manufactured goods consumed an ever-growing proportion of household income. Moreover, on smaller, more remote farms, the reach of agricultural technology in the form of irrigation, improved methods of farming, higher-yielding crop strains, and rural education was slight, and so actual productivity fell. A succession of official and semi-official reports during these years noted a marked fall in the proportion of owner-cultivators and a corresponding rise in the proportion of tenancy farmers. Under such pressure, the supply of tenant farmers exceeded demand and strengthened the hand of owner-cultivators in setting rents. The number of tenancy disputes rose rapidly, reaching a peak in 1933.

Landowners themselves were not immune from this crisis. Much of their wealth was tied up in agricultural land and produce, and many of the larger landowners used this as collateral on commercial debts. As this source of income dried up, creditors, who were mainly Japanese-run banks, foreclosed, and many former landowners became tenants on their own land. In 1931 mortgaged land was estimated at 40 per cent of total cultivated land. The income of both landlord and tenant virtually collapsed, and many fell hopelessly into high-interest debt. Although many people today believe that the Japanese dispossessed large numbers of Koreans of their land as an immediate consequence of colonisation in 1910, in fact relatively few ordinary Koreans lost their land at this stage. However, many Korean landholders could not withstand the impact of the steep decline in rice prices and, with the onset of the Great Depression, Japanese land ownership rose steeply, before levelling off in the mid-1930s.

The Government-General sought to restore the basis of the colony's economy through counter-measures which again reflected home government policy. Guided by a mixture of populism and pragmatism, it suppressed radicalism and co-opted moderate elements into the Movement of Rural Revival, which emphasised self-reliance, self-sufficiency and spiritual regeneration. It also enacted modest tenancy reform measures to check the growth in absentee landlordism and encourage resident cultivation. However, rural recovery depended on economic recovery in Japan itself, which would again open up the rice market. This began to occur in 1932, and by 1934 Korean agricultural prices had almost regained pre-1927 levels. A measure of prosperity began to return to rural Korea, although the value of rice as a cash crop still promoted the practice of famine export established during the 1920s. It is noteworthy that, despite the endemic poverty, despite the strong social division between gentry and commoner, and despite the economic division into landlord and tenant cultivation, widespread class-based conflict did not emerge in rural Korea during this period. A major reason seems to have been the shared privation of all parties, as well as the general blurring of clear-cut social and economic divisions brought about by tilling on the basis of part-ownership or part-tenancy. The great majority of landlords owned small plots, and shared the same village life with its communal patterns of work and reciprocal obligation. Studies of peasant–landlord conflicts in the 1930s therefore tend to find causes of disputes in local issues, which often defied broader socio-economic categorisation.

The Government-General also sought to alleviate the effects of the Great Depression by diversifying the colonial economy. The economic policies of the 1920s had produced a vulnerable economy which revolved around rice as the chief export and land as the chief source of wealth. However, as Korea emerged as an important rear supply base for Manchuria, Japan sought to stimulate manufacturing industry in Korea. This process began with a rapid increase in the mining of precious and non-ferrous metals such as gold, silver, lead, copper and zinc in the far north after 1932, from which a rudimentary industrial infrastructure emerged, drawing on Korean labour for mining, and Korean coal and hydroelectric power for the processing of minerals. The result was a far more diversified economy in which agriculture still figured prominently, but in which its actual contribution to gross product had declined from 60 per cent in 1931 to 32 per cent in 1942.

Under the impact of such industrialisation, a small industrial workforce came into being within Korea, eventually rising from 100,000 in 1930 to 400,000 in 1945. Hundreds of thousands more worked in industry abroad, mainly in Japan but also in Manchuria. Much of this new workforce comprised surplus rural labour; and, while many had left rural Korea to escape the hopeless cycle of tenancy and debt, as the 1930s progressed, workers were increasingly recruited and drafted by the government as the Japanese war economy took shape. A small cadre of Koreans became skilled technicians, especially as Japanese skilled workers were increasingly drafted into the military, but the bulk of this workforce comprised unskilled rural recruits who drifted in and out of industrial areas amid high turnover, high accident rates, and absenteeism. As was the case with Japanese labour, Korean labour was almost entirely unable to organise to express grievances, or to enjoy the protection of industrial legislation or regulation. The formation of a nascent Korean industrial labour force therefore took place under highly improvised, often coercive conditions.

Japanese capital dominated this process. Estimates of the Japanese share of the total paid-in industrial capital of the country by the 1940s vary between 70 per cent and 90 per cent, but capital investment is only one indicator of the dependent nature of Korean industrial development. Since Korea could produce only the most basic capital equipment, most industrial machinery was imported from Japan, while the dearth of vocational education institutions in Korea meant that most Koreans went to Japan for training in new technologies. Market structure and access was likewise determined in accordance with Japanese self-interest, for the somewhat rough-and-ready products of the new Korean industries found their markets almost exclusively in the economically underdeveloped lands of Japanese-controlled Manchuria and China.

The spread of education, the increasing regimentation, the growth of urban centres, and a marked rise in population mobility all affected Korean society. As the Government-General sought labour to exploit new opportunities to the north, immigration to Manchuria and Japan increased. The number of Koreans in Japan had risen from a mere handful in 1910, consisting mainly of students, to 419,000 in 1930. During the 1930s this population more than doubled to over a million. Similarly, the Korean population in Manchuria rose from 600,000 to 870,000 during 1930–36. With such mobility the sense that education and immigration were keys to the future also spread more rapidly in rural Korea during the 1930s. Villagers increasingly accepted that those who could afford the often sacrificial price would send their children to city schools, and they also came to realise that a growing proportion of them would not return.

Large-scale Korean emigration to Japan represented another source of social change. Under the various mobilisation measures of the late 1930s, the number of Koreans in Japan grew from 400,000 in 1930, to 690,503 in 1936, to 2,400,000 in 1945. Many Koreans originally entered Japan during the First World War boom years and stayed on amid increasing economic difficulty and often appalling social privation. The vast majority were unskilled rural people from the southern provinces, many of whom were short-term migrants. In time they formed a swelling underclass, working in the difficult, dangerous and dirty casual and day-labouring jobs which Japanese workers had abandoned as they moved to the relative comfort and security of the factory floor. It is not surprising that the Koreans gravitated towards other outcast and fringe dwellers, nor that they often became involved in radical politics. However, as the Japanese economy recovered in the early 1930s, the pattern of Korean migration became more socially stable, comprising an increasing number of whole families who stayed for extended periods. The phenomenon of second-generation Korean residents began to appear, and Koreans took advantage of their ghetto concentration in specific electorates to seek office; fifty-three Koreans were elected to local public office in Japan during 1919–39.

Postwar historians often attribute the rise of this community to forced labour or conscription, and in many cases Koreans were coerced and exploited. Nowhere was this more true than in the recruitment of 'comfort women'. Under this practice, tens of thousands of young Korean women were recruited ostensibly for regular employment in support of the Japanese war effort, then forced into service as sexual slaves in the vast chain of military-run brothels which sprang up behind Japanese front lines throughout China and South-East Asia. But, in general, Korean industrial workers in Japan responded as much to the promise of reward as to the presence of threat. Wartime conditions taxed Japanese powers of organisation and domestic surveillance to the limit, and the process of recruitment and deployment was frequently haphazard. As a result, Korean workers profited from the growing labour shortage and moved around Japan in search of better pay and conditions with surprising freedom, also figuring prominently in wartime labour disputes. Until Allied bombing of Japanese cities became a factor after June 1944, Koreans still tried to enter Japan illegally, and at war's end conscription accounted for only a minority of the resident Korean population of 2.4 million. Significant numbers of Koreans in Japan were drafted into the military after 1941, none participated in campaigns of sabotage such as those in Nazi-occupied Europe, and some 20 per cent of them ultimately elected to remain in Japan after 1945.

In the late 1930s assimilationism reached its most intense form in the policy of *naisen ittai*, or 'Japan and Korea as one body'. *Naisen ittai* sanctioned a comprehensive and diverse array of social and cultural policies, all designed to 'Japanise' Koreans. Tokyo intended that Korea would cease to be a colony and be ruled as an integral part of Japan itself. In preparation, Koreans would need to cultivate the 'Japanese spirit' that their rulers saw as an essential component of Japanese citizenship. Participation in Japanese Shintoist ceremonies and rituals associated with the cult of the Emperor became more intense, while manifestations of Korean culture were actively suppressed. The appointment of Minami Jiro as Governor-General in August 1936 marked an intensification of mobilisation and assimilation policies. Government oversight of industry became intense and detailed, encompassing allocation of raw materials, production quotas, and sale and distribution at fixed prices through sanctioned wholesaler cartels. Thus, manufacturing and industry functioned as an arm of military procurement, with human and material resources allocated to designated priority industries. Meanwhile, in imitation of practices within Japan itself, from 1937 to 1940 the remnants of the thousands of Korean social and cultural organisations which had mushroomed between 1920 and 1922 were forcibly dissolved and replaced by loyalist mass organisations which incorporated Korean farmers, workers, students, business-men and professionals into a network of associations whose overt aim was to support the Japanese war effort. In 1939 the Name Order, under which an estimated 84 per cent of Koreans were forced to adopt Japanese names, came into effect, and in August 1940 all non-official Korean language papers were closed down. However, although all vestiges of organised political protest, including farm tenancy disputes, ceased under wartime mobilisation, wartime Korean diaries and reminiscences suggest that amid the inefficiencies and exigencies of the Japanese war effort the authorities could enforce little more than surface conformity. This meant that significant numbers of Korean subjects could think, feel and even act without close Japanese oversight, and this in turn helped prepare the way for postwar radicalism.

Some argue that the 1930s mobilisation produced an incipient working class in Korea, and that this provided the basis for substantial political mobilisation in rural as well as urban areas after 1945. This remains contentious, for indices of modernisation must be taken alongside evidence of the strong persistence of tradition. Collapse of the political centre in 1910 did not mean collapse at the local level, and in the villages of Korea, where over 80 per cent of the population continued to live throughout the colonial period, many features of the traditional political culture continued to operate. Evidence from autobiographical and anthro-pological accounts of village life towards the end of this era and in the immediate post-1945 era does not suggest that the wide-ranging social and economic changes introduced by the Japanese had produced fundamental social changes at this level. New élites, defined by Japanese rule and committed to modernisation, were in the process of formation, but local communities retained a close material and spiritual attachment to land, the age-old class and status systems remained under-pinned by the enduring circumstances of occupation, family, lifestyle, education and marriage, and the penetration of new technology, communications and ideas to this level remained slight. Socially, Korea in the 1930s was a society undergoing mobilisation, not ferment.

Korean resistance

During the 1930s all Korean nationalist groups struggled against the immense power and reach of the Japanese Empire. Moderate nationalists strove for grad-ualist remedies, but their characteristic programmes of education, indigenous economic development and the reinforcement of Korean cultural identity were increasingly suppressed by the colonial authorities. During the period 1931–45, Koreans in Korea became practically powerless to organise politically. After the dissolution of the Singanhoe in 1931, moderate nationalists grew progressively less active in the face of Japanese pressure, while socialists and radicals, no longer constrained by united-front politics, sought more direct forms of action, including labour and peasant organisation and agitation within Korea and guerrilla and terrorist activities abroad.

Abroad, Korean nationalist activities were severely hampered by the lack of a foreign sanctuary. Their cause meant little or nothing to the Great Powers, including Great Britain, the United States and the Soviet Union, all of whom continued to accept the Japanese argument that Korea had lost the capacity to rule itself and that its people would benefit from Japanese colonial rule. As Japanese influence expanded in China, the Great Powers developed misgivings about Japanese policy, but this did not extend to support for Korean independence. Manchuria and later China were the major centres of Korean nationalist activity, but their fortunes declined steadily during the 1930s. The Korean Provisional Government in Shanghai became dysfunctional, while the Korean National Revolutionary Party, a radical party organised under Kim Wonbong in northern China in the mid-1930s, was in constant retreat before the Japanese advance. It eventually retreated to Chongqing, where it amalgamated with KPG remnants under Nationalist Chinese sponsorship. None of the various nationalist and communists groups gained sufficient stature to be recognised as governments-in-exile, nor were any Korean émigré groups recruited as part of the Allied war effort.

The Korean communists fared little better. Their movement first emerged against the background of the 1917 Bolshevik revolution and developed as a distinctive entity within the Korean nationalist exile movement. However, it was heterogeneous, ideologically unsophisticated, geographically dispersed and operationally ineffective. The different centres of activity rarely had contact with each other, and no leaders were widely recognised across the various sectors of the movement. Efforts at formal organisation within Korea failed with the demise of the Korean Communist Party in 1928, and henceforth the movement became a movement in exile. In Manchuria, the main theatre of operations, two main communist guerrilla groups emerged – those who remained outside the Chinese Communist Party (CCP) and those who fought under direct CCP leadership. The non-CCP guerrillas continued military operations until 1938, when they retreated deep into China and fought against the Japanese alongside the CCP. In postwar Korea they were known as the Yan'an Group, and they played a major role in the formation of the North Korean state.

The guerrillas who fought as Korean units under CCP control in Manchuria had a far more profound influence in postwar North Korea. In 1930 an 18-year-old activist named Kim Song-ju, who eventually took the name Kim Il Sung, joined the CCP in eastern Manchuria, and around 1932 became attached to one of the small guerrilla units operating in the district. Kim rose to become one of a dozen or so leading Koreans in the CCP guerrilla hierarchy, which at its height commanded some 15,000 fighters. Kim's vivid, highly selective memoirs depict small numbers of youthful, resolute fighters locked into a desperate, protracted struggle in a harsh climate against a well-equipped and ruthless enemy. For the most part they seemed in extended strategic retreat, interspersed with brief hit-and-run operations against isolated settlements and Japanese outposts, the most famous of which was the attack on the Korean border village of Bochonbo in 1937. From other contemporary sources we also learn of the subculture of guerrilla violence, involving robbery, extortion and internecine purges, in which Kim remained immersed for nearly ten years, until Japanese pressure forced the guerrillas to cease effective operations. In 1940, when Kim finally left Manchuria for the Soviet Union, he was one of the last remaining active CCP guerrilla commanders.

Conclusion

On the eve of liberation in 1945, Koreans looked at themselves primarily through the distorting prisms of colonialism and imperialism. Economically, it is hardly possible to overestimate the Japanese role in consolidating a modern educational, communication, transport, financial and local government infrastructure. Yet it is also hard to overestimate the effect of Japan's skewed economic priorities. Japan sought the economic growth of Japan in Korea, not the economic development of Korea *per se*, and it sought much of this growth for the purpose of making war. Writing in 1935, George McCune expressed a common assessment in noting that 'it is the Japanese who have, in the majority, gained the profits coming from this expansion while few of the Koreans have benefited and many are in a worse state'.

The legacy of the Japanese defence state and economy was contradictory and divisive. On the one hand it was midwife to a far-reaching modernisation process, and was also the direct antecedent government of both Korean states. However, it was also a despised and discredited régime which discriminated against and demeaned many Koreans. In contrast to government under the Choson dynasty with its heavy reliance on self regulation, the Japanese defence state legitimated the establishment of an all-embracing state administrative structure. It also acculturated Koreans to the acceptance of strong central government which intervened in selected areas of clan, family and individual life far more pervasively than its predecessor. The defence state also mandated the enforcement of semi-wartime mobilisation as the more or less normal condition for the population as a whole, and sanctioned the rigorous suppression of activities that ran counter to the government's military and industrial goals. Statistics testify to the scale of Japanese-led development, but it is perhaps more eloquent to note that within five years of liberation the North mobilised and invaded the South, then mobilised its population to effect a massive programme of recovery and industrialisation. When the South launched its own sustained programme of industrialisation in the 1960s it, too, built substantially on knowledge and expertise acquired during the 1910–45 period.

Korean society and culture changed markedly under the Japanese. As public health improved, birth rates rose, death rates declined, and the population rose from an estimated 15 million in 1910 to some 24 million in 1940. Well over half the population was still illiterate in 1945, but the Japanese had extended the education system developed by Koreans in the years leading up to 1910. More generally, cultural values had begun to change as the disestablishment of Neo-Confucianism led to more open views of social purpose, change and innovation among the élite. Economic growth stimulated the beginnings of an urbanised society, of a mass media, and of new directions in the arts and in literature. In the process of applying science and technology to agricultural production and to the large-scale exploitation of natural resources, key ideas about modernisation disseminated – that things could change for the better, and that social status, wealth and influence could be acquired through modern education and personal achievement as well as through inherited class privilege. This was the formative background of a future modernising Korean élite of businessmen, bankers, bureaucrats, soldiers and professionals imbued with the Japanese economic corporatist model of a strong state seeking high rates of economic growth, and allocating finite human and capital resources like a military high command.

Such changes came hand in hand with the ideology of assimilationism. Koreans were constantly reminded in demeaning and humiliating terms that their cultural heritage summed up all that was backward, reprehensible and useless in the modern world, and that only in Japanese culture and practice could they find what they required to become a 'modern' people. In strictly material terms many Koreans derived benefits under Japanese rule, but they remain unconsoled by such thoughts, for the Japanese did great damage to the cultural psyche. Inability to see that individual Korean identity was rooted in community and culture, and the attempted separation of Koreans from this profound and complex culture, gave expression to an ideology of racial arrogance which undergirded Japanese thoughts, feelings, policies and practices. The way rulers define subjects shapes the way they rule them. Japan did not define Koreans in terms of a shared humanity.

Because of the length and intensity of Japanese rule, in one way or another all Koreans had to reach an accommodation with the colonial order. Some went further than others and actively participated in it, raising the issue of collaboration which, broadly speaking, had two major components: attacks on individuals mainly in the immediate postwar era, and political attacks on successive ruling élites in South Korea, which incorporated elements of the former colonial élite. This issue arises primarily because by the mid-1930s most members of the Korean colonial élite had been educated and socialised almost entirely under Japanese auspices. Unless one were an exile or a guerrilla, a professional career in education, business, the civil service or the military automatically meant a close relationship with the Japanese authorities. Neutrality was rarely an option for such people, and to be a Korean and a Japanese subject represented a psychological burden which divided the self. Some resolved it through adopting the conviction that to be Korean and a loyal servant of the Empire involved little contradiction, while for others it represented an agonising conflict of loyalties. Either way, the issue remained, in Hahm Pyong-choon's words, 'a fissure in the national identity' for a generation after 1945.

Koreans were not alone in confronting this legacy. In Europe vast areas were subject to Nazi occupation during 1939–45, and in many countries collaboration became a major issue in postwar politics. Participants in Nazi war crimes and overt collaborators like the Norwegian Vidkun Quisling were tried and executed for their crimes, but most European governments assessed that the taint of collaboration adhered to almost every person who had exercised authority under Nazi occupation, and that this issue had the potential to tear their societies apart. Most therefore elected to downplay the issue and propagate the myth of heroic resistance by the majority. Only much later did revisionist historians, novelists and film-makers in Europe gain a public forum to demonstrate the manifold, widespread and complex nature of such collaboration. This has not yet happened in Korea.

In isolating Korea from international contact, in applying extreme coercion to non-loyalist Koreans, in excluding Koreans from any legislative role, in constraining not just civil society but also the meaningful expression of public opinion, and in offering Koreans only the most marginal role in bureaucratic decision-making, the Japanese left a deep and powerful legacy. In 1945, Koreans were ready to regain their independence but had no persuasive answers to the fundamental question of who among them would rule independent Korea.

Selected reading

Eckert, Carter J. 1991, *Offspring of Empire: The Koch'ang Kims and the Colonial Origins of Korean Capitalism, 1876–1945*, Seattle, WA: University of Washington Press.

Gragert, Edwin H. 1994, *Landownership under Colonial Rule: Korea's Japanese Experience, 1900–1935*, Honolulu: University of Hawaii Press.

Grajdanzev, Andrew J. 1944, *Modern Korea*, New York: The Institute of Pacific Relations/ John Day Company.

Han, Chungnim C. 1987 [1949], 'Social Organization of Upper Han Hamlet in Korea', dissertation thesis, University of Michigan, reprinted in *Transactions of the Royal Asiatic Society Korea Branch*, vol. 62, pp. 1–142.

Kim, Richard E. 1970, *Lost Names: Scenes from a Korean Boyhood*. Seoul: Sisayongo-sa Publishing Co.

McCune, George M. 1950, *Korea Today*, London: Allen & Unwin.

Shin, Gi-Wook 1996, *Peasant Protest and Social Change in Colonial Korea*, Seattle, WA: University of Washington Press.

Suh, Dae-Sook 1967, *The Korean Communist Movement 1918–1948*, Princeton, NJ: Princeton University Press.

Suh, Sang Chul 1978, *Growth and Structural Changes in the Korean Economy, 1910–1940*, Cambridge, MA: Harvard University Press.

3   Bitter liberty, 1945–48 .

Japan launched an all-out war against China in 1937 but, while the China campaign delivered large territorial gains, it also drained Japanese resources and produced no decisive military outcome. Meanwhile, increasing friction with the Western powers and the United States led to the simultaneous Japanese attacks on Pearl Harbor, French Indochina and British Malaysia on 7–8 December 1941 and the beginning of the Pacific War. Initial Japanese expansion was rapid, but within a year the US-led allies regrouped and began to apply their superior naval and industrial power to telling effect. During 1942–45 Japan suffered crippling losses and gradually yielded up all its occupied territory. On 15 August 1945 it finally accepted terms of unconditional surrender to the Allied powers after the destruction of Hiroshima and Nagasaki by atomic bombs.

The Allied powers proceeded to determine the immediate future of Korea in accordance with the Cairo Declaration of 1 December 1943, in which the US, the Soviet Union and Britain declared that Korea's independence would be restored to it upon the defeat of Japan 'in due course'. However, although this declaration signalled that sovereignty would not pass directly from the Japanese to the Koreans, Allied policy was otherwise confused, mainly because amid the immense and complex array of strategic problems which dominated wartime summit meetings Korea received only cursory attention. Ultimately, in early August 1945 the Soviet Union, which had declared war against Japan on 8 August, and the US agreed to a joint occupation of Korea to receive the Japanese surrender, with the 38th parallel of latitude fixed as the dividing line between the two forces. On 24 August the Soviets entered Pyongyang and established themselves as the military government of North Korea. On 8 September the US arrived in Seoul, and established the United States Military Government in Korea (USMGIK) in South Korea. Korea was divided into two occupation zones, and basic decision-making on the path to future independence rested with these two occupiers.

Liberation and occupation also brought about an immediate clash of aspirations between the 'liberated' Koreans and the two occupying powers. The Korean perspective was local: the major domestic political figures in the North and the South were prepared to use foreign influence to advance their various causes, but they wanted, expected and demanded to go their own independent way, however unclear that path might be and wherever it might lead. By contrast, the Soviet and US perspective was regional and global: the Koreans could govern themselves, but only by conforming with the broader strategic interests of their respective occupiers – bolstered in each case by distinct political ideologies which became increasingly rigid with the onset of the Cold War. The Great Power perspective promoted the interests of local clients who understood and agreed to abide by the new rules of the game, but ran counter to the ambitions of Korean nationalism, lending cogency to the observation that in 1945 Korea traded one occupier for two. The irony, and the seed of future tragedy, here was that, after decades of unsuccessful attempts to place the cause of Korean independence on the international agenda, Korea had now got what it thought it wanted. The 'Korean question' of the colonial era finally engaged the attention of the two superpowers, who committed themselves to the reconstitution of an independent Korea, but who rapidly became the major obstruction to Korean independence.

Foreign occupation provided the basic context for the domestic struggle for power. In theory, the outlook was promising. The pre-1910 dynastic order had vanished and was unmourned, while public rhetoric emphasised that the new nation-in-waiting would be a democratic republic, dedicated to economic development, and defined by social equality, equality of opportunity and a strong reassertion of Korean identity. Land reform was a common platform, and punishment for collaborators was the general expectation. Taken together with cultural homogeneity and the common suffering under the Japanese, these elements seemed to constitute an important foundation for national unity and common political purpose.

However, significant elements of contention were also present. Cultural homogeneity was undercut by strong local and regional traditions, people had had widely divergent experiences of Japanese colonial rule, and political groups expressed discordant views on what the guiding ideology of an independent Korea should be – capitalist, corporatist, socialist, or communist. Moreover, would-be Korean reformers still faced a profound and unacknowledged contradiction in that they sought to usher in a new political order on top of a so-called 'backward' traditional order that was still a daily reality for almost all Koreans. Thirty-five years of colonial rule had set loose the forces of urbanisation, industrialisation and modernisation, and created new political and social forces, but these forces had only spasmodically touched the 80 per cent of Korea's population which still lived in small rural communities, where a profound and intricate political culture and social hierarchy remained largely intact. At this level, community political leadership issued largely from such key attributes as age, social status and educational attainment, and so political energies and allegiances remained strongly personalistic. Such a political culture did not relate easily to politics on the national level and competing, distant, impersonal ideologies.

Local politics and experiences were a major determinant of attitudes to major issues. They determined whether people supported land reform as an instrument of class warfare aimed at destroying the landed-gentry class, as sought by the communists, or else as a milder measure of equity, as sought by leftists and centrists in general. Local experience also influenced the extent and severity of retribution that people thought appropriate for collaborators, for colonised Koreans had seen how in myriad forms daily activities had forced collaboration on them, often in ways that were painful and demeaning. These diverse experiences gave the issue a complexity during 1945–48 that could not be captured by the vengeful rhetoric of social revolutionaries and returning exiles. Moreover, much as Koreans might reject the Japanese colonial experience, for more than a generation the Japanese had been the prime agents of modernisation. Unless Koreans were to return to pre-1910 ways, they had to grapple with the challenge of determining which colonial forms, procedures, practices and technologies to accept and which to discard.

Occupying Korea: the first moves

Although politics in the Soviet and US zones provided many sharp contrasts, during 1945–48 both zones passed from military occupation government to independence through a number of common stages. These stages more or less tracked the broader stages of the disintegrating wartime alliance of the Soviet Union and the US. The first stage lasted a matter of weeks after the Japanese surrender, and during this period Koreans engaged in vigorous political mobilisation activities without occupying power interference. In the second stage, which lasted from September 1945 to January 1946, the occupying powers made concerted efforts to harness this activity to serve their respective interests. In both cases this meant promoting their clients, most of whom were returned exiles, and marginalising their clients' opponents. In the third period, which lasted from January 1946 to the proclamation of the two Korean states in 1948, the occupying powers sought – with mixed success – to fill the political vacuum they had created by giving power to clients who had limited grass-roots support. The transfer of power to a Stalinist-communist régime in the North and a rightist-conservative régime in the South created two antagonistic Korean states and established the conditions for subsequent warfare.

The US and the Soviet Union arrived at their 'in due course' 1943 Cairo formula for the postwar government of Korea amid the chaotic and improvised conditions of wartime diplomacy. When the Potsdam Conference convened in June 1945 after the final defeat of Germany and the end of the war in Europe, European affairs dominated the agenda, and the Allies merely reaffirmed the Cairo Declaration. Then, with the defeat of Japan looming, the Allied focus on Korea changed from that of a potential combat zone to that of a post-surrender occupation zone. On 10 August the US proposed to the Soviets a joint occupation to receive the Japanese surrender, with the 38th parallel dividing the two occupation zones. This boundary, hastily conceived at a late-night military planning-group session in Washington, passed north of Seoul and most other main population centres of the country. It allocated 37,055 square miles (100,790 square kilometres) and a Korean population of some 16 million to the US, and 48,191 square miles (130,115 square kilometres) with a population of some 9 million to the Soviets.

The broader relationship between these two powers did much to shape their respective Korean policies. The defeat of Germany and Japan was an absolute priority and formed the basis of a wartime alliance between the US and the Soviet

Union which of necessity papered over significant political and strategic differences. US policy was habitually guided by European priorities and experience, and therefore during 1945 it sought to uphold the wartime alliance with the Soviets and bid for their co-operation in the postwar settlement. In East Asia, US policy on Korea was strongly influenced by the Soviet factor, for in its own right the Korean peninsula was insignificant in Washington's strategic thinking. However, although the US had sought Soviet participation in the projected invasion of Japan, after the surrender of Japan it soon began to harbour doubts about the compatibility of Soviet strategic objectives in postwar Japan, and opted to exclude the Soviets from any role in the occupation of Japan. The wartime alliance disintegrated rapidly, distrust mounted, and Korea in particular fell victim to hardening, confrontationist attitudes as the Cold War began.

At this stage the Soviets had done little to define their interests in Korea. With Japan defeated, with China absorbed in civil war, and with the US having no history as an intrusive influence in Korea, many Korean public figures expected the Soviets to play a dominant role in Korean affairs. After a ruinous war, however, Soviet objectives were modest and defensive. Regionally, they sought to contain Japan and to establish a friendly buffer zone in Korea to open up transport and communication links for the Soviet Far East, for which it was essential to have access to ice-free ports such as Rajin and Wonsan on the east coast of Korea. As Stalin reportedly said at the time: 'We are closed up. We have no outlet. One should keep Japan vulnerable from all sides, north, west, south, east; then she will keep quiet.' These objectives in turn were subject to the overriding priority of avoiding unnecessary conflict with the US as the two Great Powers grappled over more important issues of postwar reconstruction. As a result, Soviet policy in Korea in 1945 was cautious and tentative, guided more by general guidelines and principles than by specific initiatives.

The speed of the Japanese collapse in August 1945 caught both occupying powers by surprise, and left neither in a position to enter Korea immediately upon the Japanese surrender. The Soviets were already in the far north of the country but did not enter Pyongyang until 24 August. The Americans did not arrive in Seoul until 8 September. Both found a situation in which the old order had disappeared, there was no in-country insurgent movement and no credible government-in-exile waiting in the wings. Immediately after the 15 August surrender, the Chosen Governor-General, Abe Nobuyuki, had reached an agreement with the veteran leftist leader Lyuh Woon-hyung for the transfer of colonial authority to an organisational framework, the Preparation Committee for Korean Independence (PCKI), which in turn had links, often quite tenuous links, with local People's Committees. These Committees had sprung up more or less spontaneously throughout the peninsula out of the highly self-regulatory framework of local communities with the major objective of ensuring law and order and the continuing operation of basic services. By the end of August some 150 of these committees had been formed.

No single political ideology dominated the PCKI. Rather, it functioned as a loosely knit united front which contained a broad spectrum of political opinion and

individuals, forced into momentary cohesion by the euphoria of liberation, and by the general unwillingness of potential leaders to make decisive moves until the future became clearer. Nevertheless, the political transformation of the country was immediate and profound. The sudden disappearance of the existing government, the deliverance from submersion in the Japanese Empire, and the cessation of the Japanese war effort removed strong driving reins. The edifice of Japanese colonialism, made to seem so permanent by authoritarian rule, rapidly disintegrated and took with it many of the restraints and attitudes of obedience and resignation. In its place new political and social forces, long suppressed under the Japanese, rose to the surface, and political activity emphasised both anti-Japanese rhetoric and the strident affirmation of principles of equal opportunity, land reform, broad access to education, social mobility and modernisation.

The sense of a slate wiped clean favoured the political left. Socialists and communists had a record of uncompromising resistance to the Japanese occupation, and their identification of the colonial wealth created by the Japanese and their Korean businessmen allies with exploitation was intrinsically persuasive, as was a programme which called for a redistribution of such wealth. Of all the PCKI's components, the most assiduous and dedicated in terms of organisation and mobilisation were domestic communists, many of whom had lately emerged from prison, hiding or inactivity. Although they were numerically small and lacked a mass base, they were skilled at political combat and, being familiar with the strategies and tactics of united front politics, they acted purposefully amid the chaos and disorder. As a result, they brought a solid organisational core to the PCKI and began to direct the process of transformation into a successor government.

In the North the Soviets were familiar with such politics, for the Korean communists were following paths which had essentially developed out of Bolshevik and Soviet experience. Consequently, when the Soviets entered Pyongyang on 24 August 1945 and found a local PCKI operating under the leadership of veteran nationalist and Presbyterian elder Cho Mansik, they designated it as their instrument of rule and set about transforming it into a local régime responsive to Soviet interests. It was relatively easy to increase communist representation, and so the twenty-member PCKI committee, which included two communists, was promptly reconstituted by the Soviets into a committee of thirty-two, which included sixteen persons of some standing within the communist movement. The Soviets also became a forceful influence throughout their zone of occupation, dissolving and reconstituting People's Committees to achieve the desirable level of communist representation.

However, the Soviet search for reliable Korean clients over the longer term was a more complicated and challenging task. To begin with, the Soviets regarded the domestic Korean communists with suspicion. Relations had been fractious in the past, and the Soviets were by instinct wary of local independent communist networks, which might not be as responsive to direct pressure from Moscow as the Soviets might wish. When they found such networks in Eastern Europe they quickly brought them under control from Moscow, and in Korea they did likewise. Moreover, by 1945 ineffective domestic leadership, lack of popular support,

Japanese repression, and lack of Soviet assistance had all combined to marginalise the Korean communist movement. The Korean Communist Party (KCP) itself ceased to exist in 1928, the Manchurian guerrilla movement petered out in the late 1930s, and the Korean communists in China proper, usually referred to as the Yan'an group, were far removed from Korea and deeply involved in the ongoing civil war against the Chinese Nationalists. In August 1945 the Soviet Union's Korean assets were therefore restricted to the remnants of a scattered underground network, a small Korean military brigade fashioned out of ex-guerrilla remnants and stationed in the Soviet Far East, members of the Yan'an group, and a community of some 400,000 ethnic Soviet-Koreans, among whom could be found many reliable, experienced, bilingual party cadres. Each group had its limitations, but the Soviets quickly blended them into a new political and administrative élite.

The role of the Soviet-Koreans in North Korea was crucial. Compatible Korean communists were either soldiers, guerrillas, or underground-movement organisers who had little experience in routine bureaucratic activity, whereas significant numbers of Soviet citizens of Korean background had career backgrounds in local government, party and security organisations. Such ethnic Koreans, whose families had mostly left Korea two or three generations previously, were initially deployed in interpreting and intermediary roles, but by the end of 1945 Soviet-Korean cadres were also placed in senior positions throughout the North Korean administration in the fields of government, education, the media, the military, party organisation, propaganda and training. Among them were cadres such as Ho Ka-i, Pak Ch'ang-ok, Pak I-wan, Nam Il and Pang Hak-se, many of whom remained at the top of the North Korean political hierarchy for many years afterward.

However, the Soviet-Koreans were Soviet citizens and could not credibly assume positions of political leadership, while most of the domestic Korean communists under Pak Hon-yong located themselves in Seoul, which they identified as the strategic nerve-centre for the postwar political struggle. Options for actual political leadership in the North were therefore limited. Local Northern communist leaders such as Hyon Chun-hyok proved unresponsive to Soviet 'guidance', the Yan'an cadres were objects of deep suspicion because of their close ties with the Chinese Communist Party, and non-communists such as Cho Mansik were not prepared to front a communist-dominated government. This was the context in which Kim Il Sung and sixty-six other Korean officers from the 88th Red Army Brigade arrived in Wonsan on 19 September 1945 and were demobilised. The guerrillas had operated outside Soviet control during the 1930s, but had been resident in the Soviet Union during 1941–45. They had trained as part of the Red Army and, although their military skills were now surplus to requirements, they offered the Soviets a solution to the leadership problem, for they could be assembled into a politically reliable indigenous leadership group.

Accordingly, on 14 October the Soviets introduced the 33-year-old Kim Il Sung to the North Korean public as a guerrilla hero and major political figure. There was substance to this claim, but it also involved considerable overstatement for although Kim had fought with courage and perseverance during the 1930s, he had fought in a remote, small-scale, Chinese communist-led campaign, and was virtually unknown not only to the general public but also to the Korean communist movement itself. Nevertheless, the Soviets soon overcame this lack of public profile by heavily promoting Kim through the Northern media. Local communists who opposed Kim's emergence were either eliminated, shunted aside or placed under the firm control of the Soviet-Koreans, and the ex-guerrillas established positions of control within the Northern branches of the Korean Communist Party, so that by 18 December 1945, when the Northern provincial committees of the Korean Communist Party combined to form a North Korean Communist Party, Kim's group was in effective control. Kim's personal power was limited, he was surrounded by strong competing factions, and the Soviets maintained basic control over political activities, but within four months the ex-Manchurian guerrilla had risen from the status of demobilised Red Army soldier to leadership of the Korean communist movement in the North.

Why Kim? The heavy cult of personality built up around Kim Il Sung in the 1950s and beyond portrayed him as a genius-hero, but no objective account from the immediate postwar era credits him with exceptional military or political ability, or with the personal charisma that might attract a following. Nor did Kim's guerrilla record automatically command a following, for there were many other nationalist figures who had fought for the same things as Kim, and who were older, better educated, better connected and far better placed to command a broader political following than Kim. However, the Soviets were innately suspicious of such qualities as charisma and grass-roots support, and seem to have been attracted to Kim as an archetypal political-military cadre in the Soviet mould – efficient, unquestioning, obedient and deferential. Moreover, Kim was well suited to the ruthless politics of mobilisation and class warfare, for his decade-long immersion in violent partisan warfare contrasted with the more cosmopolitan, intellectual struggles of the domestic Korean communists. In the final analysis, however, if it seemed less than likely that Kim might attract much allegiance in Pyongyang in 1945, it was even less likely that he needed to, for all other returning guerrillas were disarmed by the Soviets. Only the Kimists retained their weapons.

In the South, the ongoing conflict between domestic political forces was shaped definitively by the arrival in Seoul of the US occupation forces on 9 September 1945. Like the Soviets, the US authorities immediately found themselves at cross-purposes with the local Koreans. On the eve of the US arrival, the PCKI had hastily summoned local delegates to a congress in Seoul and elected a 55-member central committee, which in turn established a governmental structure called the People's Republic of Korea (PRK). The PRK claimed a mandate as the representative government of Korea, and sought recognition from the US authorities. However, the US saw itself as an occupying force and so was not prepared to recognise any provisional government. Moreover, unlike the Soviets, who well understood the advantages and possibilities of intense local political mobilisation, the US occupiers were accustomed to political behaviour which had its roots in calmer, more dispassionate forms of debate and looser forms of political organisation. The mass mobilisation of colonised subjects under leftist-nationalist leadership was an alien and disturbing form of politics to them. As a result, within a matter of weeks the USMGIK developed an antagonistic relationship with the PRK. On 10 October it described the PRK as being 'entirely without any authority, power or reality', and on 12 December it outlawed the PRK.

The PRK's united front and its quasi-revolutionary mobilisation strategies were well suited to the fluid first weeks of liberation, when it captured the mood of the country, articulated the issues and swept all before it. But it needed a vacuum to operate in, and as new, specific political structures, interests and ideologies emerged, many groups within the united front began to define separate political objectives and break away to pursue their own agendas. Initial communist influence within the PRK organisation had been low-key but as it became increasingly overt and disproportionate, conservative, moderate and non-communist leftist elements began to keep their distance and establish their own political organisations. With such newly established political parties on the scene, the PRK was no longer an effective vehicle for building a united front, and by December 1945 was a spent force.

The demise of the PRK meant the demise of united front politics in the South, and Korean politics assumed a pattern of conflict between smaller groups. Chief among these groups were members of the former Korean Provisional Government led by Kim Ku, rightist forces grouped behind the Korean Democratic Party, Lyuh Woon-Hyung's leftist Korean People's Party, the Korean Communist Party led by Pak Hon-yong, and Syngman Rhee, who was commonly recognised as the dominant personality in the ranks of the political exiles, and who had returned to Seoul from the US amid much fanfare on 16 October. In addition to these four major players, myriad smaller parties emerged. Like the Rhee camp, they were typically organised around a dominant individual rather than a distinctive political platform or ideology. By October 1945 more than fifty political parties had registered themselves, and by 1948 this number had risen to 344. The Americans moved uncertainly amid this unfamiliar political culture – untrained, unprepared, and perhaps largely uninterested in the task at hand as they attempted to fashion alliances and coalitions in a quixotic search for the coherent representative politics they themselves associated with the democratic way. This frequently led them to favour English-speaking moderates and rightists, and here the group which most closely met their idea of a viable political élite was the leadership group of the Korean Democratic Party (KDP). Founded on 16 September 1945 as a conservative opposing force to the PRK, the KDP leaders comprised mainly Japan- and US-educated intellectuals, moderate nationalists and men of property, all of whom were reasonably well disposed towards the USMGIK, and who were qualified for appointment to high positions within it.

From the outset, the USMGIK laboured under a number of disadvantages. Like the Soviets it operated within an uncertain policy framework and within an inefficient chain of command. However, unlike the Soviets the US occupation authorities had no equivalent of the Soviet-Korean cadres, Moreover, although the Soviets imposed ruthless political discipline throughout their occupation zone, the USMGIK rarely acted with purpose or authority. As a result, slowly and surely political life in the South lost coherence. Generally speaking, the groups that the US communicated with most effectively were élite groups with little mass support, while the groups they communicated with least effectively were non-élite groups which exercised considerable power at the local level. Consequently, US hostility towards the local People's Committees in particular was a major cause of political instability. These committees often reflected the balance of local political power; and, like the Soviets, the US knew little about them and had little use for them. Whereas the Soviets preserved and reconstituted this local structure to make it more responsive to the political centre, the USMGIK typically dissolved these committees and created alternative forms of representation, thus alienating people from central political authority. In many cases the Committees only ceased to exist in a formal sense, and continued to operate informally as centres of dissent and resistance against outside influence. In both occupation zones the means employed were different but the result was the same: by the end of 1945 each political centre had only a tenuous relationship with grass-roots political activity.

The Moscow Agreement and its aftermath

As the Soviets and the Americans moved to clarify the intent of the Cairo Declaration, the lines of domestic political battle were drawn with greater clarity and precision. On 27 December 1945 the wartime Allied powers met in Moscow and, among many other decisions relating to the shape of the postwar world, agreed that the Soviet Union, the United States, China and Britain should constitute a four-power trusteeship of Korea for up to five years with the object of preparing the country for independence. The agreement also provided for a Soviet–US Joint Commission to work towards the establishment of a unified provisional Korean government. In fact, by now neither the US nor the Soviets viewed trusteeship as a viable policy. The Soviets had already signalled their belief that exclusive control of North Korea was preferable to a four-party trusteeship arrangement for the entire peninsula by placing numerous Soviet-Koreans throughout the North Korean government and party organs, and by establishing an increasingly autonomous Northern branch of the Korean Communist Party. Influential parties within the US government had also reached the conclusion that trusteeship was not viable.

For the moment, however, both occupying powers publicly espoused trusteeship, and worked strenuously to pull domestic political parties and organisations into line to support it. This was no easy matter, since the Moscow accords constituted a major affront to Korean nationalist aspirations and immediately caused large-scale demonstrations and protests throughout Korea. In the North, Cho Mansik opposed trusteeship on 4 January 1946 at a meeting of the People's Committee, whereupon he swiftly disappeared into house arrest and on to an unknown fate. He was never seen in public again. Cho was the last-remaining non-communist Northern political figure with some claim to an independent political base, and in the wake of his disappearance Soviet strategy firmed in favour of establishing a friendly buffer state in the North, leaving open the option of pressing for a unified Korean state under Communist Party leadership at a later date, should the opportunity arise.

The reaction to the Moscow Agreement in the South was also vociferous and had far-reaching effects. An aroused public, in search of an issue on which to vent frustrated nationalist sentiment, backed waves of public demonstrations against the Moscow accords. The USMGIK attempted to fashion some form of representative body which could credibly speak for Koreans while at the same time supporting trusteeship, and so on 14 February created the Representative Democratic Council of South Korea. However, not only were its members drawn from a small rightist segment of the political spectrum, but even they remained far from compliant on the trusteeship issue. Meanwhile, the effect on the Korean communists in the South was profound and destructive, for although they had prepared themselves to join in the anti-trusteeship front they were quickly reined in by the Soviet Union, which for tactical reasons insisted upon unconditional support from all Korean parties for the Moscow accords. The communists complied and advocated acceptance of trusteeship, but at profound cost to their nationalist credentials. Not for the first or last time, a client communist party had its strategies and future prospects determined by the mother party, and the KCP's retreat from a party with claims to a mass support base to a small vanguard party of the revolution in the South gathered speed at this point.

After the Moscow accords the Soviet–US breach proceeded to widen rapidly. The phrase 'in due course' had come back to haunt both occupying powers for while it had quickly become clear to them that trusteeship did not fit actual conditions in Korea, sufficient sense of trust or commonality of purpose no longer existed to permit the renegotiation of wartime agreements. In March 1946 the Joint American–Soviet Commission, an outcome of the Moscow Conference, met but became stalemated almost immediately when the Soviets insisted that only those who accepted trusteeship should be consulted on the issue of Korean trusteeship and independence. By 8 May, when the Commission adjourned indefinitely, it had become clear that Korea would remain divided into two antagonistic client states indefinitely.

The popular reaction to the Moscow accords accelerated the ongoing creation of two separate régimes in the two occupation zones. In the North, a conference of parties, organisations and district provisional people's committees convened on 8 February 1946 produced a reconstituted Interim People's Committee structure which had heavy communist representation. Within weeks the economic foundations for an autonomous state and the political foundations of a socialist state in the North were laid, including the promulgation of a new basic civil law code, the achievement of rapid land reform, and the nationalisation of all remaining ex-Japanese industry and property. This was accompanied by measures both to defend and to isolate the embryonic state, including the strengthening of defence installations along the demilitarised zone (DMZ), the restriction of movement between North and South, and the intensification of communist militancy in the South.

Progress towards the creation of a one-party state in the North was also rapid. In August 1946 the NKCP and the Yan'an group's New People's Party (*Shinmindang*) amalgamated to form the North Korean Workers' Party (NKWP). In December the united front mechanism, which had been in abeyance after the demise of the PRK, was reborn in the shape of the Korean National Democratic Front (KNDF), consisting of all Northern parties and all Southern workers' parties, but under the effective control of the NKWP. When the first elections for provincial, county and city level People's Committees were held in late 1946, 97 per cent of the electorate voted for the KNDF slate. Then, in February 1947, a further Congress of People's Committees formed a People's Assembly, which was again dominated by NKWP members and allies. It ratified the actions of the previous Interim People's Committee and named a new Committee, no longer interim. Finally, at the Second Party Congress in March 1948, Kim Il Sung and his group carried out a major purge of the remaining Northern domestic communists and secured a hold over the party that he was never to relinquish. Likewise, in August 1948 the election of a new Supreme People's Assembly confirmed communist control over the government. With control over party and government secure, on 3 September a new constitution was promulgated, and the establishment of the Democratic People's Republic of Korea (DPRK) was proclaimed on 9 September.

Politics in the South were far less organised. With trusteeship effectively a dead issue after January 1946, and with a Soviet-style socialist system already being installed in the North, the USMGIK search for some form of representative government capable of ruling a united Korea centred on the increasingly forlorn hope of encouraging a coalition of 'moderates' as the first step towards national government. In effect, this called upon rightists and leftists to paper over their differences on the trusteeship issue – always unlikely given the chasm opened up by the trusteeship issue. In an effort to devolve administrative responsibility to the Korean bureaucracy and political responsibility to some form of representative assembly, in August 1946 the USMGIK resolved to establish a 90-seat Interim Legislative Assembly, to be half-elected and half-appointed. The process – it could not be called an election – took place during 17–22 October under heavy police and official supervision and in an atmosphere of communist- and leftist-led agitation and violence. Most of the elected representatives were therefore 'moderates' and rightists, as were the appointed members. However, when the Assembly convened in December 1946, it soon transpired that the USMGIK had merely created a new forum for robust factional politics. Even as an interim deliberative body, the Assembly lacked an institutional sense of purpose, such as might have transcended partisan political warfare. It also lacked broad public credibility since, although it had been charged with preparing serious legislation on electoral procedure and land reform, its debates and decisions were subject to USMGIK veto, and therefore carried little weight. This election marked an inauspicious beginning for popular representative government in South Korea.

Meanwhile, the South Korean economy deteriorated significantly. Until 1945 most of Korean industrial production had been geared either directly or indirectly to the Japanese war effort, and foreign trade was conducted almost entirely within the Japanese Empire. In August 1945 war goods production suddenly became purposeless, and the Empire's markets disappeared. As Japanese economic administration ceased, so senior technical and managerial expertise withdrew and the colonial banking and financial infrastructure collapsed, resulting in a paralysis of economic activity and control. Moreover, the economies of northern and southern Korea had always been deeply complementary, but as relations between the two occupying powers deteriorated, inter-zone trade became subject to increasing disruption. As a result, between 1944 and 1946 the number of factories still operating declined by 43.7 per cent, and those that remained in production operated at an average 20 per cent of total capacity.

The basic problem was that South Korea could not pay its own way. Some three-quarters of its revenue under the Japanese had been obtained from the operation of public utilities and government monopolies, but owing to the various dislocations this revenue now plummeted. The remainder came from tax collection, and this also became easy to avoid in the post-liberation chaos. Total revenue therefore quickly dropped to less than half basic annual expenditure at a time of rising popular expectations of government. For a while South Korea was cushioned from the impact of these factors because of the resilience of its agricultural economy. The cessation of famine export restored the stock of rice available for consumption to pre-1920 levels, but in 1946 the overall food situation again began to worsen owing to adverse weather, the lack of Japanese-produced chemical fertiliser, and an increasingly chaotic distribution system, As the Japanese wartime control system broke down, speculation and profiteering became rife. While affluent families could meet their own needs, and while the agricultural population in general was better-fed than it had been in years, the urban working population was increasingly squeezed in the process, contributing to general unrest. Subsidised grain prices were established to cushion the urban consumer against rampant inflation, but this could only be financed by printing more currency, thus fuelling inflation. Within a year of liberation, prices had outstripped wages in Seoul by a ratio of five to two. Such volatile political and economic conditions also exacerbated labour–management conflict, and increasingly trade unions became involved in broader political issues. The USMGIK and its military-trained minds were poorly suited to dealing with the demands of a radicalised labour force, and generally adopted repressive policies, often intervening to deny Korean labour the basic rights which were exercised as a matter of course in the US. In June 1946 major trade union activity was banned, forcing most union leadership underground. Over time, the only legitimate unionism in the South became little more than a rightist-controlled pro-government front.

Amid a deteriorating political and economic situation, in September 1946 the South reached what many at the time assessed as the brink of a major insurrection. Against the background of increasing violence and agitation, on 24 September a railway workers' strike began, and by 2 October the economy was paralysed as violent strikes spread to many other sectors. The issues were many and varied, and were often driven not by political ideology *per se* but by highly localised concerns. However, common country-wide threads included the high level of civil police repression and brutality, the continued employment of former collaborators within the USMGIK, and the general tolerance by the Americans of various forms of corruption and extortion by Korean in positions of authority over other Koreans. While such grievances were ever present, and were not in themselves sufficient to overthrow the government, they provided substantial momentum to the ongoing campaign of the KCP to render the South ungovernable.

The role of the civil police was especially resented. The Japanese colonial régime enforced law and order at the local level through a police force whose Korean members had acquired a reputation for their harsh methods. This system could not survive the end of Japanese rule, and as the police force melted away its functions passed to the local People's Committees. This proved effective in many areas of law enforcement where social custom and traditional community-based restraints supported self-regulation, but it was less effective in dealing with deeper forms of social and political unrest. Local communities were helpless against individuals and groups who rejected traditional constraints, or who saw revolutionary violence as a means to their ends. The level of surveillance and control in the North eliminated the need for the revival of traditional policing methods, but in the South the situation was more complex. Without Soviet-Koreans to act as organisers and go-betweens, a large gap opened between the USMGIK and the general population. Creating a policing force to maintain basic law and order with few resources for new manpower and training meant deploying a force which soon grew to over 20,000, many of whom knew and applied Japanese methods.

An escalating cycle of violence in the South resulted as this police force took as its major mission the uprooting of communist influence. As Korea passed from the humiliation of colonisation to the moral ambiguities of liberation and divided rule, violence, sabotage and rebellion became acceptable forms of revolutionary activity, while killing and torture became the normal tactics of those charged with suppressing such activity. Throughout this period it was never an easy matter to distinguish between the communist revolutionaries who were dispatched from the North, and who operated under the direct orders of the Northern authorities, and indigenous communists fighting on home ground in defence of their own political base. Cornelius Osgood, an American anthropologist living on Kanghwa Island at the time, summed up the situation when he observed that:

> 'Communist' has become a strange word in our time, and it may refer to a political philosopher, a Russian spy, a member of any other political party, a labor organizer, a traitor to one's own country, or someone who happened to be regarded as an enemy. On Kanghwa it seemed to mean just 'any young man of a village'.

This perspective illustrates how, in such circumstances, political agitation could become an anarchic blend of local feuds and broader ideological disputes, and it also highlights a key dilemma in assessing the strength of Southern communism.

'Communists' were often simply young nationalists, alienated from the practices and procedures of the USMGIK and its Korean proxies, and attracted to the leftist or socialist political programme, or else involved in the intense organisational life of People's Committees or peasant, worker and student unions without much in the way of ideological motivation.

However, although 'communist' meant many things to ordinary people, the leaders of the communist movement themselves maintained a very clear distinction in matters of policy, strategy and ideology between their party and other leftists. Communists had participated in the pre-1945 nationalist movement, but had remained a separate entity within it, wary and contemptuous of their nationalist colleagues, whom they saw as 'bourgeois nationalists'. Their own ideology constituted a fundamental break with the traditional Korean political and social structure of their parents' generation, and they saw liberation as the prelude to a second, far-reaching socialist revolution. Their self-proclaimed status as a vanguard party placed them in conflict not only with 'reactionaries', but also with bourgeois nationalists and with the non-communist Left. The core of the communist movement was more radical in essence, more polemical and violent in political language, and demanded far more personal sacrifice in action than most Koreans, bound as they were by the myriad strings of social and familial obligation to their local communities, were prepared to offer. They also accepted the discipline of deference to the Soviet 'mother party', and throughout this period KCP leaders in the South barely concealed the fact that they made periodic trips to Pyongyang for consultations.

As the impetus of the September–October violence spent itself, it became clear by the winter of 1946–47 that the communist movement in the South had undergone major change. It had adopted militant tactics in an effort to make the South ungovernable, but violence had wounded its own cause. Many communist leaders were either in prison, underground or else sheltering in the North. When the communists resumed operations with a spring labour offensive in March 1947, their impact was far more limited, and it became clear that the communist movement would not be able to approach the level of effectiveness shown in late 1946. This was mainly because the non-communist Left grew more and more unwilling to commit itself to such militancy and so, while the political Left as a whole might still seek similar ends, they could no longer pursue them through compatible means. In a period of some eighteen months the communists therefore changed – first from prime movers within the People's Republic of Korea to a significant party of the Left, and then to the status of an increasingly isolated revolutionary group. By 1948 its popular appeal was drastically curtailed, and in August its remnants moved North, where they were absorbed into the Northern branch of the party. Deprived of a power base, its leaders served as public figureheads, and many were purged during the Korean War. As a result, after 1948 leadership of Korean communism came from the North, while hopes for unification under communist rule depended upon the North.

For the USMGIK the establishment of representative government in the South was a means to the greater end of US disengagement and withdrawal from Korea.

The US had been ambivalent about its role in Korea from the start, and it soon realised that the Soviets had more fundamental basic strategic interests involved in the Korean Peninsula, to which Moscow was prepared to commit considerable resources. The development of the North as a separate socialist state and the scale of communist insurrectionism in the South made it clear that the US was not going to achieve a unified Korean government by negotiation with the Soviets. In April 1947 the US and the Soviet Union made a further attempt to reconvene the Joint American–Soviet Commission to initiate the trusteeship process and achieve a unified Korean government, but although initial signs of compromise on the issue of which Korean groups could be included in the consultation were apparent, the rightist parties in the South would not budge from their anti-trusteeship stance, mainly because their nationalist credentials and popular political base depended on such a stance. The talks finally collapsed in July 1947. Concurrently, on 19 July 1947 the last remaining hope of some form of moderate coalition politics emerging in the South effectively disappeared with the assassination of Lyuh Woon-hyung, the only political leader still actively committed to rightist–leftist dialogue. Thus, by mid-1947 the failure of the Joint Commission, the lack of any alternative means for pursuing the goal of a united Korea, frustration at their inability to grasp the working of domestic Korean politics, the absence of clear and widely accepted vital US interests in Korea, and the finite nature of US military resources caused the US to actively seek disengagement.

With the option of a coalition government embracing North and South gone, the USMGIK found that viable Southern political leadership revolved increasingly around Syngman Rhee, a person for whom the Americans harboured little enthusiasm. From the moment Rhee returned to Seoul in October 1945, the US viewed his strong public anti-communist stance as a barrier to agreement with the Soviets. This, of course, was accurate, because Rhee believed that such agreement, followed by a US withdrawal, would lead to Soviet domination of the peninsula, making a communist takeover of the South inevitable. During 1946 antagonism between Rhee and the USMGIK grew steadily, and the break became complete after Rhee refused to recognise the Interim Legislative Assembly election process of October 1946. Rhee spent much of 1947 under virtual house arrest before the USMGIK decided that hopes for leaving a coherent South Korean administration behind when they disengaged revolved around recognising the central role that Rhee would play.

The broader picture of US–Soviet relations during 1947 had considerable impact upon the decision to deal with Rhee. In March 1947, US attempts to institutionalise a postwar foreign policy which defined its national interest more clearly than had ever been possible under Franklin D. Roosevelt and the conditions of wartime diplomacy led to the enunciation of the Truman Doctrine, which pledged US support for countries threatened by 'armed minorities or by outside pressures'. Designed primarily as a response to the situation in Greece, where a civil war between communist and non-communist forces was in progress, this doctrine was a thinly veiled warning to the Soviets not to become involved in communist insurrections, and thus it marked a further step in the ongoing postwar deterioration of US–Soviet relations. The Truman Doctrine did not automatically include East Asia, where the situation was volatile and US policy was hesitant and tentative owing to the continuing civil war in China. In the phrase of then Secretary of State Dean Acheson, the US needed to 'wait for the dust to settle' before re-defining its East Asian strategy. Nevertheless, the doctrine underscored the reality that in Korea, trusteeship and the search for unified coalition government on the basis of US–Soviet co-operation were failed policies, and that agreement with the Soviets on any substantive policy matters was unlikely.

Such domestic and international considerations prompted the US to place the Korean question before the United Nations in September 1947. It may have done so more in hope than in expectation, but Washington could, and did, point out that the UN had played a significant role in reuniting Iran after a joint Soviet–US occupation. In November the UN agreed to the US resolution which sought the establishment of a UN Temporary Committee on Korea (UNTCOK) to expedite moves towards independence and to hold elections for a unified National Assembly throughout Korea not later than 31 March 1948. Subsequent negotiations between UNTCOK and the Korean government so formed would complete the transfer of power and the withdrawal of all foreign forces. No Korean representatives participated in this process. The Soviets refused to recognise UNTCOK, and this led to the momentous UN decision on 26 February 1948 to hold the elections 'in such parts of Korea as are accessible to the Commission'. This meant that, on 10 May, UN-sanctioned elections were held only in the South, and so became the basis for the declaration of the Republic of Korea. UNTCOK members and a number of leading Korean politicians held serious reservations about the wisdom of proceeding with a literally divisive election, and the communists opposed it bitterly and violently. In March an insurrection on Cheju Island began in protest against the forthcoming May elections and soon became a fully fledged insurrection. The South Korean authorities responded with savage reprisals and in the ensuing months quelled the revolt at the cost of an estimated 30,000 lives.

Against this background, on 27 May 1948 the newly elected National Assembly met to map out the process that would lead the South through to independence as the Republic of Korea. In contrast to the October 1946 Interim Legislative Assembly poll, the May 1948 election had a high turnout, and was relatively free and fair in the assessment of UNTCOK observers. It returned a highly fragmented 200-member National Assembly in which the largest bloc comprised fifty-five candidates who were elected as supporters of Syngman Rhee, while the conservative Democratic Party had the second-largest representation with twenty-nine seats. Sundry other parties and groups gained thirty-seven seats, and eighty-five were elected as independents. The size of the latter group underscored the prevailing localist and personalist basis of political power in the South.

Syngman Rhee, who was by far the most prominent politician in the South, was the near-unanimous choice as National Assembly temporary chairman, a position tantamount to president-designate. During the ensuing six weeks the Assembly debated the form of a new constitution and on 17 July adopted a document which reflected widespread democratic sentiment. However, although the ROK constitution divided power between the National Assembly and the presidency, it did not always define the respective roles of these two institutions in coherent fashion, and so the new republic featured a strong presidency with wide powers of appointment and patronage, while the National Assembly retained for itself the power to pass the budget and the power to appoint and dismiss the incumbent president. Such ambiguities worked in favour of a determined president and against a disunited legislature, and set the scene for acrimonious conflict between the two during the First Republic (1948–60).

On 20 July, Syngman Rhee was again overwhelmingly elected as the first president of the new republic, and on 15 August 1948 the Republic of Korea formally came into existence. On 12 December the United Nations General Assembly, which had initiated the process of ROK nationhood thirteen months previously, accepted the report of UNTCOK and designated the ROK as 'the only lawful government in Korea'. With the creation of the ROK the US appeared to move substantially closer to its stated goal of disengagement, but appearances were deceptive. Although it had turned over the problem of Korean unification to the UN, and although it had tacitly defined Korea as lying outside the US defensive perimeter, and withdrawn most of its troops, the ROK was no less a US client, and unification was no nearer. Washington had merely formalised a dangerous imbalance in military strength between the two Korean states.

Conclusion

In his memoirs, Dean Acheson commented on how the period 1941–52 seemed a period of great obscurity to those who lived through it. While he had in mind the improvised, often ephemeral nature of much Second World War and early Cold War diplomacy, this perspective relates well to Korea and the Koreans during 1945–48. Many of the features of the occupation years which seem obvious to people now did not seem so obvious to the principal players at the time. Accordingly, they often made crucial decisions on strategy and tactics in contexts which they themselves barely comprehended. In the case of Korea, we may say that in August 1945 many futures seemed possible for Korea, but by August 1948 options had narrowed dramatically. Centrist, moderate, left-of-centre or socialist politics could gain no foothold in either Korean state, for neither the colonial legacy, nor the immediate postwar state of Korea, nor the occupying powers' policies encouraged moderation. Politics was built on euphoric hopes for the future and sustained by past injustice, grievance, and an often mythologised resistance to foreign invasion and occupation. Korean politics gradually acquired a hard, vengeful tone, which found rich material for dispute in the always contentious record of the Japanese colonial era. Extremism of the left and right prevailed, and had its outcome in two repressive régimes, highly dependent on foreign patrons, and ostensibly driven by competing ideologies.

While some argue that the social basis for a division into north and south had been created by an uneven pattern of colonial development, in the final analysis the reality of two contending Korean states was fashioned chiefly by foreign occupation. The leaders in both states owed their rise to circumstances created by their occupiers, even though both ultimately disappointed and frustrated their patrons by the strength of their nationalism. Of course, neither occupying power initially sought the division of Korea into two separate states in 1945; but, then, again, neither was consciously committed to Korean unification, nor indeed to any sort of Korea other than one which somehow did not harm their broader strategic interests. Above all, their policies derived from the nature of their mission: they were *occupying* powers, not nation-builders. This soon developed into an over-riding need to deny each other full control over the peninsula, which in turn rapidly transformed the 38th parallel from a zone of occupation to a sphere of interest boundary. Consequently, two antagonistic Korean régimes emerged which mirrored their respective protectors' broader confrontation.

In the North, Stalinist principles of socialist mobilisation drove state formation. Like its Soviet model, many features of the North's economic and social pro-grammes were progressive – rapid and far-reaching land reform, the beginnings of industrialisation, equality and the abolition of social-status barriers, state ownership of the means of production, universal literacy, education and health care. Moreover, a centralised distribution system, the capacity of the Soviet Union speedily to assume the role formerly played by Japan in directing the operation of a command, dependency-driven economy, and the absence of the pressing food and refugee problems experienced by the South all contributed to rapid economic stabilisation and political consolidation. There is detailed and persuasive evidence of active Soviet participation in the shaping of the postwar North Korean Communist Party leadership, including intervention against local communists in North Korea who questioned Soviet objectives. Thus, while many North Koreans were well disposed towards socialism, they did not automatically support the North Korean communists, for Kim Il Sung and his colleagues carried such political liabilities as support for the trusteeship proposal, close identification with the Soviet military occupiers, extreme and militant rhetoric, and complicity in the purging of popular non-communist leaders such as Cho Man sik. The perspective least distorted by hindsight is that Kim Il Sung was not in any sense either a popular leader or an independent actor during these years.

The resolute, decisive Soviets contrasted strongly with the confused and con-fusing Americans. Poorly trained and prepared, and with little clear direction on policy from the US government, the USMGIK was overwhelmed by the constant state of emergency conditions brought about by wartime dislocation and postwar economic collapse. It lacked the manpower and the material means to carry out decisive policies and, of course, Soviet methods of authoritarian control and mobilisation were alien to it. Consequently, political authority in the South was characterised by residues of the traditional order and by techniques carried over from the colonial order. Extremist South Koreans routinely employed political violence and methodical persecution against liberal and moderate elements in society in the name of a more reactionary set of social policies: piecemeal and grudging land reform, the maintenance of a strong class-status system, sporadic education and literacy campaigns, and virtually no state-run social safety net.

In the South the USMGIK coped badly with the forces of Korean nationalism and with the workings of Korean politics as it attempted to institute what it saw as representative government. The polity was far more diverse, and US techniques of surveillance and control were far more primitive than in the North. The absence of such familiar features as competing politics and institutionalised opposition, and the presence of few political forces of note other than nebulous, localised popular forces, perplexed them. The alienation of the People's Committees and the People's Republic of Korea was a crucial early mistake, and set the pattern for the USMGIK promotion of conservative, often reactionary forces. While they strove pragmatically to meet basic human needs, and to revive the economy and the infrastructure, the USMGIK became blind to Korean demands for social reform, for the punishment of collaborators, and most of all for immediate independence. They kept looking for a colonial élite which could lead the masses, and were constantly frustrated by their inability to find it. They kept looking for a technocracy to keep basic services running but found a technocratic and bureaucratic cadre tainted by collaboration. As a result they faced increasingly violent opposition from the left and from the communists, whom they could neither placate nor control. This laid the basis for a divided polity, in which confrontation and violence could not be contained either by leadership or by repression. The USMGIK's inability to govern effectively in such a situation was less its fault than its fate.

In assessing the temper of the times in 1945 it is worth noting that Korea was not torn wholly from its past, and that amid the political convulsions on the broader political front, the intricate pattern of local village politics and its formidable restraints retained strong influence. The political agenda was ostensibly radical, but the Korean rural population was still guided by a complex set of moral, intellectual and social assumptions which reflected the centuries-old practices of village politics. The problems this tradition might present for a country committed to industrialisation and modernisation were hidden from view under the Japanese, but they quickly became clear in 1945 when government in the South was called upon to shoulder the burden of establishing strong, coherent central authority on top of the powerful forces of localist political power. The North entertained no scruples in quickly crushing opposition from this source and instituting a profoundly authoritarian government structure, but this model was not available to the South. But, while the rhetoric of revolution was in the air during 1945–48, it needed more than colonial and wartime mobilisation, economic privation, social disruption and political frustration for the South to go further. There were Korean traditions of rebellion, but no traditions of revolution. Other than inchoate nationalism, and anti-Japanese sentiment, there was no unifying revolutionary doctrine, no common body of coherent ideas, no nationwide organisation, and no contemporary leaders of stature to carry forward such a tradition. While they carried rebelliousness in their hearts, few Koreans carried revolution. No clear answer to the question of who would inherit Korea emerged during 1945–48. The question was simply too profound.

Selected reading

Cho, Soon Sung 1967, *Korea in World Politics 1940–1950: An Evaluation of American Responsibility*, Berkeley, CA: University of California Press.

Cumings, Bruce 1981, *The Origins of the Korean War: Liberation and the Emergence of Separate Regimes, 1945–1947*, Princeton, NJ: Princeton University Press.

Osgood, Cornelius 1951, *The Koreans and Their Culture*, New York: Ronald Press.

Scalapino, Robert A. and Lee, Chong-sik 1972, *Communism in Korea*, Part 1, *The Movement*, Berkeley, CA: University of California Press

Seiler, Sydney A. 1994, *Kim Il-song 1941–48: The Creation of a Legend, the Building of a Regime*, Lantham, MD: University Press of America.

4 The supreme disaster, 1948–53

Antagonism and confrontation between the two Koreas grew steadily during 1948–50 through inflammatory rhetoric, subversion, insurrection and guerrilla warfare, but the two Koreas stopped short of full-scale warfare. Despite Syngman Rhee's 'March north!' rhetoric, the South lacked even a semblance of the means to force a military solution to the reunification issue, and while the North had substantial military assets it could not be certain of success if it acted alone. From Pyongyang's perspective, full Soviet backing was vital to successful military action, but during the late 1940s Stalin was consistently reluctant to provide such backing for fear of the US response. However, during the early months of 1950 he gradually became convinced that the US would not intervene if the DPRK could achieve a swift victory, and so Soviet policy changed to support for a full-scale invasion. The new communist government in China also gave its support, and this removed the chief constraint on military action. On 25 June 1950 the North invaded the South.

The Korean War proceeded through four main stages: the initial Northern assault from June to September 1950; the intervention of US-led UN forces, the Inch'on landing and counter-attack from September 1950 to November 1950; the Chinese entry and the gradual emergence of a stable battle-front in the centre of the peninsula from November 1950 to May 1951; and finally a protracted period of engagement along this battle-line while armistice talks continued. In each period the objectives and motives of each side changed, evolved, and ultimately resulted in the Military Armistice Agreement of 27 July 1953. However, if one side actively sought war, diligently built up the means to pursue it, and duly engaged the enemy, then it did not get the war it wanted, against the enemy it wanted, on the scale it had prepared for, and with the outcome it so confidently anticipated. Whereas the DPRK sought to engage the ROK in a short, sharp campaign in order to achieve reunification, instead it engaged the United Nations in a long, protracted campaign which consolidated the division of the peninsula. This escalation of the Korean conflict from an obscure local confrontation to a major international conflict in itself underscores the uncertainties involved in the war-making process, but it also emphasises the scale of misunderstanding and miscalculation involved in its planning.

The two Koreas, 1948–50

The proclamation of the Democratic People's Republic of Korea in September 1948 had little impact on basic state policies in the North. Kim Il Sung still depended upon Soviet-Koreans, who ran most of the leading state, party and military departments and organisations, and who routinely referred major political and economic issues to Moscow. Nevertheless, Kim's authority grew steadily as he assumed command of the resources of an embryonic state. The North's media directed campaigns against enemies of the Party, its security apparatus isolated and destroyed opponents of the régime, and its armed forces grew steadily in size and strength. The nerve centre of the state remained the 800,000-strong Korean Workers' Party, which established branches in almost every neighbourhood, factory, government office and education institution in the country. The new recruits were mainly young, and were subject to increasingly rigorous ideological training and screening for class background. As they enthusiastically carried out class warfare against 'remnants of the old society', they began to establish themselves as members of the new ruling élite in the North.

Political command remained firmly in Northern hands, and the Southern communists found themselves increasingly powerless. They had gradually abandoned the unequal political struggle in the South, and with the proclamation of the Republic of Korea in August 1948 their leaders had retreated north. Those who stayed in the South either went underground, or became directly involved in guerrilla warfare in the remote mountainous areas along the east coast or in the Chirisan region, while those who went north became virtual internal exiles. In the North they no longer had their vital geographic power base, they could not reorganise themselves as a group within the Party without being castigated as 'splitists' and, like the Yan'an group, they were kept under tight surveillance and denied access to the grass-roots organisational base of the Northern party. Their leaders were given senior titles and offices, but Kim Il Sung and his Soviet-Korean allies maintained near-total control of party, government, security apparatus and army. Unless the Southerners could regain their former base, their future would be bleak. They therefore gave strong support to plans for early reunification, and their leader, Pak Hon-yong, accompanied Kim Il Sung to Moscow in March 1949 and 1950, where he made key presentations on·the favourable revolutionary outlook in the South. These presentations helped secure Soviet backing for the June 1950 attack.

Preparations for the anticipated war for the reunification of the country continued rapidly in the North. The rationale for such a war was self-evident: division was unacceptable, and no political means existed to end the division. Both the South and the North agreed on this point, but the North was in a position to act because it had clear military superiority over the South. The Korean People's Army (KPA) was formally established in February 1948, and by this time a force of some 50,000 had already been conscripted and trained in the North. Several thousand soldiers had received advanced training in the Soviet Union in order to handle the steady stream of surplus Second World War Soviet weaponry re-assigned to North Korea, while others joined comrades already fighting in the Chinese People's

Liberation Army as the Chinese civil war reached its climax. The KPA grew rapidly during 1949–50 as conscription intensified, and as an estimated 50,000 combat-hardened Koreans began to return from China. On the eve of the Korean War the North had approximately 150,000 men under arms.

This ideologically driven sense of purpose in the North contrasted strongly with the disorganisation and weakness of the South. In place of the clear-cut revolutionary ideology of the North, the South was riven by discordant sets of ideas. In place of the resolute and ruthless Soviet occupying force, which intervened deeply in Northern political affairs, during 1945–48 the South had depended upon guidance and material support from the irresolute USMGIK. Endemic corruption and economic crisis, the influx of an estimated three million refugees from the North, social divisions, political infighting, severe personality clashes between political leaders, tenuous law and order, assassinations, and ongoing violent clashes between extremists on the left and the right progressively removed what was left of moderate centrist influence in national politics. By 1948 post-liberation feelings of enthusiasm and euphoria had been replaced by fear, violence and partisan division.

It was in these circumstances that Syngman Rhee advanced to the centre stage of South Korean politics. Prior to 1945, Rhee had already been a widely known, controversial figure in the Korean nationalist exile movement. As early as 1919 he had been designated the first president of the Korean Provisional Government in Shanghai, and thereafter he settled in the United States. A graduate of Harvard and Princeton, he was a man of strong personality, considerable intellect, and personal charm. He was also a gifted public orator. These basic leadership qualities enabled him to negotiate his way through the labyrinthine and violent world of post-1945 Korean politics, and to establish himself as the dominant figure in South Korean politics. Innate gifts are often paired with innate flaws, however, and so Rhee's exceptional intellectual ability tended to arrogance, his strong will tended towards stubbornness, his inspirational oratory to demagoguery, and his visionary qualities to neglect of daily oversight. He seems to have been temperamentally incapable of working within the confines of competing party politics, and this was a major cause of the slide towards autocracy and repression in the ROK under his presidency after 1948.

Rhee's goal was an independent, non-communist Korea, but beyond this concept he lacked any structured vision of what such a Korea would look like. He did not believe that the Soviets would stop short of outright dominance of the peninsula, and he saw in the distant, rather mercurial United States the only possible guarantor of non-communist independence. However, his platform of immediate Korean independence was at odds with US support for trusteeship, and he quickly fell out with the USMGIK authorities when it became clear that he would not support any delay or interim administration before full independence. Such authorities routinely used self-contradictory adjectives such as 'stubborn' and 'erratic' to describe him, but such words also described a leader of fixed strategic purpose who displayed considerable analytical and strategic ability in making the most of his limited assets.

In fact, many aspects of Rhee's behaviour were the result of the habitual extreme weakness of the cards in his hand. South Korean politics during 1945–48 was ruthless and violent, and the new Republic of Korea had a poorly institution-alised administrative, constitutional and political order. Official salaries were low, personal patronage was a well-entrenched practice, and corruption was cor-respondingly endemic. As president, Rhee rarely commanded a majority in the legislature, nor did he have the benefit of many established political conventions to guide the conduct of politics. Many would argue that he himself further undermined such formal conventions as existed, but since he lacked a strong command structure, such as existed the North, his practical options were largely reduced to exercising raw coercive power over a poor agrarian country in a state of deep social ferment and economic crisis. Consequently, his power base remained highly personalised and dependent on his own force of personality and on his powers of rhetoric. His adversaries were constantly wrong-footed by this potent mixture of strong anti-Japanese, anti-communist rhetoric and an above-politics stance and stature, which cut at their own public stature. They were also increas-ingly subject to harassment from Rhee's political machine, which was typically run by people who were not above politics of the more common, brutal kind.

Within the first National Assembly (1948–50) the Rhee group initially com-manded only 55 of 200 seats, leaving Rhee to base his power not on the legislature but on his personal authority, on his limited command of the resources of the state, and on the collective weakness of his various opponents. His trump card was control of the bureaucracy, the police and the armed forces. He therefore allowed these three organisations wide latitude in extending their power and patronage, usually at the expense of institutions which generally sought to curb Rhee's powers, such as the judiciary, local government institutions, and the National Assembly. The police and the armed forces in particular grew powerful and corrupt. Government was in the hands of Koreans, but the powerful precedents of the Japanese colonial government were still present, and Rhee's administration remained deeply pre-occupied with self-preservation. As a result, government under Rhee rarely moved with dynamism.

Internal rebellion, economic development and land reform constituted major challenges for the new republic. Following the Cheju rebellion, in October 1948 a significant military rebellion broke out among army units based at Yosu on the south coast, and again a ruthless, insecure central government responded with ferocity, killing or executing some two thousand alleged participants. Meanwhile, the economic situation was serious. The mining industry remained depressed, transport and communication infrastructure continued to deteriorate, and elec-tricity from the North, on which the South had been highly dependent, was finally cut off in May 1948. By the end of 1948 manufacturing industry was operating at a bare 10–15 per cent of pre-liberation capacity, and fully half the workforce was unemployed. The cities of South Korea were growing rapidly with the continuing displacement of people from the North, from Japan, and from the rural South, and urban life was racked by hyper-inflation, crime, corruption, squatting, black marketeering, protection racketeering, sabotage and subversion. Amid the economic chaos US economic support was essential if the country were to avoid total breakdown, but the struggle for control of aid funds was constant and bitter. The ROK National Assembly demanded legislative oversight, while the US constantly insisted on greater presidential accountability. However, such demands conflicted increasingly with Rhee's own interest, which was to direct funds towards his core constituency in the government, armed forces and police. The drop-off in economic aid from $179 million in 1948 to $59 million in 1950 contributed further to Rhee's dilemma.

The issue of land reform also continued to shape the political agenda. As rightist parties that often had close connections with landowners became more influential, a deadlock developed between those favouring compensation for land seized and those favouring outright expropriation. The USMGIK preferred that the Koreans themselves deal with this issue, but in the face of continuing deadlock, in March 1948, in its last weeks in office, the USMGIK moved to meet wide-spread public expectations of action by making available for sale to tenant families the former Japanese land holdings which they controlled. This was followed by ROK legislation, enacted in early 1950, which effected a major redistribution of Korean-owned land. By the end of the Korean War some 3.3 million South Koreans, comprising 24 per cent of the total farm population, had gained ownership of land, and tenancy rates had fallen from over 70 per cent to approximately 30 per cent. The economic base of the former landlord class had been effectively destroyed.

On the eve of the Korean War it was by no means certain that Rhee could maintain his hold on power. His own sense of vulnerability was underlined by his efforts to postpone the scheduled May 1950 National Assembly elections; but, following US pressure, they were finally held under UN observation. This election was essentially a referendum on Rhee, given the recent defeat of Opposition efforts in the legislature to curb Rhee's power by making him subject to a cabinet-style government. In the event, most sitting members were replaced by neutral or anti-Rhee independents: out of 210 seats independents gained 126 seats, Rhee supporters gained 57 seats, and organised opposition parties gained 27 seats. But, if Rhee's own prospects were clouded, time was slowly allowing the new republic to cohere and consolidate. Substantial land reform had been carried out despite bitter landlord opposition, the government bureaucracy was becoming more coherent, and the economy was beginning to stabilise. By 1950 it was becoming clearer and clearer that South Korea, while still in turmoil, would not be overthrown by massed social forces from within, and that political authoritarianism was not the only reason for this.

The road to war

The path to most wars usually acquires clear signposts in hindsight, but these are rarely perceived at the time. In the case of the Korean War, however, while the actual timing, scale and location of the Northern assault on 25 June contained elements of surprise and conjecture, in the early months of 1950 many contemporary observers assessed that a war in Korea was growing increasingly likely. This was not simply because of the ongoing hostility between the two Koreas, but also because of the continuing deterioration in relations between the United States and the Soviet Union. The disintegration of the wartime US–Soviet alliance led to growing tension and the onset of the Cold War, a term which came into popular usage in early 1947. Declaration of the Truman Doctrine in March 1947 was followed by inauguration of the Marshall Plan for the economic rehabilitation of Europe in June 1947, and the establishment of the North Atlantic Treaty Organisation (NATO) in April 1949. In response, the Soviets rejected participation in the Marshall Plan, instituted the Berlin blockade in mid-1948, incorporated Czechoslovakia into the Soviet bloc, and replaced a number of Eastern and Central European nationalist/communist-led governments with loyalist, Stalinist régimes. By 1950, Europe was divided into two hostile political, economic and military blocs.

Events in East Asia also influenced Stalin's thinking. In October 1949 the Chinese Communist Party (CCP) achieved victory on the mainland over the Chinese Nationalist forces, and proclaimed the People's Republic of China. The Soviet Union and the new Chinese government had a legacy of past territorial, political, ideological and personality disputes, and Stalin in particular saw the Chinese communist victory as a potential threat to Soviet hegemony within the world communist movement. However, the CCP victory presented opportunity as well as threat, for as Stalin became more and more convinced that war would break out in Europe it became important to secure the Soviet Union's eastern flank, and here the Chinese had a vital role to play. Under these circumstances Moscow and Beijing engaged in extensive discussions at the leadership level during late 1949 on political, economic and military issues, culminating in the signing of the Sino-Soviet Treaty of Friendship, Alliance and Mutual Assistance on 14 February 1950.

By contrast, US policy in Korea remained indecisive. This was chiefly because during this period the Truman administration remained distracted by events in Europe and by constant dealings with a Congress anxious to accelerate the ongoing worldwide military contraction. US strategy in the event of conflict in Korea assumed that the ROK Army could hold off the North until the United Nations could act. However, underestimation of DPRK preparedness, and undersupply of materiel to the ROK armed forces – in no small part because of their misgivings about what a well-armed Rhee might do – combined to ensure that the ROK would be unable to perform this task. In October 1949 the US allocated funds to establish a 65,000-man ROK Army to cover the US withdrawal, but this level of funding was so limited that by June 1950 the ROK army had only an estimated fifteen days' worth of war supplies. Against this background, on 5 January 1950, President Truman announced the termination of US military assistance to the Chinese Nationalists, who were then anticipating the imminent invasion of their last stronghold of Taiwan. Then, on 12 January, US Secretary of State Acheson delivered a speech which pointedly excluded the Asian mainland from the US defensive perimeter in Asia. This did not enunciate a new policy, for public officials had been saying similar things for some time, but the authoritative repetition of this principle at this time influenced the thinking of the DPRK and its allies. Therefore, on 19 January 1950, when Kim Il Sung made the latest in a long series of requests to see Stalin to persuade the Soviets to back a quick strike at the South, Stalin, who had been keeping Kim at arm's length, finally agreed to discuss the matter.

Kim Il Sung and the DPRK leadership held a profound, ideologically driven conviction that the masses in the South would rally to the North if their government could be destabilised and toppled. Kim had attempted to bring this about in various ways short of open frontal assault prior to 1950; but without the assurance of Soviet support, and with US troops still in the South, he could go no further than provide support for guerrilla-warfare tactics. However, by the winter of 1949–50 it was clear that these tactics were not sufficient in themselves, and that guerrillas in the South were suffering serious losses. In January 1950, Kim was therefore more than usually anxious to persuade the Soviets to back his plan, just at a time when Stalin was prepared to be persuaded by it. In the prevailing international environment, control of the entire Korean Peninsula appealed to Stalin as a strategic objective: it would open a second front in the Cold War, expand the buffer zone along the Siberian border, apply pressure to the US position in Japan, draw military strength away from Europe, and further interdict US military capability in mainland Asia. Soviet resistance to Kim's arguments rapidly ebbed away.

On 30 March 1950, Kim and his delegation arrived in Moscow. During their subsequent talks with Stalin, the Koreans emphasised that a war with the South would be over within a matter of days. They would quickly capture Seoul, where-upon the ROK government would disintegrate and a massive pro-North uprising would occur before the US could intervene. Kim did not explain, and Stalin apparently did not press him to explain, why the ongoing guerrilla war was going so badly if such deep reservoirs of support existed in the South, but Kim's energetic presentation seems to have removed Stalin's remaining reservations. With swift US intervention unlikely, a full-scale invasion represented a low-risk strategy, and Stalin therefore sanctioned a DPRK offensive in general terms, subject to Chinese approval. Accordingly, during 13–16 April 1950, Kim visited Beijing and gave a similar presentation to Mao Zedong, who checked with Moscow and gave his approval in general terms, whereupon the Soviet Union itself took rapid steps to support Kim's plans. By the end of April, a high-ranking Soviet military team had arrived in Pyongyang to draw up detailed battle plans. On 10 June, Stalin approved these final plans, leaving the actual timing of the attack to Kim. So convinced of success were all parties that no contingency plans were made in case the initial assault failed to achieve the objective of an ROK defeat.

The commitment of the North's leadership to the invasion of the South was far from complete. Kim was the Party leader, he had control of the armed forces, and was the strongest advocate of immediate attack. The former Southern communists also supported an early attack, believing that it would restore them to their geographical power-base. On the other hand, other military leaders within the Korean People's Army harboured, and in some case expressed, doubts. Choe Yongkon, then the highest-ranking commander in the KPA, was one of these; and Kim Tu-bong, the highest-ranking civilian member of the Yan'an faction, was another. Both expressed reservations, but these had no practical effect since neither man was in the direct chain of active command. In the event, once the war began, the doubters were forced to put aside such reservations, but later revelations of such manoeuvrings underline the extent to which Kim Il Sung committed the country to war in the face of significant internal debate and contention.

The actual sequence of events at the beginning of the conflict remains unclear. Against a background of ongoing border fire-fights, on Sunday, 25 June 1950, the Korean War proper began with a pre-dawn artillery exchange on the Ongjin Peninsula in Hwanghae province, followed within hours by a large-scale invasion from the north. Aspects of Kim Il Sung's actual order to attack seem to have surprised both sides. The North was ready but not yet fully mobilised, and much Soviet materiel was still in transit. The South was in greater disarray, with many key ROK and US personnel on weekend leave or out of the country. Certainly, the North Koreans achieved almost total surprise despite many advance warnings simply because the US could not believe that the DPRK would initiate full-scale war against a UN-supported US ally. This meant that initially there was little resistance to the KPA, which proceeded to penetrate swiftly and deeply into the South.

After an initial period of confusion, the US responded rapidly. It engineered a series of UN resolutions condemning the DPRK, calling for a withdrawal, and calling upon UN members to assist the ROK, and on 30 June it entered the conflict, drawing on its 100,000-strong occupation force in Japan. On 5 July the first US troops engaged the KPA at Osan, some 100 kilometres south of Seoul, and on 7 July the UN Security Council established a unified military command under US command with the mission of restoring the *status quo ante* on the Korean Peninsula. Sixteen countries contributed forces to the United Nations Command (UNC), which was placed under the command of General Douglas MacArthur, but UN oversight was limited. While it subjected the US to international diplomatic restraint in some key areas, US strategies and objectives still determined the basic course of the war.

The North expected the South to capitulate after the capture of Seoul, and so when the conflict continued, its strategy involved little more than a highly improvised and uncoordinated hot pursuit of the ROK forces, which soon reduced ROK-controlled territory to a small perimeter in the south-east, incorporating Pusan and Taegu, which were the second- and third-largest cities in the country. However, time was the North's enemy, and by mid-August the North could advance no further owing to ROK regrouping, UNC reinforcements, UNC sea and air control, and the lack of pro-communist civilian uprisings. On 15 September 1950 the UNC broke the deadlock with a major landing behind KPA lines at Inch'on, on the west coast near Seoul. The KPA was forced into rapid retreat, and by the end of October was effectively out of the fight.

The Inch'on landing achieved total surprise and opened a new phase of the conflict, marked by a rapid KPA retreat, equally rapid UNC pursuit, and the drawing of China into the war. The Chinese had paid close attention to the course of events after 25 June, and had already concluded that Kim's failure to achieve swift victory, the strong response of the US, and the rapid northward advance of the US-led UN forces posed a serious threat to China's security. As a result, during August 1950 it began to move forces to the North Korean border, and on 30 September it issued a public warning to the UNC not to cross the 38th parallel. The UNC did not see the Chinese as a major factor in the conflict at this stage, and with the Soviets also remaining aloof from direct involvement it resolved to pursue the KPA north of the parallel. On 1 October 1950 the UNC crossed the 38th parallel, and the following day the Chinese took the momentous decision to enter the war. The Chinese leadership was far from united, but it deferred to Mao Zedong's strong arguments that China could not afford a US victory in Korea, that resolute action was necessary for domestic consolidation of the revolution, that it was important to back up the Soviet commitment, and that the Chinese could outlast the US under the favourable battlefield conditions of Korea.

The Chinese People's Volunteers (CPV) began to cross the Yalu River into North Korea in large numbers on 25 October. UNC policy in the event of such intervention was not clearly formulated beyond a general presumption of strategic withdrawal southward to a tenable military position. However, as battlefield commander, Douglas MacArthur continued to pursue the military objective of the unification of Korea, even if this involved a wider war with China and possibly the Soviet Union − a war to which he did not always appear to be averse. On 24 November the UNC therefore launched a 'home by Christmas' offensive to drive the Chinese and the KPA remnants across the Yalu River and out of North Korea. Such plans entailed a serious underestimation of Chinese military capabilities and an overestimation of the efficacy of UNC air power. The offensive provoked an overwhelming counter-attack, and the UNC troops were soon retreating rapidly from the far north of the peninsula.

The UNC retreat soon became a rout. Disdain for the Chinese as fighters, single-minded pursuit of the ill-defined goal of seeking unconditional KPA surrender, the harsh Korean winter, a dispersed and poorly coordinated army, and the creation of long, vulnerable supply-lines stretching up from the south all contributed to military disaster and headlong retreat. On 5 December the CPV retook Pyongyang, and proceeded south, where they crossed the 38th parallel on 30 December. By the year's end the UNC had suffered a series of rapid reversals. In some ways they were victims of their very success at Inch'on, which created seemingly unstoppable momentum, and perhaps contributed to hubris within MacArthur's inner circle. As the retreating UN forces again reached the 38th parallel, the territorial *status quo ante* was re-established, and this in theory opened a window for negotiation. However, as was the case with the UNC in its northern advance after Inch'on, diplomatic options were eschewed where these involved sacrificing battlefield momentum. Moreover, the US had been stung by the CPV offensive, and as an immediate consequence, on 16 December 1950, President Truman declared a national state of emergency and instituted a general call-up. The military roll-back of the years since 1945 now came to a definitive end as the US began a rapid, sustained process of rearmament. The US had nothing to gain by accepting terms in Korea before it was able to bring these new assets to bear on the situation.

Combat in the early months of 1951 presaged the long drawn-out stalemate that was to accompany the subsequent armistice negotiations period. The CPV retook Seoul on 4 January, and continued to move south, but by late January they had run out of momentum. Their efforts to resume the offensive in February failed, and amid huge casualties caused by human wave tactics the Chinese gave ground. In mid-March, when the UNC again retook a devastated Seoul, it was clear that military stalemate was imminent in Korea. There was general agreement in Washington about the need for an armistice, and that diplomatic moves should take precedence over any military action north of the 38th parallel. Although MacArthur had been advised of a pending presidential announcement on terms for a negotiated settlement, he proceeded to write his celebrated 'no substitute for victory' public letter, which instead canvassed the widening of the war to include objectives in China. These views were widely refuted in Washington, perhaps most famously by the chairman of the Joint Chiefs of Staff, Omar Bradley, who stated that war with China would involve the US 'in the wrong war, at the wrong place, at the wrong time, and with the wrong enemy'. On 11 April 1951, Truman dismissed MacArthur. The incident had little effect on the momentum towards a negotiated settlement, but reduced strain between the field command and Washington, and between the US and its allies.

Negotiations

In May 1951 the final CPV offensive came to a halt amid an estimated 70,000 casualties in human wave assaults and signs of collapsing CPV morale. With both sides exhausted and unwilling to make further battlefield sacrifices, momentum for a negotiated settlement grew. On 13 May 1951, Mao Zedong sought Stalin's support for armistice terms which demanded no more than a restoration of the prewar *status quo* along the 38th parallel. The Soviets themselves had long abandoned hope of decisive strategic gains in Korea, and now began to discuss the general outline of an armistice agreement privately with the US. In June both parties made public their willingness to discuss an armistice, and on 10 July formal negotiations began.

There were various sources of friction within the Soviet–China–DPRK alliance, but on balance these were not sufficient to deter them from a common negotiating front. The Soviets had suffered few battlefield casualties, but in strategic terms the war had nevertheless been a disaster, for they had underestimated the level of US commitment and had triggered a major global US military build-up. Moscow was therefore anxious to avoid further antagonising Washington. The Chinese were clearly less persuaded by the logic of conciliatory moves; but having pushed the US-led UNC forces well south of the Yalu, and with the DPRK ready to be reconstituted as a buffer state, moves to cut their very considerable losses and to concentrate on their overwhelming domestic problems also made sense. Kim Il

Sung sought to continue the war and to persuade his allies to make the necessary material commitment to achieve Korean reunification, but both Moscow and Beijing prevailed upon the DPRK to accept a negotiated outcome based on the continuing division of the Korean Peninsula.

On 26 July 1951 the negotiating parties, comprising representatives of United Nations Command, the Chinese People's Volunteers and the Korean People's Army agreed to an armistice negotiation agenda which included the creation of a military demarcation line, a demilitarised zone, the creation of a Military Armistice Commission to enforce the armistice, and the exchange of prisoners. However, if the military stalemate had led to negotiations, this stalemate also precluded substantial concessions by either side at these negotiations, for both sides remained deeply hostile to each other and were determined to hold firm to entrenched negotiating positions. Some issues were easier to resolve than others. For example, the lull in the fighting had enabled both sides to re-supply and reinforce the existing front line, and this simplified agreement on an armistice line. Thus, by the end of 1951 the parties had agreed on the demarcation line and its associated demilitarised zone. However, the exchange of 95,000 KPA soldiers and 20,000 CPVs for an estimated 16,000 ROK Army and UNC prisoners remained an intractable issue since the CPV and the KPA wanted total exchange and the UNC wanted voluntary exchange. The early months of 1952 brought steady progress on the overall terms of an armistice agreement, but the low number of voluntary Chinese and North Korean returnees from prison camps in the south then produced deadlock.

The election of Dwight D. Eisenhower to the US presidency in November 1952 helped to resolve this deadlock. This was because the Chinese and the North Koreans believed that Eisenhower, a Second World War leader of immense prestige and popularity, could carry out Korean policy with greater freedom than Truman, and so would apply much greater military pressure. This belief was well founded, for on 3 March 1952 a revised US strategy identified lack of sufficient military pressure as a chief reason for failure to conclude an armistice. Washington therefore resolved to extend and intensify its ongoing bombing of the North and give active consideration to the resumption of large-scale offensive military action. At this juncture, the death of Stalin in March 1953 removed a major influence for prolonging negotiations. A general unwillingness to test US resolve further led to final Soviet-brokered concessions on the POW issue in June, and to the conclusion of a Military Armistice Agreement on 27 July 1953. Again, as in 1945, a divided Korea came into being, this time through an armistice negotiated over the heads and against the will of the two Korean leaders.

The Koreans' war

Great Power military action and diplomacy are a major source of focus in the Korean War, but domestic events in both Koreas during the war reshaped political and social attitudes in important ways. Both Korean states effectively lost sovereignty in the early months of the war, and experienced the humiliation of large numbers of foreign troops fighting on their soil for strategic objectives that they themselves did not always share. Moreover, neither Korean army experienced battlefield victory of the type that might have made the sacrifice of war more palatable. Nevertheless, despite the threat to sovereignty posed by the foreign presence, and despite the threat to political power posed by lack of battlefield success, both Kim Il Sung and Syngman Rhee emerged from the war well entrenched in power.

The story of wartime DPRK politics is the story of the emergence of Kim Il Sung at the head of a reconstituted Korean Workers' Party. Six months after the war began, the KPA had been defeated and destroyed. This was a personal as well as a national disaster, because Kim had driven a divided leadership into war and had shown limited capabilities as a battlefield commander. His talents were confined to directing all-out offensives, and in this he was heir to the rigid conventional Soviet strategy evolved during the huge battles of the Second World War: relentless pursuit of the enemy, and reliance on human wave attacks in the face of superior firepower and superior technology. However, when called upon to make contingency plans, moderate or balance conflicting interests, evaluate complex situations or evolve fall-back situations, Kim was out of his depth. He placed total reliance on the flawed expectation that the war would be won if he captured Seoul, and when the resistance continued he had no fall-back position beyond relentless pursuit. In so doing, Kim remained so focused on the Pusan-Taegu perimeter that he ignored Soviet and Chinese warnings of a looming counter-attack along the west coast. Consequently, the Inch'on landing encountered little resistance and led to the effective destruction of the KPA. By the end of October 1950, Kim had been shunted aside by the Chinese and found himself openly criticised, not just by the CPV commander Peng Dehuai but also by leading figures within the KWP. However, despite such setbacks, Kim and his guerrilla group still commanded Soviet backing, as well as the still-formidable resources of the remnants of the Party apparatus.

As the battle-lines stabilised and armistice talks began in mid-1951, Kim began a major overhaul of the Party. At the first wartime Party Plenum, held in Kanggye near the Manchurian border in December 1950, he therefore went on the political offensive, purging a number of potential rivals to his leadership and reasserting his authority over a demoralised party. In many areas people had abandoned the party and had actively collaborated with the enemy. All told, during the course of the war, the Party lost up to half of its prewar membership of 700,000 through desertion, expulsion and battlefield action, but reinstatements and the enrolment of 450,000 new members brought the total Party membership up to just over 1 million by 1953. In reality, the preservation of the name 'Korea Workers' Party' obscures the fact that by 1953 the ruling party of the DPRK was a very different entity. The new party was a mass party, not an élite party; it was no longer organised and run by Soviet-Koreans in imitation of the Communist Party of the Soviet Union; and its new members comprised mainly people of poor peasant or manual-worker background who had remained loyal to the party despite enormous wartime privation and suffering. They were enrolled for their class background rather than for their grasp of ideology, and since they owed their new status in DPRK society to the Kim Il Sung group they constituted a powerful support-base for Kim within the party. Kim Il Sung's authority grew substantially, and it is at this juncture that the first signs of a strong cult of personality became visible as the party sought a new focus for loyalty.

Further major purges soon eliminated the leaders of all rival groups to Kim within the KWP. The major political casualties of the war were the Southerners. They were held to blame for the lack of any uprising in the South and, having just seen their geographical support base disappear, were in no position to defend themselves effectively. In early 1953 many leading Southern communists were publicly denounced, and in August 1953, Pak Hon-yong himself was arrested, tried and found guilty of high treason. He was executed in 1955. Other leading cadres purged at this time included Mu Chong, the most prominent military member of the Yan'an group, who was dismissed from office in late 1950 and died soon after, and Ho Ka-i, the most prominent of the Soviet-Koreans, who committed suicide in April 1953 while under political attack from within the KWP.

Outside élite circles, the human story of the North at war is predominantly the story of the many people who stayed loyal to their government and leaders despite appalling privation and suffering. As the UNC gained control of the air during 1952, exhausted, hungry and terrified soldiers and civilians were subject to a ferocious, sustained and often indiscriminate bombing campaign, but they did not break. Rather, they endured because they had already made their commitment to a communist Korea, and because most were already inured to the hardships of wartime production, barracks life, food shortages, remorseless discipline and an implacable system of reward and punishment. They also responded to the organisational life and its communal goals, to the relentless propaganda and to the constant ethos of struggle with which the guerrilla leadership was so familiar. Such high levels of mobilisation became characteristic of the DPRK after the armistice as well as during the actual war.

In the South the outbreak of the Korean War changed the fortunes of the Rhee administration dramatically. During the first year of the conflict, the battle-front changed dramatically and the final outcome remained in doubt. This prompted political forces within the ROK to rally behind Rhee as leader, at least sufficiently to enable him to head off the threatened collapse of his authority. We should be careful of exaggerating the narrow confines of Rhee's support base, for to do so would be to fall into the same kind of error that underlay Kim Il Sung's expectation that the South would rise up against Rhee when they saw a communist alternative on the horizon. Despite overwhelming military defeat in the early weeks, the government apparatus retreated to Pusan in good order and remained intact, the National Assembly continued to function, there was no disintegration of morale, nor were there any major mutinies. South Koreans did not rise up, ROK soldiers and civilians fought and endured, as did the régime itself. If the long-suffering citizens did not do so for Syngman Rhee and a specific government, they did so for the basic values that he articulated and for the time-honoured reason that the alternative was, to them, either worse or simply unimaginable.

Characteristically, Syngman Rhee felt little need to co-opt his political opponents into the war effort. Consequently, his relations with the opposition-dominated Second National Assembly (1950–54) during the war remained acrimonious, while his political power-base remained a loose minority collection of rightist political parties, organisations and independent assemblymen who needed and accepted his support to function. This base was supplemented as always by his wide powers of appointment and patronage within the bureaucracy, and by his control of the national police and paramilitary organisations such as the National Youth Corps. Since 1948, Rhee had portrayed himself as a leader who stood above the partisan and factional battles of daily politics, and this was an important element in his public image, as well as a key source of popular support. However, this stance grew steadily less effective in the face of more organised opposition groups, and in December 1951 he abandoned this position and established the Liberal Party as his instrument of power. The new party provided Rhee with a better means of gathering and distributing political funds, and of establishing a firmer base from which to seek a second term as president.

Although Syngman Rhee had provided a strong nationalist focus during the war, his administration had also demonstrated considerable inefficiency and brutality under wartime conditions. With incidents such as major National Defence Corps embezzlements and the massacre of hundreds of civilians in the village of Koch'ang during 1951 it became increasingly unlikely that the National Assembly would elect Rhee to a second term. Rhee's response was to circumvent the Assembly and seek a constitutional amendment to enable the president to be elected by direct popular vote. This was duly proposed in November 1951, but rejected by the Assembly in January 1952. The Rhee camp responded by carrying out mass arrests of opposing assemblymen before passing the required constitutional amendment in July 1952. The second ROK presidential election was immediately held on 5 August 1952, and Rhee gained 74 per cent of the vote against a slew of disorganised and demoralised opposition candidates. This use of executive power against legislative opponents curtailed the power and effectiveness of the anti-Rhee groups within the National Assembly. Never again did Rhee find it necessary to resort to mass arrests to exert control over the legislature.

Rhee's personality and profound nationalism often placed him in direct conflict with the US and the United National Command. He saw the war as a chance to unify the peninsula, and repeatedly urged this course upon his allies. From the ROK's point of view this was, of course, strategically sound, because a war that merely restored the situation before June 1950 did little to enhance ROK security. However, Rhee pursued this advocacy well past the point of diminishing returns, and well after it became clear that the total destruction of the North was no longer either achievable or desirable in the assessment of his allies. As he had done so frequently before the war, Rhee made himself the issue, and when in June 1951 the ROK launched an anti-armistice public campaign critical of any halt in the fighting short of the Yalu the major achievement of the campaign was to reinforce foreign perceptions of Rhee as an erratic and highly emotional leader who posed a threat to negotiations.

Outside politics, a major development within the ROK was that the ROK Army came of age as an army and as an important ROK institution during the Korean War. Unlike the KPA, it was not an effective fighting force in June 1950. At the beginning of the war its young conscripts were predominantly led by inexperienced officers, and their light weaponry was no match for the well-organised, well-supplied North. Despite initial heavy defeats they regrouped to play a significant role after the Inch'on landing. In this they were not helped by the habitual and corrupt diversion of military aid funds to civilian purposes, nor by the constant humiliation of fighting alongside well-supplied, well-equipped and well-fed foreigners who also determined the overall military strategy, in pursuit of which ROK soldiers had to offer their lives. The CPV often targeted ROK troops as the weakest link in their initial battlefield assaults, and it became difficult to maintain morale under such pressure. However, as the battle line steadied, the ROK Army's performance improved. The US, which had been openly sceptical about the Koreans' reliability and capability, largely resolved its misgivings and began to build up ROK forces. Training facilities were expanded, and the Korean Military Academy was reorganised along the lines of West Point. By July 1953 the ROK army had almost doubled its prewar size, and was significantly more professional in training, organisation and outlook.

The large expansion of the ROK armed forces produced significant change in ROK society. While Japan had partially mobilised Korea in support of its war effort, the 1950–53 mobilisation was more thoroughgoing. Millions of mostly young men from rural communities were pressed into army life, with its modern methods and tempo of work. They were trained to be literate, to master diverse modern technologies and to accept the command–response model of organisation, and were also brought into intense sustained contact with people from other parts of the country and other social backgrounds. Conscription became an ordeal and a rite of passage for all young Koreans, and the size of the army and especially its officer corps grew. The outlines of a distinct military ethos began to appear amid the intensely civilianised society of the South, and by virtue of their training, military men also became part of a new technological élite.

Conclusion

To many Western observers at the time, and for many years afterward, the Korean War seemed to be a highly ideological war, fought to protect a fledgling democracy from 'communist aggression'. Compared with the profound political and moral ambiguities of the later Vietnam and Iraq conflicts, the issues in Korea seemed relatively clear-cut. In time, however, the values people fight for inevitably become blurred, and the perspectives of the Korean War which remain salient today are of the confusion and recklessness that transformed the local Korean conflict into a major war, the horrifying material damage done to both Koreas but especially the North, and the complex interaction between Great Power diplomacy, competing national interests, domestic politics and individual personalities. No war is inevitable, and many factors contributed to the outbreak of the Korean War. The problem is not so much to identify such factors as to determine the hierarchy of their importance and their relationship to one another.

The mere existence of two antagonistic Korean states suggests that some form of major Korean conflict might in any case have broken out in the early 1950s, but in accounting for the actual conflict which did break out on 25 June 1950 history is likely to continue to accord major responsibility to Kim Il Sung and his supporters. Kim persuaded the Soviets and the Chinese to back an invasion, and then carried his people into war despite objections from senior colleagues and advisers. These objections were of course aimed only at the wisdom or necessity of this particular war at this particular time, for otherwise the Pyongyang leadership was of one mind that a successful war would reunify the country, consolidate the party's hegemony, remove a military threat, and restore the integrity of the pre-1945 economy. There was ample motivation in the cause of reunification alone, and this was a compelling rationale for the strategy of frontal assault, since the alternatives of subversion, insurrection and guerrilla warfare had failed to bring down the South during 1948–50. From their own perspective, the central issue was clear-cut: this was a 'good' war.

This in turn raises the question of Soviet and Chinese responsibility. Until 1950 the major deterrent to war had been the Soviet veto, which was held in place chiefly by uncertainty over the likely US response. As Stalin became convinced that Kim Il Sung could execute a short campaign to deliver an important strategic gain at little cost, he withdrew this veto. Amid a fluid regional situation and a deteriorating international situation, such a war in Korea seemed an increasingly acceptable risk. As a result, the Korean War was planned and executed by the North with close Soviet assistance, the full scale of which has only become clear after detailed study of Soviet archival material released after the fall of the Soviet Union in 1991. The issue of Chinese responsibility is less clear. To Mao in April 1950, Kim presented evidence of basic Moscow–Pyongyang agreement on an invasion, and this made it hard for China to stay out, since it was still highly dependent on the Soviets. In both Moscow and Bejing, the actual decision-making processes were hugely deficient, and so the go-ahead was given to Kim without co-ordination, without close checking of the basic guarantees given by each party, without more careful weighing of the likely US reaction, without careful analysis of Kim's assumptions, especially his claim that large numbers of people in the South would support the invasion, and without establishing any fall-back positions, should the initial assault fail.

Some observers argue that Stalin would not have given his approval for the North's military campaign had US policy towards Korea not been so ambiguous. Those who argue that confusing US signals led to this miscalculation often cite the January 1950 Acheson speech, and despite Acheson's vigorous defence that the speech did not signal any change of policy it seems clear that he gave an unintended emphasis to the already-established US position not to become militarily involved in Korea in the event of war. On the other hand, as we have already suggested, Stalin's shift was still consistent with overall Soviet strategic vision, and the uncertainties and ambiguities in the US position ran much deeper than the Acheson speech. US strategic thinking was in fact poorly developed, not least because it placed too much reliance on the belief that Kim was under effective restraint and would not attack a UN-sponsored US ally. But, while it is arguable that less ambiguity might have reduced the likelihood of conflict at that time and in that place, the Cold War itself had established conditions of distrust and antagonism in which a Soviet misreading of US intentions was always likely.

Other observers also argue the need to seek causes not just in the events of 25 June, but also in all that happened in Korea after 1945. From this perspective the actual war was the escalation of an ongoing civil and revolutionary conflict which had been fought in one way or another with increasing levels of organisation between communists and non-communists since 1945. Here we may affirm that the events of 1945–50 on the Korean Peninsula are important, just as events in Europe during 1935–39 are important for understanding the origins of the Second World War. They help us understand the substantial civil dimensions of a conflict in which Koreans killed each other in large numbers across a battle-line. However, while such explanations are an important part of the background of the war, the various political divisions and conflicts in Korea during 1945–50, whether in the North or in the South, cannot be separated from the environment of massive foreign intervention. Without such intervention, it seems far-fetched to suggest that the complex, contradictory, highly localised political forces which emerged after 1945 could of themselves have provided the basis for the two specific régimes of the DPRK and ROK, each with distinct social underpinnings, a clear state ideology, a clear geographical base of support, and a clear *casus belli*.

The civil dimensions of the Korean conflict also tell us little about the actual course of the war, its outcome, its effect on the two Koreas and on international politics. This is chiefly because the actual war which began on 25 June 1950 placed the many sources of prewar intra-Korean conflict in an entirely new dimension of scale and involvement. The initial assault was made possible by the Soviet interest, and its plan of battle was drawn up in the Russian language by Soviet military officers. Within months both Korean leaders had been shunted aside, and the fighting was led not by Koreans for Korean ends, but by Americans, Soviets and Chinese for American, Soviet and Chinese ends. This wholesale re-entry of foreign forces into Korea itself emphasises the international origins and dimensions of the conflict.

What, then, were the major consequences of the Korean War? The Korean War took approximately 750,000 military and 800,000 civilian lives. At the end of the Korean War almost 300,000 KPA troops, 227,000 ROK Army troops, 200,000 CPVs, and 57,440 UN troops, of whom more than 33,000 were American, were dead. The North lost over 11 per cent of its population, and in the South there was also massive loss of life and property. Beyond the immediate picture of suffering, the war had important effects on the Soviet Union, China, the United States and their respective allies, and more generally on the international economic and political system. These repercussions are still being felt today.

The world cannot draw much comfort from the Korean conflict, but arguably it contributed to the evolution of a more stable Cold War order by standardising

Cold War rules of superpower engagement. As the US, the Soviet Union and China meditated on their mistakes and miscalculations, they concluded that, although they would continue to fight smaller conflicts through local proxies, they would not again confront each other so directly on the battlefield. No more Berlin blockades occurred, and not until Afghanistan in 1979 would the Soviets again offer major military support to a foreign client.

The Korean War also marked the emergence of the US as a peacetime global power, and also marked the onset of a stable bipolar international order which endured for a further thirty-five years. In June 1950 the US was still retreating from international involvement and dismantling much of its Second World War fighting capabilities. However, the Korean War brought US troops back into battle against Soviet-backed forces, and gave focus to a powerful coalition of legislative and military interests in Washington which committed the US to a sustained military build-up. During the course of the Korean War the US defence budget nearly quadrupled, and these high levels of spending were maintained after 1953. In Europe the Korean War led to the consolidation of NATO and the reintegration of West Germany into the European economic and strategic framework. Meanwhile, in Asia it led to a permanent US military presence throughout the East Asian region, a revival of the Japanese economy based on military procurement of the UNC forces in Korea, the full rehabilitation of Japan as a United States ally, an enduring commitment to the defence of Taiwan, and US support for, and eventual inheritance of, the French role in Indochina. The US held off the enemy in Korea and preserved its security arrangements in Japan, but it also adopted rigid policies of confrontation and resistance to communist-nationalist movements in East Asia. This constituted a prelude to the later calamitous search for a military solution in Vietnam.

The Soviet Union played a major part in establishing the conditions for the North Korean attack, but it was spared major loss. At war's end the DPRK was still a Soviet buffer state, actual Soviet casualties were negligible, and much of the financial burden had been borne by the Chinese. But these were short-term gains, for in the longer term the Korean War did major damage to Soviet strategic interests. In particular, the sustained emergence of the US as a global power brought enormous continuing economic and military pressure to bear on Moscow, and ultimately this pressure became a substantial factor in the decline and fall of the Soviet system and the end of the Cold War. The war also damaged Soviet interests by creating a major fracture in the international communist movement, for the Chinese felt duped by Stalin's promises of massive material assistance in support of the CPV, and retained a keen recollection of unnecessarily high casualties and stiff payments for Soviet materiel. The wounded pride they nursed as a result was an important factor in prolonging armistice negotiations, and their wartime experience of Soviet 'diplomacy' later contributed to the Sino-Soviet split of the late 1950s.

The Chinese emerged from the Korean War as a major regional military and political influence, but they also paid a heavy price for their involvement, in terms of loss of life, damage to the economy, radicalisation of ideology, and international isolation. Although the CCP leadership resolved never again to send troops to fight in a foreign war, the US assessment of the Chinese as a dangerous, erratic power with whom dialogue was impossible remained fixed for many years to come. Chinese relations with the US entered a state of acute confrontation which lasted for a further twenty years.

The effects of this sustained conflict on the two Koreas themselves were, of course, momentous. In the North, the destruction of the KWP communist oligarchy which began during the Korean War was a turning-point in the history of the DPRK, for it directly stimulated the Party's transformation from a broad cross-section of the Korean communist movement to a narrow party led by Kim's guerrilla group. Cadres from other sections of the prewar Korean communist move-ment – the Northern and Southern domestic Korean communists, the Yan'an group, the Soviet-Koreans – disappeared from the senior ranks of the Party, and with their departure the support base of the party narrowed markedly. As a result, the post-Korean War ideological and policy framework in the DPRK increasingly came to reflect the tastes, prejudices and experiences of the Manchurian guerrilla mindset – militarist, Spartan, anti-intellectual and xenophobic.

In the South, the Korean War may well have saved the political career of Syngman Rhee, but its major effects were social. Many Koreans gravitated to the new urban environments which grew rapidly during the war. In 1949 only 18.3 per cent of the population lived in cities of 50,000 or more, but by 1955 this had grown to 25.3 per cent. Exposure to urbanisation also meant increased exposure to mass media, to new methods of work, and to advanced education, and in turn this led to increased social awareness, expectations and demands. Coupled with refugee movements from the North, such major movements of population sepa-rated many people from their extended families, their ancestral clan villages and the restrictions of traditional society. They not only scattered tightly knit village communities but also divided and separated families, and although the traditional social structure had proved remarkably resilient during the previous twenty years, it could not withstand this massive assault. While status and hierarchy remained key elements in Korean social organisation, they were no longer strictly geared to the demands of the village and the agricultural life. The catastrophe of war thus produced a significant levelling of the traditional social structure, and social egalitarianism became a prominent feature of the emerging mass society. In this manner the war removed important psychological and attitudinal barriers to modernisation.

The key consequence of the war was that it sealed the status of Korea as a divided nation. Geopolitically, the Soviets, the Chinese and the USA tacitly accepted a relatively stable regional order based on the *status quo* of a divided Korea, while domestically both the DPRK and the ROK gained legitimacy simply by surviving the war, for this helped to vindicate and consecrate the enormous individual sacrifices Koreans had made for their respective causes. Neither Korea could accept either the division itself, nor the implied rebuke and threat of an alternative political system and ideology presented by the continuing existence of the other. But while each side claimed the right to lead a unified Korea, and while continuing division posed enormous political and economic problems for both Koreas, what had seemed unbearable in 1950 was more bearable in 1953.

Selected reading

Foot, Rosemary 1985, *The Wrong War: American Policy and the Dimensions of the Korean Conflict, 1950–53*, Ithaca, NY: Cornell University Press.

Goncharov, Sergei N., Lewis, John W., and Xue, Litai 1993, *Uncertain Partners: Stalin, Mao, and the Korean War*, Stanford, CA: Stanford University Press.

Halliday, Jon and Cumings, Bruce 1988, *Korea: The Unknown War*, London: Viking Press.

Hastings, Max 1987, *The Korean War*. London: Michael Joseph.

Henderson, Gregory 1968, *Korea: The Politics of the Vortex*, Cambridge, MA: Harvard University Press.

Scalapino, Robert A. and Lee, Chong-sik 1972, *Communism in Korea*, Part 1, *The Movement*, Berkeley, CA: University of California Press.

Stueck, William 1995, *The Korean War: An International History*, Princeton, NJ: Princeton University Press.

5   The mastery of despair, 1953–71

At the conclusion of the Korean War the division of Korea was an accomplished fact. It was reinforced by two mutually exclusive political and economic systems, by the nature of the foreign alliances which guaranteed each Korean state's security, by massive shifts of population – 10–12 per cent of the southern population was now of northern origin and a lesser but still significant number of southerners had gone north – by reciprocal bloodshed and atrocity, and by two competing and irreconcilable claims to represent and speak for all Koreans. In the decades ahead Koreans continued to argue that their common history until 1945 and their profound historical and cultural sense of unity would eventually bring about reunification. Meanwhile, however, the countervailing profound sense of historical and cultural separateness which had developed since 1945 ensured that the division would continue, and that both Koreas would develop as modern states with the threat – or, indeed, *promise* to some – of a resumption of war influencing political thinking and state policy at almost every turn.

The tightly centralised system of the North enforced political conformity and enabled a more rapid postwar recovery than the looser system of the South. Kim Il Sung's wartime reconstruction of the shattered Korean Workers' Party had eliminated many members of competing factions from positions of effective power, and this process continued during the immediate postwar years until Kim and his supporters had achieved domination of party and state. This ushered in a new phase of the DPRK revolution, characterised by rigorous isolation of the population from foreign contact, continuing stress on ideological struggle, high levels of military expenditure and preparedness, a sustained cultural revolution, the development and maintenance of an extensive coercive apparatus, a radically anti-imperialist foreign policy, and the development of Kim's personality cult to the level of absolutist personal autocracy.

In the South, the search for political stability was more elusive. Although Syngman Rhee retained his hold on the presidency, opposition grew as he became progressively more ineffective in the face of mounting postwar social and economic demands. Eventually, in April 1960, widespread demonstrations following a massive vote-rigging scandal forced him from office and into exile. In the elections which followed his departure the Democratic Party, which had been the major opposition party during 1955–60, took office. However, within a matter of months the stresses and opportunities of government fractured the party and rendered it ineffective in office. It was in these circumstances that elements of the ROK Army staged a *coup d'état* on 16 May 1961, and proceeded to consolidate power. The *coup*-makers and their leader, Park Chung-hee, were driven by complex motives, the most salient of which was a conviction that the security of the ROK could only be guaranteed by a strong state capable of mobilising the population in pursuit of military strength and rapid economic growth. As their policies took hold in the mid-1960s, the country began to undergo a major transformation.

The nature of the two Koreas' foreign relationships during this period influenced domestic policy in fundamental ways. Both Korean leaderships depended on their major foreign allies, but they also made crucial distinctions between their interests and those of their allies. The North derived basic security guarantees from the Soviet Union and China, but neither ally backed a resumption of armed conflict. This was not in Pyongyang's interest, as it meant the acceptance of an indefinitely divided Korea. As a result, Kim Il Sung concluded that he would have to rely on the North's own military assets to achieve reunification. In the early 1960s this led to the adoption of the policies of extreme military mobilisation, self-reliance and isolationism, known collectively as Juche, or 'self-reliance'. Juche policies had strong roots in Korean nationalism but, more significantly, in the fundamental differences of policy and perspective on Korean reunification between the DPRK and its allies.

The South was almost entirely dependent for its security on the United States and on the other states that had supported the US-led UN intervention in Korea in 1950. But while these allies were powerful they were also geographically distant, and shared no historical or cultural affinity with the ROK. Memories of the confusion and ambivalence of US pre-1950 policies were also vivid enough for Seoul to conclude that a policy of indefinite, near-total reliance on such allies was inherently risky for a country surrounded by two ideologically hostile neighbours in China and the Soviet Union, and by Japan, its former colonial tormentor. Gratitude and uneasiness at this state of affairs jostled in the South Korean mind, and the pursuit of a balance between the need for international engagement and the need to control their own destiny became elusive and complex.

After the war: the DPRK

As a result of a devastating wartime UNC bombing campaign, after the July 1953 armistice the North faced reconstruction of basic housing, schools, factories, government facilities, power-generating capacity, roads, bridges, ports, mines, irrigation and flood-control dikes, dams and channels. Agricultural and industrial production had dropped well below prewar levels, while the population was war-weary and had been psychologically battered by the sustained bombardment. Most people were without adequate food or clothing, and found shelter in a variety of improvised shanty dwellings. The country subsisted through massive Soviet-bloc aid and was in urgent need of policies of relief and rehabilitation.

The KWP leadership was divided on the issue of postwar recovery. On the one hand, Kim Il Sung and the ex-Manchurian guerrillas sought the early acceleration of socialism, of heavy industrialisation, and of the restoration of the war-making capacity of the DPRK. On the other hand, bureaucrat-technocrat elements led by the Soviet-Koreans had little interest in resurrecting a war economy, and so advocated more gradualist policies which gave priority to the restoration of agriculture and light industry. Beneath the surface of this policy debate lay a far more profound ideological struggle, similar to the 'red versus expert' conflicts which occurred in other communist states at similar periods of their development – Stalin versus Bukharin in the Soviet Union during the 1930s, Mao Zedong versus Liu Shaoqi in China during the early 1960s – and seemingly for similar reasons: leaders such as Stalin, Mao and Kim were suited by temperament and training to seizing power and running highly mobilised, ideologically militant régimes. They had little time for the humdrum daily bureaucratic tasks that rapid economic transformation required, and constantly sought to re-create the conditions of ideological mobilisation in which they felt more at home.

During 1953–58, Kim Il Sung's position on postwar strategy gradually became state policy. As a result, the DPRK placed a major, overriding priority on the reconstruction of heavy industry, and a correspondingly lesser priority on light industry and agriculture. These policies called for high levels of state control and social mobilisation, since effectively they called upon the North Korean people to labour day and night to rebuild steel mills, machine-tool factories, roads and rail infrastructure at a time when most people were without adequate food, clothing or shelter, and had no immediate prospects of gaining access to basic consumer goods. The successful implementation of such policies also underlined the strength of the dictatorship Kim had fashioned. Although he had led his country into a disastrous war, by the time of the July 1953 armistice he was actually in a stronger position within the Korean Workers' Party than ever before. He was the leader of a highly centralised party, government and security apparatus, which he routinely used to isolate and eliminate internal opponents. Outside the party, the population at large was too preoccupied with daily survival to have any real awareness of internal party politics, and even if it did, people had no base from which to voice dissenting opinions. Nor was any opposition from outside the country possible, since neither the Soviets nor the Chinese were prepared to intervene in this struggle.

The initial issues in this intra-party conflict were economic, but the struggle soon spread from the economic to the cultural arena as Kim intensified his attacks on the predominantly Soviet-Korean advocates of gradualism. Contrasting the latter's external ties with the Soviet Union with his own background, for the first time Kim began to stress the virtues of self-reliance and Korean self-identity. This was a high-risk policy, because in the immediate postwar period he was still surrounded by Soviet-Korean cadres, most of whom were responsive to the post-Stalin thaw, and also more able and experienced in the routine business of government than his own supporters. Nevertheless, in December 1955 he began to stress the principle of self-reliance in ideological matters, and then to assert his right to apply the universal truths of Marxism–Leninism to the DPRK's domestic realities as he saw fit. In the process, he first made systematic use of the term

'Juche' to denote state policies of self-reliance, thus foreshadowing the later elevation of Juche to the level of dominant state ideology.

By the time of the April 1955 Party Plenum Kim was able to announce the 'acceleration of socialism'. At the same time, he now openly castigated Soviet-Korean influence within the party in a way that had not been possible before. In December 1955 he criticised the leading Soviet-Korean cadre and leading economic planner, Pak Ch'ang-ok, by name, and in January 1956 removed him as chairman of the State Economic Planning Commission. It was in this atmosphere of ongoing rivalry that the KWP held its Third Congress in April 1956, the first such gathering of the leadership since 1948. The public documents of such congresses provide valuable snapshots of the current and emerging DPRK power élite, and the 1956 Congress confirmed a major transformation of party at both the leadership and grass-roots levels. The Southern communists had been almost entirely eliminated from the politburo, which was the highest organ of the Party, and although some senior Soviet-Korean and Yan'an group cadres retained their formal positions their influence at senior levels of the Party was sharply reduced. Over half the Congress delegates had joined after 1950 as a result of the wartime organisational drive, most were under 40 years of age, and most had limited formal education. Veteran party cadres whose political experience extended back into the pre-1945 era represented a mere 8 per cent of the total. These figures reflected the emerging élite of a guerrilla state: a generation of workers and peasants which had been tempered by war and rewarded for their loyalty in its aftermath, limited in education and without significant foreign connections, even elsewhere within the communist world.

There was little overt sign of internal party struggle at the 1956 Congress, but three months later, in August 1956, the intra-party debate came to a head. Strengthened and encouraged by Soviet leader Nikita Khrushchev's recent denunciation of Stalin and many policies of the Stalin era, including cult of personality politics and the pervasive use of terror and execution, members of the KWP leadership met while Kim was absent abroad, and adopted resolutions criticising Kim for dictatorial tendencies, personality cult leadership and harsh economic policies. However, the opponents had overestimated their strength, and when Kim returned to Pyongyang he prevailed in the subsequent showdown, depriving the ringleaders of the last vestiges of their power. After a protracted grass-roots campaign, by early 1958 the last significant source of opposition to Kim within the Party had been purged, and Kim Il Sung and his group exercised near-total control. Some idea of the severity of the purges conducted during this era may be gained from the fact that they terminated the careers of roughly 70 per cent of the members of the KWP Central Committee, the body which constituted the inner core of the Party.

Kimist control was reflected in the growing emphasis on Kim Il Sung's cult of personality. For a further ten years or so, the Party continued to witness wide-ranging purges, but a significant change had already taken place. Whereas before 1958 the contending groups represented distinct traditions and outlooks drawn from their heritage within the Korean communist movement, after 1958 the division was between those whose loyalty to Kim was direct and unconditional, and those who still continued to argue their case against a leader who increasingly claimed to be the only authoritative source of guidance in the affairs of state. With the elimination of the remaining moderates and other independently minded cadres, public debate on policy and ideology effectively ceased, the KWP ceased to become a political movement as such, and instead became an instrument for carrying out the instructions of the Great Leader. Throughout the 1960s these instructions mandated an intensified drive for heavy industrialisation and rearmament, and growing isolation within the communist bloc. The slogan 'Learn from the Soviet Union!', in use for much of the 1950s, was replaced by the slogan 'Learn from the glorious revolutionary tradition founded by Kim Il Sung and his anti-Japanese partisans!', and this evocation of the anti-Japanese guerrilla tradition was more than a mere slogan. It described an outlook on politics and life which came to dominate virtually all facets of DPRK life – isolated, xenophobic, ruthless, profoundly disciplined, inured to hardship, and committed to unrelenting struggle in a hostile world.

One key result of the demise of the Soviet-Koreans was that the DPRK became isolated from post-Stalin developments in the Soviet bloc. As a result, while aspects of the Stalinist legacy were being widely disavowed elsewhere, Stalin remained revered in Pyongyang and the influence of Stalinism remained profound. A major reason for this was that, while Kim could draw on his guerrilla days as a source for homilies on the need for perseverance, loyalty and discipline, these guerrilla experiences offered little practical guidance in the actual building of an industrialised socialist state. Since there was no precedent in Korea and no body of theoretical writing by Korean communists to offer signposts, the architects of the DPRK state relied profoundly on the Stalinist model of socialist construction and conscientiously applied Stalinist methods in almost every major area of North Korean life. The structure and practices of the Korean Workers' Party closely resembled Stalinist practice, as did the style and detail of Kim's personality cult and the extreme and often abusive language of political debate. The economic structure, with its severe collectivisation of agriculture, unrelenting drive for heavy industrialisation and military strength, was closely modelled on Stalinist policy, as was the almost total lack of interest in consumer production. In ideological matters Kim placed emphasis on remoulding human nature and creating a new 'Juche-type man', which he described in virtually identical terms to Stalin's 'New Soviet Man'. The use of family relationships and imagery (e.g. 'the Fatherly Leader') to describe and validate the leader's unlimited authority over the people was based directly on Stalinist practice, as was Kim's claim to be a genius-leader whose every utterance provided infallible guidance on a wide range of issues, from architecture to zoology. In the choice of political imagery, in themes of propaganda, in the precise laudatory titles bestowed on the Great Leader, and in countless other ways great and small, Stalinist ideas and practices provided the leadership of the DPRK with almost daily guidance in the overturning of Korean tradition and the reshaping of North Korean society.

In economic policy, by 1959 the state owned the entire means of production, while private ownership, whether of land or business, had ceased to exist. The market economy, as such, had also disappeared as centralised bureaucratic management determined output and supply quotas, prices and wages throughout the economy. The DPRK economy grew to be the antithesis of the ROK's export economy, for economic planners instituted a government foreign trade monopoly which excluded foreign investment and reduced trade outside the Soviet bloc largely to the procurement of luxury goods and services for the party élite. Military-style mobilisation became the most prominent feature of civilian working life in the DPRK through a series of production campaigns, beginning with the Chollima movement in 1958, and continuing through various 'speed campaigns' to this day.

However, even as Kim began to mobilise the resources of the DPRK in pursuit of reunification, in the late 1950s international developments began to conspire against his chosen strategy for reunification. Whereas the Stalinist world-view centred on a global struggle to the death between socialism and capitalism, after 1956 the Soviet Union under Nikita Khrushchev spoke increasingly of the possibilities of peaceful coexistence with the West. By the early 1960s, DPRK hopes that the Soviet Union would somehow turn away from this growing trend of peaceful coexistence with the US and resume the resolute confrontation of the Stalinist era had begun to fade. The outcome to the Cuban missile crisis in October 1962, in which the Soviets backed away from their attempts to establish missile sites in Cuba, produced further profound disillusionment in Pyongyang, causing Kim finally to abandon all realistic hope of decisive Soviet support for the militant pursuit of Korean reunification, and with this came the realisation that the DPRK would have to effect a drastic increase in the level of its own mobilisation.

This formed the background to the KWP's adoption of a series of policies at its December 1962 Party Plenum, two months after the Cuban crisis, which gave equal emphasis to the military and civilian economies. Under the slogan 'Arms in one hand and a hammer and sickle in the other!', the KWP effectively placed the entire country on a permanent semi-war footing, and in the process soon drastically transformed the economy, the leadership, and ultimately the nature of the DPRK state itself. The Plenum established four basic military policies: arming the entire population, providing extensive additional training for existing soldiers, converting the entire country into a fortress, and modernising the armed forces. As it implemented these policies in the following three years, the allocation of economic resources to military production rose rapidly from an estimated 6 per cent to 30 per cent, far higher than equivalent rates in the Soviet Union or in China. The effect of this major redirection of resources on the civilian economy was drastic, for it soon proved impossible for the state to serve the needs of ongoing economic development as well accelerate the country's military build-up. As military expenditure stabilised at around 30 per cent, the economy ceased its rapid growth trajectory and stagnated. The economic decline of the DPRK and the later economic catastrophe of the 1990s had profound roots in these developments.

A particular effect of Equal Emphasis was to enforce rigorous censorship over virtually all significant economic and social data. In contrast to the avalanche of statistics that continued to emerge from the ROK, reliable information about the DPRK, including even basic economic data such as GNP, and basic social indices such as population and demographics, went unreported in the media and were unavailable for reasons of 'military security'. Nevertheless, it is clear that by 1965 the economy was experiencing severe strains, and the party leadership was beginning to divide on the issue of moderating the military build-up. Like the 1953–56 debate on postwar economic priorities, this issue pitted unconditional supporters of the build-up, mainly Kim and the military, against others, mainly technocrats and economic managers, who doubted that the economy could stand the strain. In such a personalised system, disputes over policy were difficult to separate from disputes over leadership, and so behind the debate lay the question of whether the Party should place unconditional faith in Kim's judgement, or whether it should continue to argue out policy positions. This question was resolved in emphatic fashion at a special party conference in October 1966 when Kim ended the careers of nine of the sixteen members of the Politburo, including six who were responsible for economic management, replacing them with people whose unconditional and personal loyalty was not in doubt. This move marked the last time that the KWP experienced a significant leadership purge, for henceforth the ideology of the Party and the state policies that resulted from it derived exclusively from the teachings of Kim Il Sung, while unflinching personal loyalty to Kim became a necessary condition for physical as well as political survival for the party élite.

The 1966 purge removed the last doubters from the inner circle, and the triumph of the true believers fuelled an unprecedented display of militancy towards the South. Significant DMZ incidents increased eleven-fold in 1967, and in January 1968 a KPA commando unit infiltrated Seoul and launched an attack on the ROK presidential compound known as the Blue House. Almost simultaneously, the DPRK navy seized the US surveillance vessel *Pueblo* in international waters off its east coast, and in October 1968 teams of Northern guerrillas landed on the east coast of the ROK in an apparent effort to establish a base for guerrilla warfare in the sparsely populated and impoverished hinterland. While it is difficult to assess DPRK motivation with precision, these operations seem to have been designed to apply pressure to the ROK and the US at a time when both were deeply involved in the Vietnam War. However, while such actions brought the two Koreas to the brink of conflict once more, the results seem to have disappointed the North, and by 1969 the number and scale of military incidents fell away again as Pyongyang reconsidered its options.

By 1970 the Korean Workers' Party had extensively remoulded DPRK society in accordance with Juche ideology. A powerful, intrusive party and state extended their reach deeply into society, and closely supervised all political activity. Such staple groups in civil society as the technocracy, the intelligentsia, trade unions, the farming population, youth, and women's organisations all spoke through party-controlled representative organisations, and their utterances were usually confined to offering lavish, robotic praise to the leadership of Kim Il Sung. In addition, individual citizens themselves were subject to a formidable reward–punishment system and a ruthless, coercive state apparatus. In a small geographical area the Kimist system went further than its Soviet and Chinese counterparts in penetrating and organising civil society. It gave no role to private economic initiative beyond black and grey market activities; and, while the rule of law in the sense of rules of procedure in public matters continued to exist, it ceased to be a body of rules which could restrain or inhibit the state in dealing with its citizens.

Revolutionary change also sustained a high level of social mobility during the 1950s and 1960s. Against a background of war, successive political and ideological shakeups, and rapid economic mobilisation, life changed profoundly for many people. The worker-peasant members of the post-1953 mass KWP used their new status to enter into new urban environments, new jobs, new organisations, where they encountered new production and management technologies. Workers and peasants became bureaucrats and sometimes technocrats, and all faced the shock of the new. Their new status had a legal basis in the formal three-level classification by the party of DPRK citizens as either loyal to the party, wavering, or potentially disloyal by reason of their class background. Such a classification system determined access to education, employment and housing, and to Party membership, which alone could ensure a reasonable level of material comfort.

Although ties based on kinship, place of origin, school class and military service were tolerated among the loyal party élite, where nepotism flourished from the very top down, such tendencies were heavily discouraged elsewhere in society. The Korean clan and family system was effectively repressed, people ceased to observe ritual festival days such as the autumn harvest thanksgiving festival of Chusok, and ancestral graves ceased to be tended. Meaningful organised religion, whether Buddhist, Confucian or Christian, also ceased to exist. In a rare description of his country's religious life to a Japanese delegation in 1971, Kim Il Sung described how younger people had all received a 'modern education' and were no longer interested in Buddhism or Confucianism. Christianity had ceased to exist in his country, he maintained, when Christians lost their faith as a result of US bombing during the Korean War.

The almost total lack of a consumer economy meant the almost total dependence of citizens on the government for the distribution of even basic items of food and clothing. By 1970 there was still barely enough to go round, for despite strong rates of economic growth the benefits had been ploughed back into military expenditure, into increasing the means of production, and into providing a very basic level of health care, education and welfare. Material incentives were limited, and the régime placed major importance on ideological incentives, constantly assuring people that an age of prosperity was close at hand, and urging them to make sacrifices for socialist construction and for the liberation of the South. The concept of citizens as individuals with certain basic human rights was dismissed as a 'bourgeois' notion, unnecessary in the DPRK where all people were taken care of as 'children' of the benevolent Great Leader. In time this became a deeply embedded concept, but the illusion of benevolence masked a more complicated relationship of fear and dependency between leader and people. Their voices could not be heard except as affirmative choruses to official sloganeering; and, as many later defectors confirmed, lack of basic decision-making control over their lives was a source of constant anxiety and frustration. Paradoxically, but perhaps predictably, the more monolithic the claims of the Party, the more its institutional base in society became brittle through the lack of strong, autonomous social bonds between ordinary people in their daily dealings with each other.

The Party maintained tight control over the workforce. It remained suspicious of the emergence of a distinct managerial and specialist outlook in the course of industrialisation, and therefore devoted much energy to the superimposition of party control over all workplaces. The major factory-floor-level instrument for this was Kim's Taean Work System, instituted in 1960. This system took management of factories and other industrial economic units away from a single technician-manager and vested it in the unit's Party political committee. As many economic managers elsewhere in socialist countries had discovered before them, gains in loyalty required measurement against loss of efficiency and technological backwardness. Similarly, Kim's Chongsan-ri Method organised agricultural work along the lines of industrial work. Essentially, farmers were organised along the lines of workers in factories, and so resources and time available for private agricultural production became almost nonexistent. Isolated by primitive communication and by restrictions on internal movement, the rural dweller remained almost dependent on the political centre and a centralised distribution system. This arrangement was to have catastrophic results in the famine-ravaged 1990s.

By the early 1970s the DPRK had achieved compulsory eleven-year schooling (age 5–16) through nearly ten thousand primary and secondary schools and 4,809 secondary schools. In addition, over 200 universities, colleges and specialised colleges had been established. The quality was variable, but the organisational achievement was noteworthy. Beginning in kindergarten, the Party-mandated curriculum featured a heavy ideological component which reflected the guerrilla outlook of the élite. The students themselves were subject to a daily routine that was not only highly regimented but also overtly militarised. Habitual marching in step both inside and outside the school, military songs, games, drills, and even playground apparatus modelled on military equipment prepared children for their adult military responsibilities. Formal academic instruction was also supplemented by a pervasive programme of extracurricular education designed to inculcate political loyalty. The number and range of such activities and organisations included pre-school institutions such as nurseries and kindergartens, after-school activities, youth groups, extended daily workplace and neighbourhood study sessions, and military-political education within the armed forces. In addition, the mass media, art, literature and music were all pressed into service to produce 'new, Juche-type citizens'. Essentially, what the Party sought, and by all indications achieved, was a new generation raised to emulate the lifestyle of the prewar guerrilla generation.

Despite the growth in education, the political system continued to exclude the intelligentsia from political power and policy-making, while also depriving them of a creative voice. The Party remained continually uneasy about its relations with 'intellectuals', and maintained tight surveillance and ideological control over them. In his public pronouncements Kim Il Sung made clear his own profound distrust of intellectuals, whom he suspected of such ideological crimes as 'individualism' and the harbouring of bourgeois thought. In fact, intellectual activity in an environment where all ideas and concepts had to be sanctioned by Kim before they could be circulated in the public sphere became profoundly derivative. At the level of university and beyond, the effects of isolation and heavy ideological content became increasingly apparent as the standard of published DPRK scholarship declined drastically. Moreover, intellectuals were, of course, major casualties of party warfare; and by 1970, of the forty or so top party officials, only Yun Gi Bok and Hwang Jang Yop could claim to have worked in an intellectual environment for any length of time.

The spread of monolithic Kimist ideology also brought with it the tightening of control over art and culture. The state exercised absolute power in determining the subject matter, themes, and techniques of expression, and Kim Il Song gave periodic public guidance to writers on their craft. Following the basic principles of Socialist Realism which evolved in the Soviet Union under Stalin, the task of DPRK writers was to portray the revolutionary struggle and the 'joy of life' under socialism, to avoid the subjectivism, individualism and 'negativism' of bourgeois literature, and to place one's creative life at the service of the collective. Art was created by trained propagandists – 'engineers of human souls' in Zhdanov's famous phrase – and aimed at uplifting the masses, inspiring them first by the deeds of socialist heroes, and increasingly by the heroic deeds of Kim Il Sung himself as guerrilla fighter and nation-builder. By 1970 individual authorship had all but ceased, and creative literature, as the term is commonly defined, had been replaced by literary propaganda which exalted the inspirational leadership of Kim Il Sung. Not only were the paths which the creative artist might follow subject to severe oversight, but the creative impulse and the individual point of view were themselves also discouraged.

After the war: the ROK

In the South the war strengthened the Rhee administration. While Rhee faced continuing pressure from opponents within the National Assembly in the immediate aftermath of the war, the population as a whole offered little challenge to his continuing rule. This was due, in varying degrees, to the enervating effect of wartime suffering, to the daily struggle for survival, to Rhee's personal popularity, to a sense of national unity based on anti-communism, and to the effects of political repression. Civil society was far from quiescent, but its energies were directed primarily towards family and clan affairs, rather than towards public life, and so it did not support the development of strong social or political alliances which might have challenged the state. Well over half the population still lived in rural villages where family and clan exercised effective social and political control over the individual, and where the reach of the outside world was limited. Thus, any portrait of ROK society in the 1950s needs to take account of two co-existing, strongly contrasting social systems: the rural villages, which were ruled in accordance with the age-old prerogatives of patriarchal and clan custom, and the cities, which were governed by an altogether different set of institutions and élites – bureaucratic, Japanised as much as Westernised, and increasingly egalitarian as much as hierarchical.

Land reform on the eve of the war converted many tenant and predominantly tenant farmers into landowners. It removed landlords from their traditional source of wealth and status, while rampant postwar inflation quickly eroded the financial compensation they had received. Meanwhile, the new owner-cultivators struggled against a new set of economic difficulties. The landlords had been the source of operating capital for tenant farmers in a relationship which was characterised not just by exploitation but also by reciprocal obligation. With the demise of the landlords, the small farmer, hard-pressed for cash, was forced to turn to local merchants as moneylenders, pledging land as collateral. As defaults occurred, there was a new fragmentation of land holdings, resulting in the emergence of a new land-owning class. Meanwhile, however, land ownership itself lost much of its significance as an arbiter of social status because new channels of social advancement began to emerge in the bureaucracy, the fast-growing education sector, and the military. Rural-gentry status increasingly described a style and a tradition, not a political or economic base.

The Rhee autocracy reached its height in the immediate postwar period. Through a combination of police harassment and restrictive electoral laws aimed at the major opposition candidates of the Democratic Nationalist Party (DNP), Rhee's political organisation strengthened its control over the Assembly at the Third National Assembly elections in May 1954. Rhee's Liberals gained 114 seats, an increase of some 57, while the number of DNP seats fell from 40 to 15. Ostensibly, the always-numerous independent members held the balance of power, but collectively they had little perception of their own role as a check on presidential power. They lacked funds to maintain their local political profile, and this made them vulnerable to the large-scale practice of money politics by the Liberals, who proceeded to recruit nominal independents with a view to pushing through a further constitutional amendment allowing Rhee to seek a third term in 1956. In November 1954 this amendment was carried amid high farce when 135 out of 203 members voted for it. Under heavy pressure, the presiding Vice-Speaker declared that since a two-thirds majority consisted of 135.3 members he would disregard the one-third and declare the bill carried. The DNP opposition was demoralised by its inability to withstand this constitutional *coup*, and in September 1955 gave way to a new major opposition party, the Democratic Party, which was formed on the basis of unity among all anti-Rhee forces. Such a basis was of course expedient and tenuous, and defined the Democrats' subsequent identity as a vehicle for the ambitions of its component faction leaders.

As the process of postwar recovery took hold, the rapid expansion of education and the growth of urban culture marked a growing sophistication in ROK society and politics, which in the longer term eroded the foundations of Rhee's autocracy. The presidential election of May 1956 provided the first strong indication of a changing political mood. Although Rhee was re-elected, he gained only 56 per cent of the vote, down from 72 per cent in the 1952 election. The real level of electoral support was probably substantially lower, given the government's command of the electoral process, and given the absence of an opponent after the death of Shin Ik-hui from a heart attack during the campaign. Moreover, in the separate vice-presidential election, the opposition candidate Chang Myon defeated Rhee's protégé and anointed successor Yi Ki-bung, out-polling him 41.7 per cent to 39.6 per cent overall, and winning by a margin of almost three to one in urban areas. Rhee gained a third four-year term, but the human and material resources required to maintain political control continued to drain his administration and distract it from addressing fundamental economic and social issues.

Meanwhile, the pace of economic recovery remained slow. In addition to the loss of manpower and the disruption to infrastructure, much of the ROK's industrial capacity had been destroyed in the Korean War, while the population had been swollen by a further north–south refugee flow. In 1953 the ROK produced sub-stantially less than its constituent southern provinces did in 1940. Exports totalled $40 million, but imports of $347 million emphasised the indigent status of the country. By 1958 the government had accomplished the basic reconstruction of industry and infrastructure, and price stabilisation policies created a platform for modest economic growth during 1958–60. However, land reform had produced a fragmented pattern of land holdings in which the social and political gains were offset by economic inefficiency. Manufacturing industry was chiefly oriented towards the production of consumer items behind high tariff barriers, while the business sector depended on a close and often corrupt relationship with the government sector, from which flowed such benefits as the acquisition of foreign exchange at undervalued official rates, exclusive import licences, public contracts, aid funds and materials, and inexpensive bank loans, all of which discouraged more efficient business activities. The sum of all these factors was slow growth rates, far too slow to satisfy rising popular expectations. In structure and output, the ROK economy in 1960 still closely resembled that of the southern provinces in 1940.

The Fourth National Assembly elections in May 1958 emphasised the con-tinuing decline of the Rhee administration. The Liberal Party could gain only 38.7 per cent of the vote despite extensive electoral fraud and harassment of the Democratic Party, which gained 29.5 per cent of the vote, largely at the expense of independent candidates. The discipline of a two-party system was beginning to take hold, and the overwhelming centring of the Democrats' strength in the cities underscored a growing urban–rural cleavage. The election resulted in a stronger opposition within the National Assembly, to which the administration responded with further repression, culminating in the passage of a series of national security bills in December 1958, the provisions of which amounted to a virtual suspension of the remaining vestiges of the democratic process.

By the time of the fourth presidential election in March 1960 the First Republic had seriously lost coherence. The Rhee camp had no viable means of achieving victory other than by electoral fraud on an unprecedented scale. Conversely, opposition forces had no viable means of achieving the removal of Rhee other than by palace *coup* or popular revolt. Syngman Rhee himself was in his mid-eighties and failing intellectually, while his adopted son and political heir, Yi Ki-bung, was not only widely disliked and feared, but was also debilitated by serious illness. In many ways Yi symbolised the decline of the Rhee machine. He was a key figure in maintaining the coercive power of the régime but was so deeply unpopular in Seoul that he was forced to seek a rural electorate to gain election to the National Assembly. In the fourth ROK presidential election of 15 March 1960, Rhee was declared elected with 88.7 per cent of the vote, while the result gave Yi Ki-bung a similar margin over Chang Myon for the vice-presidency. Vote rigging on this scale revealed a leadership which had seriously lost touch with reality, and waves of protest followed. These were led chiefly by university students, and amid growing police brutality the turning-point came when police fired on demonstrating Koryo University students in Seoul on 19 April. This turned protest into an insurrection which spread to other major cities and took the lives of an estimated four hundred students. On 25 April university professors, most of whom were themselves Rhee appointees, joined the ranks of the demonstrators, and when the government called upon the army to restore order the commanders made it clear that they would not fire on unarmed demonstrators. The régime then quickly crumbled. On 26 April, Rhee resigned, and on 29 May he left Korea for exile in Hawaii, where he died in 1965. Rather than face certain and extreme humiliation and retribution, on 28 April, Yi Ki-bung and his family committed suicide together.

Rhee left a mixed legacy. He had lived most of his life abroad, and so never got to practise the politics he preached among his fellow countrymen until he was well past his prime. In the mean-time, the liberal convictions of his early political career had become increasingly reactionary. By the end of the Korean War, Rhee was nearly 80 years old, and as the 1950s wore on his response to the overwhelming problems of postwar reconstruction grew progressively feeble. Nevertheless, in some respects, he laid much of the groundwork for the years of rapid economic growth from the mid-1960s on. The conservative political interests he represented dragged their heels over land reform, but ultimately it took place, and the dispossession of the rural gentry removed an important barrier to social mobility – and hence to industrial mobilisation. Within the bureaucracy, Rhee maintained close control of the politically sensitive portfolios, but he also placed a talented cadre of technocrats in positions of authority to administer the post-1953 recovery, and they in turn recruited many of the younger, task-oriented professionals who were so influential in government from the 1960s on. The Rhee administration established the Economic Development Council in 1958, which was the forerunner of the Economic Planning Board and the first government department devoted to long-range economic planning. It also oversaw the establishment of much of the training infrastructure for the future technocracy, and such infrastructure became a valuable asset to Park Chung-hee when the ROK adopted a series of Five-Year Economic Plans after 1961, for it provided much of the human capital and expertise for rapid modernisation.

However, such foresight existed alongside serious political shortcomings. In the final analysis, while Rhee fought passionately for Korean independence, and while he understood the desperate consequences of the asymmetrical commitments of the Soviet Union and the US to Korea, he had little sense of what an independent Korea might look like, other than that it should be anti-communist and somehow 'free'. He often treated issues of economic and social policy dismissively, as though he expected such issues to be resolved by the fact of independence. Rhee's feel for politics was sure, but his understanding of the forces of modernisation was limited. To Rhee, national destiny seemed ultimately determined by national spirit regardless of material circumstances, and his grasp of public policy was limited accordingly. Rhee often displayed keen insights, especially in his criticisms of US aid policy, but these were undermined by his tolerance of corruption and repression, by the counter-productive anti-Japanese rhetoric which encased so many of his economic pronouncements, and by the inability of his administration to develop effective state planning and joint aid administration mechanisms to match his economic ambitions. As a result, economic recovery was slow, and aid dependency remained high. The ambition to achieve rapid industrialisation was present, but the country lacked the basic infrastructure, governmental planning mechanisms, managerial, technical and marketing skills, and access to capital. Moreover, it was continually overwhelmed by immediate human need, with a destitute population requiring that a major proportion of the country's available resources be allocated to relief and rehabilitation.

Long after Rhee's demise, Korean public-opinion polls have continued to rank him as one of the ROK's most effective leaders, but his effect on Korean politics was also dispiriting. Even after noting that social, cultural, material and political conditions during the First Republic were far from ideal for maintaining a commitment to democratic practices, Rhee presided over a system in which the constitution, the electoral process, and the nation's democratic institutions were corrupted, civil rights and the due process of law frequently disregarded, freedom of expression restricted, and political opposition suppressed and discouraged. Caught between conflicting progressive and reactionary inclinations, Rhee weakened popular support for democratic, civilian-led modernisation, and this helped prepare the way for military leadership and authoritarian politics.

The Second Republic

One of Syngman Rhee's last acts in office was to effect an orderly succession of government by appointing an old colleague, Ho Chong, as prime minister and acting president. Ho was not implicated in the excesses of Liberal Party rule, and he quickly established an interim government comprising eminent persons with a similar reputation for impartiality. On 15 June 1960 the Ho administration promulgated a new constitution which created a new, bicameral National Assembly, re-established a system of cabinet government, and sought to avoid a repetition of the Rhee presidential autocracy by significantly reducing the powers of the president, who was henceforth to be chosen by the National Assembly and not by direct popular election. In the National Assembly elections which followed on 29 July, the Democratic Party, which had been the main opposition party under Rhee during 1955–60, gained 175 of 233 seats in the lower house, and set about forming a government. However, far from confirming the Democratic Party as the new majority party, electoral success exposed the party's essential identity as a coalition of mutually hostile political bosses drawn together by their opposition to Rhee. During weeks of post-election manoeuvring over the choice of prime minister, the major factions of Yun Posun and Chang Myon fell out with each other, and when Chang secured the numbers for election to the position the 86 members of the Yun faction left the Democratic Party. Chang began his term of office having lost nearly half of his National Assembly seats as well as valuable momentum and goodwill.

The Chang Myon government did little to persuade the electorate that it could meet widespread demands for strong national defence, basic law and order, and economic progress. Corruption remained endemic, while the demise of Rhee's national police brought about a deterioration of law and order, especially in urban areas. Endemic demonstrations were an important sign of the new democracy, but as the months passed they grew more shrill and even fatuous, and so also raised questions about the government's authority. Perceptions of weakness in all these fields provided the background to a military *coup* on 16 May 1961. Carefully planned and engineered mainly by junior generals and colonels, the *coup* involved some 3,500 soldiers assembled around a core of 250 officers within a 500,000-man army. On 17 May the *coup* leader, Park Chung-hee, dissolved the National Assembly, prohibited indefinitely all political activity, and announced the formation of a junta of thirty colonels and brigadier-generals. The era of the Third Republic began.

Many factors contributed to the downfall of the Second Republic. In the absence of the broad unwritten political conventions which underlie mature parliamentary democracy, the chances for successful government depended foremost on the letter of the new constitution, on the effectiveness of the political parties, and on the performance of the leading individuals involved. As we have noted, the framers of the new constitution were mindful – perhaps overly so – of the Syngman Rhee experience, and so they established a weak executive under the firm control of a nominally strong legislature. However, this strengthened legislature could not provide effective government under prevailing conditions. Its members were typically elected by virtue of their personal standing in local electorates, rather than as the candidates of a disciplined party organisation, and their instincts were parochial, not national. They required significant financial resources to maintain their local standing, and so arrived in the National Assembly as quasi-independent legislators with few practical skills to offer government, but with a powerful in-built need to share in the spoils of office. Since they owed little to the Democratic Party organisation, the party had to bid constantly for their allegiance. The demands for a share of the spoils of office soon grew shrill, corruption flourished, and the legislature became increasingly ineffective. In this manner, the constitution was out of touch with grass-roots realities, and could not restrain a legislature which was neither decisive nor, indeed, always responsible in its actions.

The constitution and the practical responsibility of office also ruthlessly exposed the shortcomings of the Democratic Party. As a party and as a government, it had its roots in the past, and drew its leadership primarily from members of the Seoul élite who had first risen to prominence in the late 1940s. These were men of the past who had all headed their own political organisations, but who in 1955 had united into a single party on the basis that Rhee was their common enemy. With Rhee gone, the underlying rationale for a united opposition also disappeared, and the discipline of office was not sufficient to save the party from factionalism and disunity. The violence and upheaval which had accompanied the final downfall of Rhee tended to obscure the minimal change that had actually occurred: this was change *within* the élite, not *of* the élite. As a result, the Democrats were the somewhat startled beneficiaries of a change in government and a change in the public mood which had been brought about by new social forces which they did not fully comprehend. They had few contacts with such groups as the student movement, younger intellectuals, organised labour or the military. For such politicians, the challenge of coping simultaneously with internal division, a new political system, new political forces and new constitutional procedures, let alone of harnessing these forces to deal with pressing matters of state, was overwhelming.

These shortcomings imposed powerful constraints on the leadership. Prime Minister Chang Myon's mandate seemed overwhelming, and yet it was still limited. The major issue as far as public opinion was concerned was the re-establishment of democracy, but subsequent support for the new democracy depended on the extent to which it served practical interests such as clean government, public order, and economic progress. In seeking to meet such demands Chang was under powerful constraints. The early split in the Democratic Party weakened his authority, and his defeated rivals became powerful and implacable factional enemies, opposed to many government policies. Chang could not act decisively to call former Rhee officials to account, because he still needed the support of many former Rhee appointees to make the armed forces and the bureaucracy function. Nor could he either placate or bring to heel the largely leaderless student movement, for although their initiative in leading the demonstrations against Rhee gained them prestige and respect, their leftist politics and demands for radical, far-reaching reform commanded little discernible public support.

Lack of effective economic policy also undermined support for the government. At a time of widespread demands for economic relief, the continuing political strife worked against effective economic planning. The new government sought to implement systematic development plans using the planning infrastructure which had been established in the last years of the Rhee administration, but political turmoil proved to be a constant distraction. By May 1961 it still had little to show for its efforts, apart from curbing inflation and otherwise imposing the type of fiscal responsibility which meant a good deal of economic pain and sacrifice in the short term – an option that did not find much public favour. It took the government seven months to produce a substantial economic agenda document, and a promised Five-Year Plan had not yet emerged by the time of its overthrow.

Chang was also constrained by the inevitable revitalisation of political debates long repressed under Rhee. The freer political atmosphere encouraged contention between radicals and conservatives but, as with the political debates of the pre-Rhee period, the degree of polarisation and acrimony made it difficult to find middle ground. The absence of a settled political and intellectual community, the highly localised and personalised dimension to Korean politics, and a yawning generation-gap often meant that terms such as 'radical' or 'conservative' explained little about the nature of political debate. In the context of the ROK in 1960, to be radical generally meant to be young, to be more analytical about the nature of society and politics, to be more preoccupied with issues of social and class conflict, to be alienated from the existing socio-economic order, though not necessarily to advocate a socialist alternative, to oppose state-directed repression, to have a much greater commitment towards dialogue with the North and reunification, to have a more nationalistic, self-reliant attitude to foreign policy, and to be critical of the ROK's close reliance on the US. Style was as significant as substance in such matters, and so radicals tended to be more idealistic and intellectual in their approach to public policy. Their natural milieu was the education sector, and their objective was comprehensive reform. The 'conservative' viewpoint was less intellectual or analytical in approach. Whether through innate acceptance of Confucian-derived values or through intellectual conviction, conservatives stressed the continuing relevance of a loose set of principles which they somehow felt to be representative of 'traditional' Korean values. The anti-communist struggle was prominent in conservative thinking, and they were pessimistic about the chances of constructive dialogue with the North. Conservative leaders also tended to be more élitist and internationalist in outlook, and hence were more comfortable with the US alliance. Their natural milieu was the bureaucratic-administrative élite and their objective was incremental change.

The student movement was an important spearhead of radicalism. Students had played a leading role in Rhee's downfall, although collectively they had in mind a different Second Republic from the one which ultimately emerged. Better educated than their parents' generation, they were less worn down by war and repression, and more sensitive to economic and social issues. They themselves could not make a revolution, and so their political role was essentially that of a catalyst for political forces within the élite. Their role during this and other crises to come was determined chiefly by the fact that they did not represent any material interest. Rather, their activism devolved from their age-group and life-style, which consisted of youth, gathered together in a single place of education with freedom and ease of assembly, pausing to enjoy a period of leftist political activism – to take what their more cynical elders sometimes called a 'pink shower' – before proceeding to a brutal and demanding period of national service, then settling down to a solid and apolitical middle-class working life. For a brief period in their lives they stood free of material responsibility and were shielded from the complex and inhibiting responsibilities of adulthood. They were also the first to reflect new ways of thinking and feeling particular to post-1953 ROK society, and were largely removed from the dimension of pre-1950 memory and comparative experience.

Few people rose to defend the Second Republic from the murky future foreshadowed by the 16 May *coup*-makers. The long years of military-dominated authoritarian rule which have caused many to pass lightly over the shortcomings of the Chang administration, but to contemporaries its shortcomings were obvious and severe, and its passing inspired little regret. Given more time it might have addressed these shortcomings with greater assurance, but its own failings ensured that it did not receive this opportunity. Few blamed the actual leaders, and public surveys revealed a dominant, self-critical Korean attitude that they were somehow 'not ready for democracy'. To the extent that this attitude highlighted the often contradictory demands of rapid modernisation and participatory democracy, this was a shrewd assessment. Liberal politics was vulnerable because, to most people other than the urban-based élite, representative democracy seemed an unconvincing way of running the state. As both democratically elected representatives and members of the élite, the Chang administration believed that its right to rule was self-evident, and so it mistook legitimacy for credibility. It did not seem to have seriously believed that more ruthless, extra-constitutional forces would not accept this claim. Meanwhile, to the extent that the Second Republic further undermined many Koreans' faith in constitutional, representative government and political institutions, it pointed with foreboding to the future.

However, while the achievements of the Second Republic were generally passed over at the time, they were considerable. The events of April 1960 put an end to Syngman Rhee's political machine, and to the dominance of the bureaucracy by the colonial Japanese-educated élite. An important break with what had become an increasingly dead weight of the past inspired the development of a more future-oriented outlook. This inspired a more vigorous and creative intellectual life, much of whose energy was devoted to gaining wealth and power as much as to defining its social values. Meanwhile, the April 1960 student revolution reaffirmed and added contemporary relevance to that portion of the Korean political tradition which emphasised the importance of popular resistance to repression in pursuit of political freedom and justice.

Park Chung-hee and the beginnings of the ROK industrial state

The 16 May *coup*-makers made their move because they believed that few people would stand and defend the Second Republic, and this assessment proved accurate. President Yun Posun agreed to remain in office under the new leaders, leading media such as the *Donga Ilbo* and *Sasang-gye* gave support to the *coup*, and many other opinion leaders either reserved judgement or reacted positively to the proposed programmes of the new government, which were announced in resonant, patriotic terms. The new leaders would protect the nation from the 'false' democracy practised by inefficient, corrupt civilian politicians, and implement 'administrative democracy', whereby popular needs and expectations would be met through the functioning of an efficient, public-spirited government committed to progress. They would also wean the economy off aid dependency and lead it towards rapid independent economic development. They would also do away with corrupt and 'backward' social practices which stood in the way of the building of an efficient modern society.

A strong sense of imminent threat to the state underlay this programme. Since the ROK was engaged in an ongoing war with the North, most citizens needed little convincing of the need for a strong, effective military. Moreover, an additional challenge had also emerged with the rapid economic recovery of Japan, which threatened to turn the South into an economic dependency once more. Only eight years had passed since the end of the Korean War, and the argument that disorderly government, political corruption, unruly public demonstrations and the spread of radical ideologies might tempt the North to believe that significant support for communism existed in the South and to resume military action still carried substantial weight. However, the ROK military's perception of threat went further than military invasion to include industrial and technological backwardness. A central objective of the new rulers was therefore the rapid building of a modern state which would close the military gap with the North and the economic gap with Japan and the West as rapidly as possible.

In the context of the Republic of Korea in 1961, this was a revolutionary programme, conceived and implemented by a new élite which represented a sharp break with the élites of the First and Second Republic. The new rulers were generally men of lower social origin than the Seoul élites, and in time the common background of being raised and educated in and around Taegu, North Kyongsang Province – the 'T–K' link – became prominent. They were mostly under 40 years of age, and were products of the isolated, disciplined world of the Korean military. Many had also trained under the Japanese in the Manchurian Military Academy, had graduated from the eighth graduating class of the Korean Military Academy, and had worked in military intelligence. Older officers such as Park Chung-hee were strongly influenced by their exposure to the methods of the Japanese Empire during 1931–45. To such men, state-directed capitalism, operating in an atmosphere free of the constraints of societal pressure and electoral politics, represented an efficient means of effecting rapid economic transformation. The younger officers who comprised the majority of the new junta members lacked exposure to the Japanese model, but while they were more familiar with Western military technology, management and command structures as a result of US training, they had had little exposure to Western values. In fact, their own set of personal experiences, drawn from political chaos, war and inert, inefficient civilian bureaucratic rule, alienated them from the practices of the older civilian political leaders and gave them a similar outlook to their senior colleagues. To such men strong government and social discipline were the very cornerstones of a successful economy and state, and so many remained hostile to political and economic liberalism.

Although the new rulers received significant support for their *coup* from sections of the Seoul political élite, most members of this élite regarded them as outsiders and usurpers. The *coup*-makers therefore faced continuing resistance from the forces they had displaced – mainly from the civilian politicians, but also from the students and intellectuals who had played such a key role in the overthrow of Rhee. Establishing their legitimacy in the eyes of such forces constituted a key issue, and this they attempted to do with a mixture of force and more subtle pressure. On 19 May 1961, Park Chung-hee reorganised his junta and proceeded to rule the country through a Supreme Council for National Reconstruction. On 6 June 1961 the Supreme Council promulgated a Law for National Reconstruction, which gave it effective control over all branches of government and in all spheres of political activity. Under this law the National Assembly was dissolved, Chang Myon and most of his colleagues were temporarily detained, approximately 17,000 civil servants and 2,000 military officers were dismissed, an estimated two-thirds of all publications were closed, and all elected local government discontinued. Street-level law and order, by general consent a strong popular demand and a key Second Republic failing in the urban areas, was enforced by the summary rounding up of gangs and other 'anti-social elements'.

This initial wholesale application of military methods to civil government helped the new rulers to achieve some of their immediate social and economic objectives, but they could not establish legitimacy or longer-term stability, nor could they satisfy the expectations of their foreign allies, without a reversion to civilian rule. Consequently, in August 1961, Park Chung-hee announced that the Council would restore civilian rule by May 1963. In December 1962 a new constitution was drafted whose major outlines resembled the First Republic in re-establishing a strong presidency and a weak, unicameral legislature, and the following month the government lifted its wide-ranging ban on political activities. In February 1963 the *coup* leaders positioned themselves to dominate the restored civilian administration and institutionalise their power-base by inaugurating the Democratic Republican Party (DRP), and in May 1963, after various manoeuvres, Park was endorsed as the DRP candidate for president. In October 1963, Park was elected with 46.5 per cent of the vote over Yun Posun (45 per cent).

The restoration of key features of representative government went some way towards broadening the base of the régime. It also reflected an often tacit recognition by the new rulers that the command–response model of military hierarchy could not be applied wholesale to ROK civil society, as had occurred in the North. But, if wholesale repression of political and social forces was not an option, co-opting various civilian sectors and claiming a mandate on the basis of effective economic performance and good public order was. Thus, a complicated alliance of convenience began to take shape, comprising a rejuvenated bureaucracy as the source of macro-economic planning expertise, the business sector as the source of the requisite expertise for building a modern economy, and the military as the enforcers of political and social discipline in the name of effective economic planning. This alliance achieved the co-ordination of political aims and economic means, and in time delivered to the military a measure of tolerance and acceptance in the business, academic, intellectual and bureaucratic communities. Over all, however, relations between these two very distinct branches of the new élite remained uneasy throughout the Park era.

Park Chung-hee stood at the head of the Third Republic, uneasily combining the roles of military command and civilian leadership. More than most, Park could claim to be a self-made man. Taciturn and with few confidants, his achievement is clear, but the workings of his mind and personality are the subject of continuing speculation and theory. He was born in 1917 to a poor peasant family in North Kyongsang Province, the youngest of seven children. He displayed exceptional academic ability to gain entrance to the élite Taegu Normal School in 1932. There he adopted the pragmatic values current in Japanised Korea, rejected the 'backwardness' of traditional Korean society, and made his way successfully through the Japanese-controlled education system with no trace of interest, much less involvement, in nationalist politics. After graduation, Park became a schoolteacher for three years before heading north to the new horizons of Japanese-controlled Manchukuo, where he enrolled in the Manchukuo Military Academy. In 1944 he was commissioned as a second lieutenant in the Imperial Japanese Army, and after demobilisation returned to Korea in 1946, where he was soon re-commissioned as a captain. In 1948 he was implicated in the Yosu military rebellion, sentenced to life imprisonment, reprieved, dismissed from the Army, rehired as a civilian, and then reinstated after the outbreak of the Korean War. He finished the war as a brigadier-general, but thereafter promotions became slow. By May 1961 he had advanced only to the rank of major-general.

Small in stature and undemonstrative in personality, Park possessed the abilities normally expected in an able senior military officer: a tidy, quick, and decisive mind, a strong work ethic, and a commitment to order and hierarchy. But beyond this he possessed some uncommon qualities. In his upbringing and early life he seems to have acquired a strong sense of self-identity, clear values, and a coherent view of the times in which he lived and of his country's place in the world. This gave an underlying consistency to his life and thought. He was, of course, opportunistic in seizing the advantages which came his way, but he retained fixed goals to the end of his life. During the 1950s he did not actively participate in any of the ubiquitous army fraternities and factional groups. This aloofness, combined with a frugal lifestyle and a reputation for honesty amid widespread corruption, gave him an air of intensity, inscrutability and command. Park did not inspire affection but usually gained the respect of those whose support he needed. Such people tended to respect Park as a leader driven by clear principles and objectives, and possessed of obvious, if somewhat unfathomable, intellectual ability, who used words sparingly and with precision, usually to convey clear orders and outline practical courses of action.

Park seems to have been content to wait until the opportunity for power found him, but once in power he was anything but ambivalent in exercising it. In office he proved to be a shrewd and ruthless handler of men. The labyrinthine, overlapping agencies of the ROK government had hampered Rhee, then brought the Second Republic to virtual administrative gridlock, but under Park they functioned with an efficiency rarely seen either before or since. Driven by a profound conviction that time was against the ROK, Park was an interventionist leader, though judiciously so. His role was therefore more as a co-ordinating chief of staff than as an activist field general, which was the role adopted by Kim Il Sung. Thus, he oversaw the effective deployment of economic specialists and entre-preneurs, while also ensuring that these chosen spearheads of modernisation were protected from the political consequences of policies which were often coercive and unpopular. In pursuing his objectives he also showed two priceless assets of leadership: discerning judgement and a capacity to listen and learn from specialist advice.

Although Park presided over the foundation of the modern ROK economy, he himself had little formal economic training, and his relationship with the business sector was therefore usually strained. In his lifetime he had witnessed commercial life in the two very different settings of the Japanese Empire and the Rhee admin-istration. In both these settings business was firmly subordinated to government, but the Japanese example was dynamic and wealth-producing while the Rhee example was passive and parasitic. Park therefore developed a relationship with leading entrepreneurs which aimed at adapting the best aspects of the Japanese model to the circumstances of the ROK, whereby the military-backed state enlisted and subordinated business in the pursuit of broader state goals.

There were few elements of grand economic design in the early economic measures adopted by the Third Republic. Rural debt relief and rice price-support measures were enacted to provide some limited relief from the extreme rural poverty which still afflicted well over half the entire population. The govern-ment also enacted measures to reorganise and effect recovery in the nation's tiny industrial and manufacturing sector, including the establishment in August 1961 of the Federation of Korean Industries (FKI), which grew to be a key and powerful institution in the years that followed. More important was the empowerment of the longer-term planning mechanisms first conceived under the Rhee government.

However, as the new régime consolidated power, it adopted more far-reaching policies. It announced a Five-Year Economic Development Plan to be enacted from January 1962, and simultaneously set about creating a major new institution, the Economic Planning Board, to effect the planning and execution of the Plan. The significance of the Plan was as much symbolic as actual, for it amounted to little more than a broad outline of costs and outputs in key targeted sectors. The econ-omic dividend of tight political control was expected to accrue through severe restrictions on consumption and a high savings rate, enabling strong investment in infrastructure to advance key manufacturing industries. Measures to stimulate exports such as cheap loans, tax benefits, export compensation schemes and various administrative supports were a notable indicator of future directions. The Plan sought 7.1 per cent annual growth during 1962–66 and exceeded most expectations in achieving rapid expansion of both output and exports. GNP rose from 4.1 per cent in 1962 to 9.3 per cent in 1963 and thereafter consistently remained above 8.0 per cent.

The vital component in the ROK's economic development strategy in the early 1960s was the international economy, for the marshalling of domestic economic forces would of itself have been of little use if the ROK could not gain access to foreign markets. The 1960s fell in the middle of what historian Eric Hobsbawm has called 'the Golden Age of the capitalist world economy'. After decades marked by war, protectionism, depression, and war again, a vibrant international economic system gradually took shape after 1945, driven by favourable conditions for international trade, capital movements and currency convertability. This rapid growth pattern was fed by many forces, many of which were closely noted and studied in the ROK. First, the postwar international economy acquired a clear leader in the United States, which asserted itself in defence of its traditional free-trade principles and also in reaction to its traditional fear of the spread of communism. Second, the redirection of West German and Japanese entrepreneurial skill from war-making activities to market-enhancing activities fuelled a major, regionally balanced upsurge in global production. Third, the quality of political, economic and technocratic leadership in many key states seems in retrospect to have been extraordinarily high, as evidenced by the rise of the European Community and the rapid recovery of West Germany and Japan. The development of economics as a science and the practical experience of the wartime economy were only two of a number of factors which contributed to a far more sophisticated understanding of practical economics, and to the emergence of a cadre of flexible, pragmatic economic policy-makers in the finance ministries of the industrialised world whose major legacy was the substantial restructuring and reform of capitalism. Their most important contribution was the tempering of free-market ideology with the striking of social contracts between labour and industry, aimed foremost at sustaining growth through the linkage of wages to productivity. The rapid development of new technologies during the 1950s contributed substantially to this process, and caused a marked increase in production which was matched by the growth of disposable income. The result was a sustained consumer boom in the industrialised world.

In the ROK, most economic thinkers had long concluded that the prospects for self-reliant economic growth were bleak for a country with few natural resources, limited arable land and relatively high population density, On the other hand, the ROK looked out on a booming world economy where US free-trade ideology inhibited protectionism in manufactures, where Cold War politics gave ideological clarity to economic policy thinking, where sustained economic growth in the industrialised world was opening up huge consumer markets, and where the cost of acquiring the basic technology to exploit many of these markets was relatively low. A well-organised state which was able to deploy an educated, well-organised, low-wage workforce in a targeted fashion was therefore in a position of strong comparative advantage in these markets. Moreover, if such assessments seemed somewhat theoretical to some Koreans, then they needed only to observe current Japanese economic performance in order to find a compelling example of the benefits which might accrue from the skilful exploitation of the possibilities of an export-led economic growth model.

Close linkages to the Japanese and US economies as sources of investment, markets and technology, while unpalatable to the Korean sense of nationalism, were cornerstones for the development of an export economy. Against a background of sustained, vociferous domestic protest again led by students, in 1965 the ROK government therefore concluded an agreement normalising relations with Japan. This agreement brought with it a large compensation payout, which enabled the ROK to generate the investment funds required to sustain its economic momentum. The ROK applied similar pragmatism to its relations with the United States. The US had originally reacted to the military *coup* with alarm, since the *coup* represented the overthrow of constitutional government by a shadowy group of officers of evident energy and intensity who used strong nationalist rhetoric. Unlikely as it sounds in retrospect, some US officials feared strong leftist influence among the *coup* leaders. However, the perspectives that united the two countries were greater than those which divided them, and relations gradually improved, especially after the ROK agreed to participate in the ongoing escalation of the US war effort in Vietnam by dispatching an initial 20,000-man force in 1965. Strong anti-communist ideology, the satisfying sense of participating in a broader coalition of allies in a significant war, and important economic spin-offs all combined to make this a popular move, and in 1966 revenues from the war, especially from civilian construction contracts, comprised 40 per cent of the ROK's total foreign exchange earnings.

These developments gave a sense of momentum to the government and enhanced its profile leading up to the 1967 presidential election. Although in this election the opposition was more united than in 1963, Park benefited from a more efficient, united and well-funded political machine, increasing his share of the vote to 51.4 per cent; while Yun Posun, who was again Park's principal opponent, gained 41 per cent. In fact, this election marked the high-water mark in the Third Republic's rather half-hearted quest for legitimacy through the ballot box, for between 1967 and 1971 Park and his advisers firmed in their view that they could not continue to hold power within the existing constitutional framework. In the first place, under this constitution Park was barred from seeking a third term. In addition, the ongoing rapid urbanisation of the country was rapidly eating away at the core of the régime's support. Moreover, by both temperament and training the military mind found it difficult, if not impossible, to work within the confines of a democratic system, while they also shared the ideological conviction that strong central control was more important than the establishment of parliamentary democracy. Such views were all the more profoundly held because they were both self-serving and pragmatic, and the end result was that in 1969 Park decided to seek a constitutional amendment to run for a third term – as Rhee had done in 1954. Within the ruling party there was a general perception that replacing Park would induce instability in the leadership, and so they laboured long and hard to have the amendment approved in a referendum. On 17 October 1968, 65.1 per cent of the electorate voted in favour. The head of state now stood effectively above the political process.

During 1970–71 the régime again approached a watershed as foreign-policy, political and economic setbacks converged. In Vietnam the US essentially lost its will to force a military solution after the Vietcong Tet offensive in early 1968, and this had a demoralising effect on the US military worldwide. Meanwhile, the redefining of US foreign-policy goals in East Asia under the Nixon Doctrine to emphasise the need for countries in the region to become more militarily self-reliant, and the beginnings of US rapprochement with China all raised serious questions in Seoul about the US commitment to defend the ROK. Domestically, the 1969 constitutional amendment campaign had been successful, but had seriously depleted Park's remaining political capital, from within the party by dissenters who did not want to see Park retain office indefinitely, and more generally by opposition forces. Moreover, the strategy of rapid economic development came under pressure with the tapering off of income generated by the Vietnam War, by ongoing reductions in US aid and food assistance, and by the US imposition of import quotas on strategic ROK manufactures such as textiles. While the underlying international economic climate remained sound, these various minor tremors had important cumulative effects, for the strategy of rapid economic growth was basically a high-risk policy which required the continual generation of substantial export earnings to service a sizeable foreign debt and to deal with ever-increasing social pressures and demands. Rising labour unrest, continuing rapid urbanisation, the re-emergence of student demonstrations, the first signs of a significant dissident movement, and endemic restlessness within the ruling party all combined to bring significant pressure to bear on Park. As a result, the atmosphere of the 1971 presidential election was significantly different from that of the 1967 election. Park gained 51.2 per cent of the vote against Kim Dae Jung (43.6 per cent) but drew little comfort from the result. The opposition had grown in strength and intellectual awareness, and the broader public consensus which had backed Park's policies in the 1960s was fraying. These issues came to a head when Park declared a state of national emergency in December 1971, then engineered the Shiwol Yushin constitutional *coup* of October 1972 which brought the Third Republic to an end.

By this time the Third Republic had already presided over far-reaching changes in ROK society. In fact, the transformation of rural Korea had begun in earnest in 1950 with the enacting of comprehensive land reform legislation, and had continued through the Korean War with its mass population movements, and the subjecting of almost the entire young population to organisational life in the military. After 1953 many rural dwellers did not return to the villages, but instead entered a new urban environment, where an urban-oriented mass media and education system increasingly exposed them and their children to notions of social equality, political democracy, market economics and contractual relationships.

In the 1960s rural poverty transformed the rural exodus into a flood. The population of Seoul more than doubled during the 1960s, from 2.5 million in 1960 to 5.5 million in 1970, out of a total population of 31 million, while other major cities such as Pusan also experienced sharp growth. In 1970, 17.5 per cent of the entire ROK population lived in Seoul, compared with 9.9 per cent in 1960 and 13 per cent in 1966. The newcomers rapidly overwhelmed available services, and as the supply of housing became exhausted they increasingly assembled in transient

squatter settlements and slums. Initially, few migrants found jobs in the new manufacturing industries. More characteristically they endured unemployment or else engaged in small-scale servicing or commerce and peddling. Only 18.3 per cent of the Seoul population engaged in manufacturing in 1970. Nevertheless, their income, diet and access to both necessities of life and luxuries soon compared very favourably to their rural counterparts, and women in particular grew to experience undreamed-of freedom in their new surroundings. There were losses as well as gains, for urban dwellers not only shed their grinding rural poverty, but also lost the coherent community life of country villages, since this could not be re-created amid the vast, amorphous dormitory suburbs of the city. Moreover, although economic growth was creating an urban society, the newcomers were not readily transformed into modern urban dwellers. The overwhelming numbers in which they came, and the close ties they maintained with their home towns and villages, ensured that Seoul retained the flavour and ambience of a massive rural community, rather than a cosmopolitan centre.

Social values were also undergoing change. Although the traditional social system was still largely intact in 1970, it was under severe threat from the massive drain of young people to the city, and from a greater awareness of the outside world among those who stayed. The influence of modern ideas was far more restrained in the villages which the migrants had left behind, but such ideas nevertheless spread through rural media, and through the continuing close family and clan contacts such as the regular ritual occasions which brought city-dwelling family members and relatives back to the ancestral village. The sense of class distinction between gentry and commoner became increasingly hazy, but the attributes of age, education, and general reputation for upright social behaviour, provided a basis for assessments about local community standing which contained important residues of older social attitudes. Many aspects of Confucian tradition were increasingly dismissed as intellectually feeble and irrelevant, yet somehow selective retention of Confucian mores still provided the moral cement of a society in the midst of major transformation. In the new ROK, 'Confucianism' now described a purpose, a style and a design for leadership, combining austerity, restraint and rigorous hierarchy. It also provided a sense of place and social identity for the masses, most of whom saw themselves and their descendants as potential members of the new meritocratic élite. The vibrancy of this conservative force helps explain how South Korean society retained a sense of equilibrium despite division, war and poverty.

Conclusion

Although by 1970 the respective paths of the two Koreas had diverged sharply, the ruling élites in both states could rightfully claim to have mastered the despair of wartime destruction and to have carried out major reconstruction. Both élites were strongly oriented towards building powerful modern states. They therefore built powerful central government structures which brought the myriad, formerly self-sufficient and self-regulatory local communities under firm central control through universal education, an expanding transport and communication network, and the provision of government services such as health, public works and agricultural extension work. In both countries the operations of a powerful military, a civil bureaucracy, and a ruthless police and security network further kept the population under tight control. Such links wore away traditional rural self-sufficiency, and created channels of advancement and social mobility which steadily transformed both societies.

By 1970 the two Koreas were also often perceived internationally in much the same way as the two Germanys – as advertisements for their respective political and economic systems. In fact, such a vantage-point entailed significant distortions, for not only had the two Koreas already deviated substantially from their assigned polarities as 'communist' and 'free' but they had also diverged into two systems so utterly unlike each other as to render most comparisons of limited value. Increasingly the DPRK had become imprisoned by the inbuilt conservatism of its revolutionary model. It was dismissive of social and political demands other than those generated by the leadership itself, and in applying successively tighter forms of regimentation to the population it grew more and more rigid and unable to sustain the momentum for revolutionary change. The lack of foreign contact, the lack of internal feedback and an isolated leadership all contributed to an increasingly stagnant polity and economy. By contrast, the military revolutionaries of the South did not aim at a total reshaping of state and society. They dominated politics, but allowed for the expression of opposing political views and often agreed to be bound by the consensual process in important social policy areas such as education. They dominated the operation of the national economy, but encouraged private and semi-public market economic activity. They also continued to preside, albeit uneasily, over a vigorous civil society which they had neither the means nor the will to repress to anything approaching the level achieved in the North.

The choice of economic model was crucial to the development of each Korean state. To the North, international capitalism was a doomed system, and so it withdrew into isolation within the Soviet bloc. Such isolation discouraged foreign education and training, stifled innovation, and deprived the country of even basic industrial and manufacturing technologies. The turning-point came with the adoption of the Kimist Equal Emphasis policies in December 1962, for this set the pattern for the steady cannibalisation of the civilian economy by the military. Five years later, the extension of the Seven-Year Plan (1961–67) to ten years for completion made it clear that the economy was encountering significant problems under such policies, but countermanding or significant modification remained out of the question. The political strains generated primarily by faltering economic performance resulted in the removal of over half the Politburo in 1966, but few outsiders were aware that during 1966–67 the DPRK had effected a fundamental change to its system of government by replacing rule by the party with absolute personal rule by Kim Il Sung. Fewer still could see that near-total reliance on the judgement of one man of limited intellect and experience of the world would have such dire consequences for the country.

DPRK policies were driven by a highly developed sense of threat, which stemmed from a number of ideological, institutional and political factors. First, the régime had its origins in tiny, unstable conspiratorial groups dedicated to the overthrow of the existing international political and economic orders – the Japanese colonial régime in particular and imperialism in general. The Manchurian guerrilla mindset required a finely honed sense of threat for sheer survival, and discounted trust and mutual confidence as a basis for coexistence. Second, the Stalinist model in its full-blown phase from the mid-1930s on mandated rigorous surveillance and justified political terror by portraying the Soviet state as constantly under threat from internal 'enemies'. The DPRK internal security system modelled itself on the Soviet system, and was in fact headed by a Soviet citizen of Korean background until the late 1950s. Third, the DPRK had initiated war in 1950 and suffered massive retaliation. As a war-making state committed to reversing the verdict of 1950–53, it was naturally fearful that it might pay a similar price in the process.

Ambivalence sometimes characterised the ROK's external vision during the 1960s for, like Meiji Japan, its rulers sought Western technology but were uneasy with Western values. Nevertheless, the country became substantially open to international politics and economics. Such linkages encouraged foreign education, the absorption of ever greater levels of foreign technology, innovative practices and freedom of information, though of course not freedom of expression. Even so, in 1970 it was by no means clear that the ROK could sustain its drive to become an advanced industrial economy. During the 1960s the growing manufacturing sector surpassed the primary sector, but in 1970 the country still remained in the very early stages of industrialisation with its largest export earners low value-added products such as textiles, plywood, wigs and soft toys. Despite the continuing favourable conditions for international trade, the mature economies of Western Europe and North America still accounted for over 70 per cent of gross world output and almost 80 per cent of the world's industrial output. For the ROK, the gradient to membership in this exclusive group remained steep, and the task of developing the industries which were the mainstays of such economies, such as shipbuilding, advanced machine industries, electronics, and mass automobile production remained daunting.

Selected reading

Brandt, Vincent S. R. 1971, *A Korean Village between Farm and Sea*, Cambridge, MA: Harvard University Press.

Chung, Joseph S. 1974, *The North Korean Economy: Structure and Development*, Stanford, CA: Hoover Institution Press.

Earhart, H. Byron 1974, 'The New Religions of Korea: A Preliminary Interpretation.' *Transactions of the Royal Asiatic Society Korea Branch*, vol. 49, pp. 7–25.

Han, Sung-joo 1974, *The Failure of Democracy in South Korea*, Berkeley, CA: University of California Press.

Kim, Alexander Joungwon 1975, *Divided Korea: The Politics of Development 1945–1972*,

Cambridge, MA: East Asian Research Center, Harvard University/Harvard University Press.

Lee, Hahn-Been 1968, *Korea: Time, Change, and Administration*, Honolulu: East–West Center Press, University of Hawaii.

Pak, Chi-Young 1980, *Political Opposition in Korea 1945–1960*, Seoul: Seoul National University Press.

Pak, Ki-Hyuk with Gamble, Sidney D. 1975, *The Changing Korean Village*, Seoul: Shin-hung Press.

Rutt, Richard 1964, *Korean Works and Days*, Seoul: Park's Company.

Scalapino, Robert A. and Lee, Chong-sik 1972, *Communism in Korea*, Part 1, *The Movement*, Berkeley, CA: University of California Press.

Scalapino, Robert A. and Lee, Chong-sik 1972, *Communism in Korea*, Part 2, *The Society*, Berkeley, CA: University of California Press.

Suh, Dae-Sook 1988, *Kim Il Sung: The North Korean Leader*, New York: Columbia University Press.

6   Reversal of fortunes, 1971–80

When the Fifth KWP Congress opened in Pyongyang on 2 November 1970, it confirmed the absolute supremacy of Kim Il Sung. The Party had left its collectivist phase behind and now celebrated its dependence on the wisdom and judgement of Kim as its genius-leader. Kim reached this position of supreme power at a time when the DPRK faced a number of significant challenges to its basic state policies. The stagnating economy represented a growing dilemma, for by the early 1970s new inputs of investment and technology, and more sophisticated, decentralised economic decision-making, were essential if the country were to address the serious shortcomimgs which had emerged during the 1960s. Similarly, the foundations of the DPRK's foreign policy were severely challenged by Sino-US rapprochement and Soviet–US détente. These processes strengthened the commitment of the DPRK's major allies to peace and stability on the Korean peninsula, and hence to a continuing division which remained unacceptable to the DPRK.

The basic decisions and strategies adopted by Kim in the period immediately after 1970 had a profound effect on the country. Kim elected to deal with fundamental economic problems by further strengthening the DPRK's basic reliance on strictly centralised economic planning and ideological incentives. The centrepiece in this strategy was a sustained nationwide ideological movement known as the Three Revolutions Teams Movement, which was launched in 1974 under the leadership of his son, Kim Jong Il. This and subsequent similar Kimist campaigns stressed the primacy of ideology over pragmatism in economic activity, and so exacerbated an economic decline which presaged the calamities of the 1990s. Meanwhile, in foreign policy the DPRK world-view continued to be dominated by anti-imperialist struggle, and took little account of such developments as China's emergence from isolationism or the development of Soviet–US détente. To its interlocutors, the DPRK insisted that its circumstances had not changed, and that the division of Korea mandated a continuing militant struggle against the USA and the South Korean 'puppets'. During the 1970s these policies became uncomfortable reminders of an era its chief backers were rapidly leaving behind them, and as Pyongyang's relations with Moscow and Beijing began to grow distant its diplomacy became less and less effective.

The ROK also faced major challenges in the 1970s. It had achieved substantial momentum for rapid economic growth during the 1960s, but the task of sustaining this momentum required the mobilisation of human and material resources on an ever-growing scale. The state, not society, directed much of this process, and during the 1970s the ROK government exercised increasing authoritarian control over political and economic activity in ways which polarised domestic politics and attracted international criticism. In October 1972, Park Chung-hee instituted the authoritarian Yushin constitutional amendments which perpetuated his hold on power, but at the same time gave strength and purpose to significant forces of opposition and dissidence. In fact, the Park authoritarian state coexisted with a civil society which remained vibrant and, on occasions, assertive. This phenomenon, often called the 'strong state–contentious society' paradox, arose essentially because the régime's commitment to rapid economic growth outweighed its commitment to ideological control. As a result, millions of Korean workers gravitated towards the new urban centres with their huge dormitory suburbs in numbers that the government could barely keep track of, let alone control. Churches, universities and workplaces provided gathering-places and increasingly became the focus for opposition and dissident activities. The superstructure of authoritarian rule stretched uneasily across such a society.

Against this background, significant developments occurred in relations between the two Koreas. The North's tactics of direct confrontation reached a high point in 1968, but such tactics did not induce unrest in the South, nor did they win any support from Pyongyang's major allies. Accordingly, in 1969 the level of violence on the DMZ began to drop. Meanwhile, a fundamental shift began to emerge in the major Great Power alignments in East Asia. The key was the Sino-Soviet split of the late 1950s and the subsequent deterioration of Sino-Soviet relations to the point of military skirmishes on their long common border during the late 1960s. Despite its official, anti-imperialist rhetoric, the Chinese leaders realised that they could not withstand the sustained enmity of the two global superpowers, and so in the late 1960s they cautiously sought to improve relations with the US as the lesser of the two threats. The US, demoralised by military and political failure in Vietnam, reciprocated and shifted from its previous hostile assessment of China. By 1971 the new US–China *entente* was strong enough for both to urge their respective Korean patrons to seek a negotiated settlement to the Korean question, and in 1971 face-to-face negotiations began between Seoul and Pyongyang. In July 1972 the two Koreas announced a joint formula for eventual reunification, and during the following year held a series of high-level negotiations.

This inter-Korean dialogue produced few short-term benefits but, on the whole, international developments during the 1970s favoured ROK interests. Seoul's alliances with Japan and the US were not free from strain, but they provided basic, stable security guarantees. Equally important, alliance with the two most power-ful economies in the world opened up access to the capital, technology and human resource training needed to sustain rapid economic growth. Moreover, from the point of view of the ROK and her allies, Sino-US co-operation, Soviet–US détente and Sino-Japanese reconciliation were all positive developments which marked a steady shift away from Great Power confrontation over Korea towards negotiation and settlement.

The talks begin

Following the successful outcome of secret diplomacy conducted by US National Security Advisor Henry Kissinger, on 16 July 1971 President Nixon announced that he would visit Beijing in February 1972. In the ROK this confirmation of far-reaching change in US foreign policy in East Asia reinforced long-held fears about US reliability, while to the DPRK the Nixon visit represented, as Kim Il Sung described it, 'a trip of the defeated, fully reflecting the destiny of US imperialism which is like a sun sinking in the western sky'. The announcement also reflected the desire of both the US and China to resolve long-standing issues of dispute – including, of course, the Korean question – and both parties brought pressure to bear on their respective Korean allies to begin negotiations. As a result, the first post-1953 face-to-face inter-Korean negotiations began with talks on humanitarian issues between the national Red Cross committees of the two Koreas in August 1971, and by March 1972 the dialogue had progressed to the point where the two sides were exchanging high-level secret envoys. Finally, on 4 July 1972, they released a joint communiqué which set forth the principles under which they would negotiate peaceful reunification: reunification would be pursued independently without outside interference; it would be pursued peacefully; and 'a great national unity, as a homogeneous people, transcending differences in ideas, ideologies and systems', would provide the basis for union.

The 1972–73 inter-Korean talks developed into two distinct areas of negotiation. On the one hand, the two parties sought agreements on humanitarian issues through Red Cross talks, while on the other hand they sought to resolve political issues through high-level government-to-government negotiations. The humanitarian talks agenda included locating dispersed families, facilitating family reunions, and arranging postal exchanges, while the political talks sought to give effect to the 4 July communiqué. However, subsequent negotiations soon revealed significant differences in approach. The DPRK maintained that if the two sides reached agreement on broader issues first, then humanitarian issues would more or less resolve themselves. Thus, Pyongyang interpreted the joint commitment to independent reunification as signifying the priority withdrawal of US forces from the ROK and the signing of a DPRK–US peace treaty to replace the 1953 Military Armistice Agreement. Since the North saw the US as the real belligerent on the Southern side and the major source of support for the 'puppet' government of the South, it believed that such a withdrawal would remove a major impediment to reunification and facilitate a political settlement. On the other hand, the ROK stressed the importance of people-to-people contacts as a prelude to substantive political negotiation at the leadership level. Only after positive outcomes at this level would the ROK contemplate changes to its basic security posture. In the months that followed, the two sides attempted to find ways and means of implementing the Joint Declaration, but could not identify common ground. In early 1973 the talks stalled, and then effectively ceased in the face of DPRK demands for far-reaching political changes in the South as a prelude to discussion of humanitarian issues. The two sides met again briefly in 1980 in the wake of Park

Chung-hee's assassination, but no further significant negotiations took place until 1984.

The 1972–73 negotiations established a pattern which remained consistent during the decades which followed. Since the opening of Red Cross talks in 1971, and since the holding of the first full-scale political talks in 1972, the two sides have conducted humanitarian, political and economic talks in a variety of official, unofficial, open and secret processes. However, to date almost all significant negotiation has taken place during four short periods – 1972–73, 1984–85, 1990–91 and 2000–01 – while the intervening periods have witnessed high levels of confrontation and recrimination. The two sides have signed various agreements, but these have remained dead letters owing to differing interpretations of the wording, and also owing to an inability to move beyond procedural issues. The various conflicting dimensions of history, self-identity, legitimacy, territoriality, dispossession and ideology continued to turn aside the countervailing simple conviction of Koreans everywhere that Korean ethnicity and Korean nationalism of themselves should provide a viable basis for reunification.

In their approach to dialogue, both Koreas have always aimed at steering negotiations dialogue into areas where they believed their strength lay. In this early phase of talks, the DPRK's major asset was a tight political mobilisation system backed up by substantial military assets in forward deployment. This enabled it to support its negotiating positions with a credible military threat, and to engage and withdraw from negotiation at will, without reference to interests outside the leadership circle. On the other hand, its major weakness was a declining economic base, and a rigid ideology which insisted on an increasingly anachronistic portrayal of the ROK as a US 'puppet' possessing an unstable, dependent 'bubble' economy. The DPRK's economic enfeeblement led to a growing disparity in state power between the two Koreas during the 1970s, and to Pyongyang's increasing reliance on military assets as an equaliser, while its dysfunctional ideology provided the basis for increasingly unrealistic negotiating positions.

By contrast, the ROK's major asset was economic dynamism, which steadily increased the reach of ROK diplomacy and the scale of ROK military power. In the decades which followed this proved to be a decisive factor, but it is worth remembering that during the 1970s the ROK still dealt from a position of geopolitical weakness, for not only was its economy still in the early stages of rapid growth, but also, in contrast to the DPRK's two powerful, contiguous allies, Seoul depended primarily on the more distant and mercurial support of the USA. A further, significant asset for the ROK was the growing strength of its own civil society, for growing levels of public accountability pushed the government towards realistic negotiating positions. On the other side of this coin, growing pressure from civil society meant that the government did not possess the same tactical flexibility as the North.

The DPRK in the 1970s

Militancy towards the ROK during 1967–68 reflected the triumph of the Kimists in gaining decisive control of the KWP. The fallout from this struggle within the Party became clear when the Fifth KWP Congress convened in November 1970: of the sixteen leading members of the KWP Politburo elected in 1961, only four were reappointed in 1970, while only 39 of the 172 members of the 1961 Central Committee were reappointed. Preservation of the outward forms of the KWP tended to disguise the fact that, as in 1951–53, Kim had again virtually destroyed the party he himself had built and had again created a new party. This new party was almost totally dominated by former Manchurian guerrilla comrades, their relatives, and their children, all of whom gave explicit, unquestioning loyalty to the Great Leader. Kim chose his new colleagues well because, in contrast to the high turnover in senior cadres before 1970, fully thirteen of the fifteen Politburo members appointed in 1970 were still members at the time of Kim Il Sung's death in 1994.

This final Kimist triumph had a stultifying effect on policy, for it led to a party and government dominated by ageing military men who were limited in education and generally intolerant of intellectuals and technocrats. Like Kim Il Sung himself, they regarded such cadres with suspicion and worked hard to subordinate them. As a result, Kim became the Party's only approved ideologue and theorist; while the technocrat, or 'expert', was replaced by a cadre of 'red' economic managers whose major task was to apply techniques of military-style mass mobilisation to the operation of the economy. This was a party which controlled all facets of organisational life in the DPRK, from the parade ground to the classroom, from the factory to the farm.

One immediate consequence was continued militancy on reunification. Later UN statistics revealed that during the 1970s the DPRK's armed forces increased from about 400,000 in 1970 to 700,000 in 1975 to nearly 1 million in the late 1970s, while a major build-up of offensive weapons such as tanks, field artillery pieces, and armoured personnel-carriers also occurred. Estimates of the military strength and intentions of adversaries are, of course, always susceptible to exaggeration and purposeful misinterpretation. In the case of the North, however, the discovery in November 1974 of the first of a series of elaborate infiltration tunnels under the DMZ, each capable of placing thousands of KPA troops behind enemy lines within a short period of time, persuaded many in the South that despite the talks the military confrontation with the North remained serious and ongoing, especially as it seemed clear that the tunnels were under construction throughout the period of the 1972–73 talks. To the extent that people identified strong security with military-backed authoritarianism, this increased support for the Park régime.

As Kim Il Sung consolidated his personal autocracy, he also moved to advance his son, Kim Jong Il, to a position of leadership within the party. The younger Kim was born in the Soviet Union on 16 February 1942 to Kim Chong-suk, Kim Il Sung's first wife who died in 1949, and graduated from Kimilsung University in 1964. He then entered the party organisation, and emerged as the director of a major ideological campaign, the Three Revolutions Teams Movement, in 1974. In imitation of the Maoist Chinese Red Guards during the period of the Cultural

Revolution, this campaign dispatched teams of young revolutionaries to mines, factories and other significant workplaces with the aim of increasing output by rekindling 'revolutionary fervour'. As the campaign progressed, a cult of personality began to form around the younger Kim, featuring songs of loyalty and study sessions on his writings. High-level defectors later reported that he was appointed to the KWP politburo in 1974, but throughout this period the DPRK media made no mention of either this appointment or even his name. In fact, until the Sixth Party Congress in 1980 formally introduced him to the public as a senior party cadre in his own right, the media referred to him only as 'the Party Centre' (*Tang chungang*). The emergence of the world's first hereditary communist leadership seemed incredible to many at the time, but it was a logical option which flowed from well-entrenched nepotism and the ever-narrowing base of the DPRK leadership. Kim Il Sung had become convinced that only a ruling party controlled by ex-Manchurian guerrillas under the leadership of his son could preserve and continue his life's work. Thus, Kim Jong Il was promoted as a 'model revolutionary' who would consolidate the ideology of his father's generation and forestall any attempts at revisionism by the younger generation.

The growing stability of the post-1968 Kimist autocracy was reflected in the promulgation of a new constitution in 1972. This constitution superseded the 1948 constitution, and reflected many of the changes in the balance of state and party power which had occurred in the 1950s and 1960s. The intervening years had seen the emergence of Kim's personal autocracy, and so the new constitution was notable for its vaguer language and unclear processes, which could only be made coherent through the exercise of personal power. Thus, it featured a powerful state presidency, which was endowed with the formal functions and powers that Kim had already come to hold, but it did not make provision for any constitutional succession process. This reflected the expectation, already widespread within the party at this time, that Kim Jong Il would succeed his father and rule as personal autocrat in much the same way.

Meanwhile, during the 1970s the DPRK faced increasingly debilitating economic problems. At the Fifth KWP Congress in 1970, Kim Il Sung had proclaimed the successful completion of the First Seven-Year Plan (1961–67) after a three-year extension (1967–70), and then announced the beginning of a new Six-Year Plan (1971–76). This plan sought to maintain the high growth rates and heavy industrialisation policies of the 1960s, but by the early 1970s hallmark policies of international isolation, extreme administrative centralisation, predominant reliance on ideological incentives, and the constant mass mobilisation of labour had exhausted their usefulness. Under Kim Jong Il's direction, the Three Revolutions Teams Movement further entrenched the existing unproductive methods of work, and although mass mobilisation enabled the rapid construction of key projects, continuing emphasis on quantitative production resulted in low construction standards, poor-quality goods, declining productivity, and technological backwardness.

During 1972–74 the DPRK attempted to break out of the growing pattern of stagnation through massive purchases on credit of Western plant and machinery, including petrochemical, textile, concrete, steel, wood pulp and paper manufacturing plants. In some ways, this strategy was similar to the underlying strategy of the ROK: purchase on credit and repay with the export revenue generated from the new industries. However, economic circumstances in the DPRK worked against this strategy. Part of the problem was timing: the DPRK purchases coincided with the onset of the oil shocks of 1974 and the resultant global recession, but the major reason was that the DPRK economy did not possess the planning capacities, building-technology skills, infrastructural sophistication or managerial and tradesman skills to absorb this level of technology. Factories could not meet the precise building standards needed to house sophisticated machines, the power grid could not service the new plants adequately, the workers did not have the training to operate or maintain them, and the state could not market their output effectively. In 1974 the DPRK stopped such purchases and, without the means to pay for them, became a chronic debtor nation. As time went by, Pyongyang became increasingly unable and unwilling to negotiate a satisfactory settlement of its debts and so was cut off from further access to foreign investment and advanced technology. Starved of investment, and subject to the ongoing ideological assaults of Kim Jong Il's Three Revolutions Teams Movement, the non-military economy relied increasingly on obsolete technology, and could add little value to raw and semi-processed materials, which comprised a steady 80 per cent of exports. The DPRK economy stalled at its semi-industrialised stage of development.

Pyongyang also faced major challenges in foreign relations during the 1970s. At the beginning of the decade, Kim Il Sung proclaimed publicly that US imperialism was in full retreat from South-East Asia, and this almost certainly reflected his personal conviction. In particular, he believed that the US defeat in Indochina would – and should – lead to the revival of the international anti-imperialist coalition, capable of providing backing for his reunification strategy, and enabling successful military action against the ROK. Therefore, after the fall of South Vietnam in April 1974, Kim made an immediate visit to Beijing where he argued strenuously, but unsuccessfully, for Chinese support for a military strike against the ROK. Prospects for such backing then evaporated as the Maoist era gave way to the era of Deng Xiaoping, and as a more pragmatic China first concluded a peace treaty with the Japanese in September 1978, then normalised relations with the US in January 1979. Meanwhile, although the Soviet Union continued to offer support for the DPRK stance on reunification, it became increasingly wary of Pyongyang's brinkmanship. As a result, it withheld advanced weaponry and offered increasingly tepid diplomatic support.

As the gulf between the DPRK and its major allies continued to widen, Pyongyang began to attach greater importance to the Non-Aligned Movement (NAM). This group of seventy or so mainly Third World countries began to coalesce during the 1950s under the leadership of India and Indonesia at a time when newly independent countries found themselves under strong pressure to side with either the US or the USSR in the Cold War. By the 1970s the NAM had developed into an international body whose size, diversity of interest, and consensus style produced a loose agenda which was primarily focused on international economic and trade issues. Although Pyongyang's formal military treaties with the Soviet Union and China were explicit, NAM membership requirements were elastic to admit the DPRK as a full member in 1975.

Kim saw the movement as a valuable means of rallying international support for the DPRK's stance on reunification, and also for promoting his own image as a significant international communist leader. However, although the NAM gave the DPRK valuable support in United Nations debates during 1975–76, this support soon dwindled. Many NAM members were uncomfortable with Pyongyang's highly political agenda and its militancy, and the continuing high levels of tension on the DMZ. The DPRK's declining economy and erratic handling of its foreign debt deprived it of the means of courting support through foreign aid and economic diplomacy; and, while Kim's regimented, militarised model of self-reliance appealed to some leaders, such as Romania's Nicolai Ceaucescu, who were anxious to perpetuate their personal hold on power, it generally attracted little interest abroad. By the late 1970s Pyongyang had gained little benefit from its NAM diplomacy, while its exposure to the glare of international diplomacy during the 1970s reinforced the general international perception of a country and leader seriously out of touch with international political and economic realities.

In 1970, Kim Il Sung had considerable grounds for believing that he was making progress on all three fronts of the Korean revolution – domestic, inter-Korean and international – but by 1980 the tide had turned on all these fronts. Kim had continued a substantial military build-up, and maintained a credible military threat, but his economic base was failing. The military–industrial sector had grown into an almost separate economy, accounting for nearly half the country's total industrial output, and cannibalising the civilian economy with its priority call on scarce raw materials, technical knowhow and infrastructure. Moreover, the entire economy was still under rigid centralised control and run by increasingly obsolete methods which emphasised quantitative output and discouraged significant technological innovation. With little to offer the outside world, self-reliance was no longer a policy option but a practical necessity.

The Yushin years in the ROK: Park's authoritarian state

On 17 October 1972, President Park declared a state of martial law, dismissed the ROK National Assembly, shut down the nation's universities, and enforced strict censorship of the media in a series of moves known collectively as the *Shiwol yushin*, or October Revitalising Reforms. The stated purpose was the need to strengthen executive power to deal more effectively with reunification and economic issues. Accordingly, in a referendum held on 21 November, a compliant electorate approved a radically revised constitution which gave the president sweeping emergency powers, guaranteed him control over the legislature by empowering him to appoint one-third of the National Assembly, and guaranteed the president more or less indefinite tenure of office through a system of indirect election by an electoral college of some 2,300 directly elected delegates. These changes inaugurated the period of the Fourth Republic (1972–79), more commonly referred to as the Yushin era.

Although the outward shape of politics changed radically, Yushin preserved a basic continuity with the Third Republic in terms of its key personnel, their philosophical outlook, their underlying faith in military-backed authoritarian government and their corresponding lack of faith in the democratic decision-making process. The Yushin constitutional amendments themselves reflected Park's assessment of a changing domestic and international situation. They were enacted in the context of a rapidly industrialising society which was becoming increasingly complex and difficult to rule, and against a background of deep uncertainty in international affairs. Under Park's supervision, the Presidential Secretariat and the Korean Central Intelligence Agency (KCIA) became major counterbalances to the bureaucracy and significant centres of power in wide areas of domestic policy. They aimed at re-establishing tight control over the country, and at limiting the susceptibility of the government to popular political pressure. This was particularly true of the KCIA, an immensely powerful and deeply corrupt institution which had long overstepped the original bounds of its national security mandate to become routinely engaged in extortion and the harassment of the régime's opponents. Such activities reached a crisis point in August 1973, when KCIA operatives abducted the self-exiled Kim Dae Jung from a hotel room in Japan, and were about to dump him at sea when last-minute US intervention saved him.

The Yushin system soon came under challenge from the parliamentary opposition, from university student demonstrations, and from a growing dissident movement. The parliamentary opposition was only intermittently effective because it remained divided between the major factions of Kim Dae Jung, Kim Yong Sam and Lee Chul Seung. It was disunited on tactics and susceptible to a wide range of carrot-and-stick government pressures. Kim Dae Jung had been abroad when the Yushin constitution came into effect, and after his abduction was forcibly repatriated, deprived of his civil rights, and placed under house arrest where he remained the symbolic leader of the dissident movement, but from where he could exercise little influence on political affairs. In Kim's absence, Kim Young Sam became leader of the main opposition New Democratic Party (NDP) in August 1974, and signalled that the NDP would confront the government on fundamental issues of democracy and human rights. However, Kim could not sustain his leadership and in 1976 was replaced by the more Yushin-compliant Lee Chul Seung. It was not part of Lee's agenda to confront the government in any serious or sustained manner, and he was eventually replaced once more by Kim Young Sam in September 1979.

The second source of opposition to Yushin came from the nation's universities. University campuses remained one of the only places where people could assemble for political rallies, and such activities were an integral part of campus life. A tradition of protest, the bloodshed on 19 April 1960, and the muzzling of most alternative forms of protest all gave students a sense of opportunity and mission.

Moreover, as members of the future élite, they already enjoyed an embryonic sense of status, which to some extent protected them from the brutality with which the government met other forms of resistance, such as labour activism. During 1974 students once again emerged as a significant factor in ROK politics through their sustained anti-Yushin protests. Within a year student demonstrations in Seoul had forced the premature closure of many campuses, and thereafter campus demonstrations became a regular occurrence during the Yushin years. However, the students could not advance beyond their traditional role as catalysts for more substantial opposition activity, and in the absence of such activity they remained a vocal but containable force.

Student protest was complemented by the emergence of a significant dissident movement. This movement was loosely organised, and espoused diverse ideologies and programmes. It included one former president (Yun Posun) and a future president (Kim Dae Jung). Some confined their agenda to the curbing of the Yushin system by a reversion to presidential election by direct popular vote; others called for a far-reaching reorganisation of politics, national security and the entire economic distributive system; while others sought social justice and a spiritual renewal of the state. Many important figures in this movement emerged from university faculties and the Christian churches, and they shared the common experience of constant surveillance and harassment, sometimes leading to arrest, brutalisation and imprisonment by the KCIA. Beyond this, however, they had little in common with each other, and despite compatible aims they rarely crossed each other's path. Their influence on the actual course of politics was arguably weak, for the Yushin system remained uncompromisingly in place, but their influence on the intellectual life of the ROK was immense.

In assessing the mood of the times, it is also important to note that the major challenge to Yushin continued to come from a relatively small group of activists, rather than from the population at large. The ability of the government to sustain rapid economic growth helped to secure a grudging public mandate, while the argument that Yushin was a valid response to a difficult regional and international situation also carried some weight. The breakdown of the 1972–73 talks, the discovery in 1974 of evidence of large-scale DPRK tunnelling activity under the DMZ, and the fall of South Vietnam in April 1975 all helped to maintain a domestic consensus on the need for strong leadership and a strong defence posture. The outcome in Vietnam particularly alarmed the ROK, which in many ways had empathised with the South Vietnamese as the anti-communist half of a divided nation, dependent on an uncertain alliance with the US. Such uncertainties were compounded during the Carter administration (1976–80), with its major campaign pledge to reduce US forces in the ROK substantially. Eventually, and reluctantly, Carter abandoned this pledge, but meanwhile the strained ROK–US relationship exacerbated the ROK sense of insecurity, and to many people seemed to provide a strong rationale for Yushin.

In January 1974, Park Chung-hee responded to growing opposition by enacting the first of a series of emergency decrees aimed at curtailing political protest and criticism of the Yushin system. However, in the process he inaugurated a cycle of repression–dissidence–further repression–stronger dissidence which continued throughout the 1970s. With the passage of time, Park became progressively more rigid, and this was reflected in his increasingly inflexible response to opposition and dissidence. Park had attracted ambivalent popular support at best; and, since much of his mandate depended on sustained economic growth, when the ROK economy encountered a sharp downturn in 1979 pressures began to mount on the régime. The main opposition NDP, long emasculated under Yushin, again found voice, and in September 1979; Kim Young Sam regained the NDP leadership and revitalised parliamentary opposition. Park responded by having Kim expelled from the National Assembly on 4 October. This extreme measure, coupled with ongoing labour unrest, provoked widespread anti-government rioting in Kim's regional power-base of Pusan-Masan in the far south-east.

Amid gathering tension and uncertainty, on 26 October 1979, Park was shot dead at a private dinner by KCIA Director Kim Chae-gyu, reportedly as a reaction to Park's repeated taunts about Kim's inability to control the Pusan-Masan situation. Kim had no discernible motive beyond personal pique, and after some hours of confusion was taken into custody and later executed. Almost the entire government apparatus had either actively served in, or at least acquiesced in, the Yushin system, but Park had been its driving force, and his death brought it to an immediate end. Amid hopes that the nation might revert to a substantially democratic order, and also amid fears that the military would again take over, Prime Minister Choi Kyu Hah, a technocrat with no party-political base, became acting president and a new, largely apolitical cabinet took office, comprising members who collectively presented a more moderate, liberal profile than had been seen at any time since the early 1960s.

At Park's death the Yushin system was fraying, but was still holding. Taken together with other political and economic developments, the Pusan-Masan riots represented a serious challenge to Park's authority, but there was no indication that he had irretrievably lost his grip on power. Nevertheless, in their sum, the many and varied judgements about the last years of the Park administration suggest a man whom time had begun to leave behind, and who was unlikely to reinvent himself for the benefit of his country. On this judgement, while the actual circumstance of his death was ignominious, it probably preserved more of his good reputation among many Koreans than might have been the case had he lived. Since the mid-1990s his reputation in the ROK has risen steadily, not just out of nostalgia for the simpler past he symbolised but also from recognition of the more complex present he helped to fashion.

Park Chung-hee left behind a mixed, contradictory legacy, whereby he accelerated the economic growth and retarded the political growth of his country. While he ruled as an authoritarian leader, he remained self-effacing. His portrait hung only in the obligatory official halls and offices; no grandiose public statues or monuments served to remind South Koreans of his achievements; no laudatory songs or public sycophancy flattered his ego; and no distinct ideology bore his name, beyond the promotion of such conventional Confucian platitudes as filial piety (*hyo*), loyalty to one's betters (*ch'ung*) and proper social etiquette (*ye*). This relative anonymity was perhaps fitting, for when one observes the durability of the modern economy over whose creation he presided, it is clear that his achievement transcended the personal.

On the more positive side, Park articulated and put into effect the vision of a rich state and strong military which was widely shared among Koreans, not just in the military but also among the younger technocracy, the business sector and the rural sector, as well as among ordinary citizens. Most South Koreans were touched only indirectly by political repression, and generally tolerated what many at the time termed 'hot-house' economic development and its accompanying authoritarian leadership. Moreover, although Park was not averse to exploiting the threat from the North, this did not make the substance of that threat any less real. His own perception of this threat was profound, and this added to his credibility as an effective commander-in-chief. As we examine the phenomenon of Yushin and the nature of the forces which helped create and sustain it, it is worth noting that later on, in the presidential election held in December 1987 after the collapse of military authoritarian rule, some 36 per cent of the population still voted for Roh Tae Woo, a man quite deeply identified with the former authoritarian system.

The ROK economy in the 1970s

The proclamation of the Yushin Constitution coincided with a further intensification of the industrialisation drive. In early 1973 the government designated five key areas in the heavy and chemical industry (HCI) sector for priority in financial loans, special depreciation allowances, low tax rates, and general infrastructure support. This priority constituted the core of ROK economic policy during the 1970s, and mandated even greater government involvement in determining such matters as the sites, infrastructural needs, capacities, building and operating contractors, and management structures of the new plants. The ROK expanded as an export-driven economy, typically exporting approximately one-third of its GNP during this period, whereas for most other industrialised states the figure was 15 per cent or less. Selected manufacturers were given generous access to bank loans, which they used to exploit the comparative advantage of cheap, controlled labour. Such industries added substantial value to their commodity imports and aggressively marketed them, repaying the bank loans with their earnings. The ROK strategy was to make foreign capital work with enough efficiency to enable it to repay debts and make further, larger borrowings. By the late 1970s foreign capital accounted for 30 per cent of total ROK domestic investment, while the economy had one of the highest debt ratios in the world.

The Yushin system produced significant distortions of the economy, fundamentally because the business–government nexus drew on the past colonial and Rhee models of close, often corrupt co-operation. While Park himself was seen as relatively honest, he presided as a cynical pragmatist over an increasingly corrupt system in which often staggering sums of money were extracted from major business and found their way into individual pockets or else were used for further influence-peddling. In return, large business corporations were protected from the social fallout of operating low-wage and often environmentally damaging companies, and gained performance-based privileges from the government, enabling them to amass great wealth. Local commercial banks directed a large proportion of their loan volume to the large export customers favoured by government policy, and so they became accustomed to a culture in which they would be shielded from the consequences of such loan decisions.

State organisation of the economy on this scale favoured the rise of large manufacturing firms, capable of achieving the economies of scale enjoyed by their Japanese rivals and counterparts, and competing effectively in the international marketplace. Such companies could deploy still-scarce human resources and pursue large export targets. As the industrialisation process continued at a rapid rate, large and increasingly diversified business groups, usually owned and operated by family-based management and known as *chaebol*, became a dominant and distinctive feature of the ROK economy. In their basic outlines, the roots of *chaebol* stretched back to the Japanese colonial period, where Korean capitalism developed through diverse, family-controlled businesses working in close collaboration with the colonial government, and dependent on the colonial financial and banking system. Under Syngman Rhee, basic features of family management and close relations with government grew more salient, and many of the future major *chaebol* came into being through the acquisition of confiscated Japanese assets, through the gaining of lucrative import trading licences, and through preferential access to bank loans. The advent of the Third Republic with its strong commitment to economic growth opened up possibilities of major expansion for these still-small companies. This was largely because they already exercised a monopoly over the entrepreneurial resources of the economy. Almost alone outside the government, their key personnel were well educated, trained, and experienced in manufacturing and international marketing. These *chaebol* of the future were also trained to be responsive to government policy and direction, and to accept such active oversight as the price of access to capital. They were therefore well tooled to thrive in an environment where economic horizons were boundless, but where actual economic resources were limited.

The relentless drive to transform the ROK into a major international economic power bore down hard on small and medium business. In their own right they produced many of the basic items for daily consumption, including food, clothing, and household goods, while their contribution to exports through such industries as soft toys, textiles, garments and footwear was enormous. However, their capital structure remained insecure, and they were often forced on to the high-interest curb market to raise investment capital. They were especially vulnerable in their dealings with larger firms amid the economic fluctuations of a high-inflation, rapid-growth economy, in which the cancellation of contracts and orders could spell ruin. They were also in cut-throat competition with each other, and this reduced profit margins, wages and conditions to a bare minimum. Collectively, they were major employers, but they had little influence on macro-economic policy, while their employees received lower wages, enjoyed far fewer benefits, and endured far greater insecurity than workers in the *chaebol*.

The development process also bore down hard on the rural sector; but, as the full social and economic consequences of rural poverty became evident, in 1971 the government also initiated policies to relieve rural poverty. In order to reduce the rural–urban migration flow, the government initiated a major movement, the Saemaul Undong, or New Community Movement, which aimed primarily at mobilising rural communities to shake off their 'backward' ways and make positive efforts to improve their material lives. In fact, already in the 1960s farming households demonstrated that they needed little invitation to seek out a better life by moving in droves to the cities, despite the uncertain economic prospects there. Key aspects of the new rural policy were the mobilisation of local government in support of Saemaul initiatives, the substantial raising of the government-set grain prices, the introduction of new strains of rice, and the unprecedented availability of investment funds and material goods for the purpose of local community projects aimed at raising incomes. Saemaul emphasised self-help and a transformation of values and attitudes, but the extent to which these contributed to the growing impact of the movement remained debatable. Rural policy did not change human behaviour, but the larger workings of the ROK economy and some judicious agricultural policy measures brought the new influences of growing infrastructure, access to city markets, market information, technology and capital investment to bear upon the rural sector with overall positive results.

The ROK economy also had to contend with adverse developments in the international economy. In particular, basic economic strategy was badly undermined by the fourfold increase in the price of oil at the end of 1973. The ROK economy was almost totally dependent on oil imports for energy supply, and almost overnight it faced a calamitous rise in the cost of its oil imports. This oil shock produced 40 per cent inflation in 1974, and caused substantial modification of heavy industrialisation plans, involving a retreat from involvement in high energy consumption industries such as non-ferrous metals, fertilisers and pulp manufacture to concentrate on steel, shipbuilding, heavy machinery, electronics and automobiles. Nevertheless, effective domestic cost-cutting, continuing productivity gains, and a resumption of rapid export growth aided recovery from the immediate impact of the crisis, and annual GNP actually expanded from its average of 9.5 per cent during 1960–75 to 12.3 per cent during 1975–78. Meanwhile, the 1973–74 oil crisis released large amounts of so-called petrodollars on to world financial markets, providing the ROK with access to cheaper investment funds. The ROK aggressively pursued such oil money, and as the oil-producing countries invested their new wealth in massive infrastructure projects, foreign construction earnings, especially in the Middle East, became an important feature of the ROK economy.

In the late 1970s the ROK economy suffered a series of reversals, and in 1980 suffered its first actual decline in real GNP since 1956. Domestic and foreign factors were both involved in what constituted a serious challenge to the fundamental premises of the ROK economic structure. Domestically, the ROK had averaged annual GNP growth of 8.1 per cent during the 1970s. This growth had been far from even, and its most significant feature had been the surge of investment which occurred following the 1974–75 recession. However, by 1979 aggregate domestic demand was fuelling excessive inflation, and was threatening the fragile structure of the export-led economy. Reflecting declining competitiveness, export growth itself slowed down markedly in 1979, and GNP growth slowed to 6.4 per cent as the economy was further shaken by the second round of oil shocks in early 1979. While the Blue House remained committed to rapid-growth economic settings, economists within the Economic Planning Board argued for a tight money policy to induce stabilisation. The death of Park Chung-hee removed a key influence against stabilisation policies, and the government soon adopted orthodox economic policies of holding down money supply and raising interest rates. In 1981 the economy emerged from its downturn. A devalued won boosted ROK exports, the re-establishment of authoritarian government again suppressed labour activism, and the economy as a whole absorbed the impact of the steep rise in oil prices. This opened the way for the economy to resume its rapid-growth trajectory during the 1980s.

ROK society in the 1970s

In the 1970s the ROK displayed the seemingly contradictory traits of a strong authoritarian state which none the less existed alongside a vibrant, occasionally assertive civil society. In fact, pre-modern era Korea had always possessed a strong civil society, and lurking beneath images of royal despotism there always existed a high self-regulatory and vigorous civil society. Moreover, the Park (and later Chun) administration, while coercive, offered no thoroughgoing social blue-print. On the contrary, they seem to have tacitly accepted the limitations imposed on them by their support-base among the urban élite and middle class. Their reach into society could be deep at times, but it was also indirect and selective, relating chiefly to the facilitation of economic development.

During the 1970s the agricultural workforce continued to decline, from 61.4 per cent in 1960 to 50.9 per cent in 1970 to 37.8 per cent in 1980, as South Koreans became highly urbanised and regimented into an industrialised workforce. Urbanisation created a new working class, comprising industrial workers, trades-people, shopkeepers and petty merchants, drivers, repairmen and service people, whose daily routine involved direct contact with the regulatory and coercive powers of the authoritarian state as never before. Their income and conditions of work were almost totally dependent upon the calculations of macro-economic planning and the fortunes of the ROK economy as a whole, which generally left them not far above subsistence level. Attempts at labour organisation, whether linked with leftist ideology or Christian social activism, met with strong government repression. However, the new workers were still materially better off than in their recent rural lives, and while they generally felt little attachment to the government which imposed their burdens and deprived them of a voice of even mild protest, memories of the greater poverty and the exhausting daily round they had recently left behind, and a certain optimism that the country was heading towards better days all favoured quiescence.

As the economic and physical environment of the ROK itself began to be transformed by rapid growth in the 1970s, a new élite comprising technocrats, businessmen and generals began to wield power and influence. The technocrats comprised senior government administrators who directed the working of the new economy. Under Syngman Rhee their influence had been limited, but under Park they held senior cabinet posts, and one of their number, Choi Kyu Hah, served as president for some months in 1979–80 following the assassination of Park Chung-hee. They remained outside the inner circle of politics, but as the masters of policy detail and institutional memory they retained broad prerogatives, and as a result of élite recruitment they stood above the general population, answerable to the president and his staff but to few others.

The business and managerial class also advanced to the front ranks of the new élite. As the economy grew, so did the sheer number of Korean entrepreneurs, and in the larger companies they gained undreamed-of wealth. Close relations with regulatory authorities, with whom they jointly planned entry into new industries, gave leading businessmen almost insider status with the government, while commercial success and generous political donations brought easy access to the Blue House. Such people tended to be better educated, more-travelled, and generally more pragmatic and cosmopolitan than many members of the military élite, and perhaps for this reason they remained firmly under the control of a government which from Park Chung-hee downward mistrusted them. Although they gained respect in some quarters, and although they generally used their formidable wealth to raise their profile in such diverse fields as charitable foundations, the funding of universities, sports teams, culture and the arts, more generally they were viewed with disdain by the general population for the corruption they fostered, for their limitless access to capital at the expense of potential small-to-medium industry and consumer borrowers, for their predatory attitude to subcontractors, harsh attitude to labour and general insensitivity to issues of environmental protection and social justice.

The military dominated élite circles in the Third and Fourth Republics. Through their control of the presidential secretariat, the KCIA and other military-security organs of government, they retained a pervasive grip on power, while their influence also penetrated deeply into the economy as many senior officers left the armed forces to become senior bureaucrats or to enter the business world. At the height of military influence on civil government during the 1970s and early 1980s, nearly half of all senior bureaucrats possessed a substantial military background. However, general social attitudes towards the military remained ambivalent. The atmosphere of continuing threat from the North and the transparent, meritocratic character of the armed forces below the very senior ranks gained for them a measure of public support, but their presence in politics as chief backers of a repressive government apparatus was deeply resented. In this respect, while the country was technically at war, ROK society remained highly civilianised.

Below the élite, industrialisation in the 1960s and 1970s brought about a sharp increase in the size of the middle class. By the mid-1970s more than half the population classified themselves as 'middle class', though such self-classification represented aspiration as much as reality. Even where such relatively objective factors as income and occupation were applied, they shed little light on the impact this burgeoning class had on politics and society. Politically, the middle class offered little opposition to the government, for it accepted political authoritarianism in return for material prosperity, public law and order, and effective national security. They were materialistic and acquisitive, though their taste to acquire the goods which reflected their rising status was limited by the general austerity enforced by the government. The key to their status remained education. The transparent and meritocratic *shihom chiok* ('examination hell') system rewarded high-school students for their rote-learning capacity, and granted places in élite universities such as Seoul National University, Yonsei University and Koryo University not only to the best and the brightest but also to those with the greatest stamina and persistence. Graduates of these universities proceeded to form a new bureaucratic and managerial élite as they entered the civil service, the legal profession, the banks and major *chaebol*. Although ROK educators continued to argue that this system impeded creativity, innovation and entrepreneurship, it was also arguable that this system had facilitated industrialisation by means of its relentless insistence upon performance and upon compliance with the demands and disciplines of modern working life.

Sandwiched between the extreme pressure of university entrance study and working life, university life constituted a relatively calm period of personal growth. The adult world tended either to ignore students or to treat them dismissively as a transient group, which in effect they were. Yet there was substance to their self-styled role as 'conscience of the nation', for they alone were relatively free to organise politically. Within the campus the formal curriculum remained undemanding, but the informal curriculum pushed by student-run study and discussion groups advanced a more radical agenda on issues such as reunification, democracy and social equity. However, such radicalism rarely influenced national politics, for the major political parties and figures showed little interest in the student movement. Meanwhile the students themselves felt little affinity with the much older political bosses and their parties.

Upon graduation most students settled into the discipline of national service and then working life. Few displayed any continuing commitment to radical politics, but those who did generally found employment in the academic or intellectual world. As in many other countries, Korean academics and intellectuals tended to preserve a distinct outlook on public issues. They saw themselves, and were often also seen by the public at large, as 'guardians of the national spirit', and as arbiters of taste in the arts. In the 1970s they still formed a small, somewhat privileged group which was geographically concentrated in Seoul and generally isolated from international contact. The relationship between intellectuals and the Yushin government was, of course, never easy. The government recruited many of the best and the brightest, but otherwise remained basically distrustful of intellectuals as a group. Although they were closely integrated into Korean society, the nature of Yushin left the dissidents among them facing a hostile régime which could, and often did, unleash the KCIA to pull targeted members into line.

The most vibrant and influential intellectual movement of the 1970s was the *minjung* cultural movement. People tended to apply their own subjective meaning to this term, which denoted a focus on the Korean people, or masses, as opposed to the ruling élites, but the main elements comprised an attitude of resistance towards political repression, and an assertion of the role of non-élite people in shaping Korean history and tradition. The *minjung* movement fostered works of art, literature, and especially commentary on social and political issues in which a sense of Korean transcendence over past humiliation and current repression had particular meaning for political activists. It also gave voice to a burgeoning sense of ethnic pride in Korean achievement after decades of poverty and foreign political and cultural domination.

Conclusion

In both economic and strategic terms, the trend of DPRK decline and ROK ascendancy became clear during the 1970s. In 1970 the ROK economy was roughly twice the size of the DPRK economy, and the two economies were roughly comparable on a GNP-per-capita basis. However, by 1980 the ROK economy had grown to more than four times the size of the DPRK economy. Meanwhile, the ROK made important gains in regional security during this period. Not only did its economic growth increase the reach of its diplomacy; among its chief allies, the United States recovered from its Vietnam débâcle and established a more limited, stable presence in East Asia, while Japan began to exercise diplomatic influence more appropriate to its status as a major regional and global economic power in ways that were generally of benefit to the ROK. On the other hand, the DPRK's alliances were weakened by its own economic stagnation and by its inability to adapt to trends towards détente in the Soviet Union, and to recognise the decline of Maoism and its militant, ideological commitment to DPRK security. Limited gains within the Non-Aligned Movement could only partly offset these losses.

The significance of many of these trends seemed clear to practically all regional actors except the DPRK, whose response was curiously minimalist. DPRK policies in the 1970s acquired some new overlays but essentially remained in the accustomed mould of the 1960s. A major reason for this seems to have been Kim Il Sung's unshakeable conviction that the reunification of Korea under the leadership of the KWP was an inevitable outcome of the Party's 'correct' policies, and that economic and diplomatic setbacks could only be temporary in nature. In his public utterances and recorded private meetings throughout this period, he displayed little awareness of the magnitude or implications of the country's disastrous debt situation, while the key cadres who implemented the policies which produced this debt retained their high offices. In foreign policy Kim's public response to the challenges of the 1970s reflected his profound conviction that world socialism was locked in a titanic struggle with the forces of US-led imperialism, and that the forces of socialism would triumph. The expulsion of the US forces and the reunification of Korea under the KWP was an integral part of that struggle, and the North gave every indication that it would pursue this struggle to the bitter end.

As the DPRK's economic and diplomatic assets diminished substantially during the 1970s, so the country became increasingly dedicated to the task of acquiring new military assets with which to pursue independent Korean reunification. By now, however, the only counter-measure that offered a long-term prospect of halting a further deterioration in the DPRK's military position was the development of nuclear weapons. Accordingly, in 1980 the DPRK began construction at Yongbyon of a 5 megawatt reactor fuelled with natural uranium and moderated with graphite. This reactor became the cause of a major confrontation between the US and the DPRK during the 1990s, and in turn initiated an extended period of nuclear diplomacy between the two countries.

It is not easy to account for DPRK policies during the 1970s, for they seem so ill-conceived and counter-productive. In Kim's case, it may help to recall that he was now an ageing man, having turned 60 in 1972. As he aged he seems to have increasingly become the prisoner of strong ideological convictions, while also suffering from a fundamental loss of perspective as a result of long years of exercising absolute power without accountability. Successive purges had left him cut off from meaningful policy debate and expert advice, and left him dependent on an inner circle of ageing, poorly educated, blindly loyal comrades. Kim possessed absolute faith in his ability to read the course of events and to arouse the revolutionary potential of the Korean people – in both the North and the South. He apparently felt he had little to learn from either the Party or the general populace, and in turn he assigned them no role other than as obedient followers.

The policy failures of the DPRK were in turn emphasised by the substantial, though flawed, successes of the ROK. The transition in 1972 to the Yushin system has been described by some as a transition from 'soft' authoritarianism to 'hard' authoritarianism, and it inaugurated a period of protracted political confrontation. The national security perspective was central to Yushin, and from the comparative safety of later years it is not always easy to recall that during the 1960s and 1970s many foreign commentators and even governments openly doubted the ROK's chances of survival in an era marked by the vibrancy of communist national liberation movements and by the militancy of established communist governments in the region. The response of Park and his circle focused not only upon political repression, but also upon export-oriented development. Aggressive borrowing, building up of *chaebol*, and pursuing growth over economic stability were not simply the result of blind obsession, but an integral part of a vision which believed that time was working against the ROK.

The extent of ROK government control of the economy in the 1970s has remained a matter for keen debate. It is beyond dispute that the government employed a wide range of incentives to ensure that the business sector operated in support of government-designated objectives. Financial subsidies, export credits, exchange and interest rate control, favourable tariffs, special tax measures, the close supervision and rationing of credit, a supporting framework of laws and regulations including price and wage controls, control of land zoning and use, the provision of infrastructure all constituted formal – and formidable – instruments of incentive for the growth of the export economy. Moreover, where such positive incentives were deemed inefficient, the government also deployed a formidable array of coercive and punitive measures, including tax audits, the withholding of credit, the recalling of loans, the disconnecting of basic services, and even physical intimidation of prominent business figures. Yet, although the government was at times more an independent decision maker than a framework provider, it was also pragmatic enough to seek for itself a role which did not dominate market and distribution, but rather performed some of the entrepreneurial, financial and managerial roles which ROK industry by itself was arguably too inexperienced to undertake at this stage of its development. The level of government economic control was also limited by economic policies which were internationalist and market-oriented, for this mandated substantial interaction with the international economic system and substantial reliance on bureaucrats and economists, many of whom who were trained in Western institutions.

Unlike in the North, significant restraints on authoritarianism existed in the South. They derived partly from the underlying political culture with its abhorrence of excessive centralism, while in the political sphere no comprehensive ideology to mandate dictatorship by any one individual, group or class existed. Authoritarianism remained a pragmatic means of pursuing set goals, rather than an all-embracing vision of the future. Moreover, notwithstanding censorship, basic freedom of information continued to prevail within the ROK, which also remained open to the substantial international scrutiny of foreign governments and organisations, especially in the area of human rights. As a result, a vigorous civil society continued to function and to challenge the government. For all the theorising about authoritarianism as an integral feature of the Korean political tradition, South Koreans had a well-developed, if seldom articulated, sense of civil and human rights. Thus, while the Yushin system placed formidable obstacles in the path to democracy, within the macro-economic and internal security constraints of the régime, people were sufficiently free in their movements, choice of occupation and choice of association to release considerable economic energy. Growth promoted stability, not the other way around.

Selected reading

Buzo, Adrian 1999, *The Guerrilla Dynasty: Politics and Leadership in North Korea*, London/New York: I. B. Tauris, 1999.

Chang, Dal-joong 1985, *Economic Control and Political Authoritarianism: The Role of Japanese Corporations in Korean Politics 1965–1979*, Seoul: Sogang University Press.

Clifford, Mark 1994, *Troubled Tiger: Businessmen, Bureaucrats, and Generals in South Korea*, Armonk, NY: M. E. Sharpe.

Kim, Kwang-ok 1984, 'Some Aspects of Korean Political Behaviour: Traditional and Modern Context,' *Korean Social Science Journal*, vol. 11, pp. 100–16.

Song, Byung-Nak 1990, *The Rise of the Korean Economy*, Hong Kong: Oxford University Press.

Yang, Sung-Chul 1994, *The North and South Korean Political Systems: A Comparative Analysis*, Seoul: Westview Press/Seoul Press.

7 Divergent courses, 1980–92

During the 1980s the pressures and contradictions which had marked both Koreas in the 1970s grew more acute. In the North pressures arose from a failing economy and an ageing guerrilla leadership which continued to reject the trends towards reform and restructuring widely practised in other socialist economies, most notably in China. In October 1980 the Sixth KWP Congress publicly acclaimed Kim Jong Il as Kim Il Sung's successor, and in the years that followed the younger Kim's ideological works were accorded the reverent, canonical status previously reserved for his father. Meanwhile, a deteriorating economy and balance of foreign trade led to efforts to boost light industry and streamline the foreign trade bureaucracy in 1984. Whether such policies might have eventually led Pyongyang towards liberalisation is moot, however, because the leadership soon countermanded them in favour of a major revival of economic and strategic ties with the Soviet Union. During 1985–89 the Soviet Union provided massive economic assistance to the DPRK in return for military concessions, but this undertaking to renovate the DPRK economy was both costly and ineffective. As the Soviet Union entered its terminal phase in the late 1980s, Moscow began to retreat from its commitments to the DPRK, and this exposed major weaknesses in the unreformed economy of the North. The cost to the country and its people of this continuing decline grew steadily as the Kimist guerrilla state grew less and less able to provide for the basic needs of its citizens. Meanwhile, as the DPRK fell further and further behind the South in economic and military assets, the option of achieving reunification through conventional military assault faded. This led its leaders to turn their attention more and more to irregular warfare and to weapons of mass destruction, not so much as instruments of coherent strategy, but rather as a means to keep its adversaries off balance and at least to buy time.

Meanwhile, in the ROK, the interregnum which followed Park Chung-hee's assassination came to a decisive end in May 1980 when General Chun Doo Hwan declared martial law and formally seized power. However, although Chun successfully consolidated his rule, in time he came under increasing domestic political challenge. His administration began with the bloody repression of a civilian insurrection in the city of Kwangju, and soon encountered major corruption scandals, some involving his wife and her immediate family, which further undermined his claim to legitimacy. Chun sought to offset these liabilities by performance in office, but in this he was only partly successful. He began to reform and rationalise the corporatist economy he had inherited, and by a mixture of good luck and good management led the ROK economy into unprecedented boom years during the mid-1980s. In his early years Chun displayed vigour and adroitness in domestic politics, and a disorganised, demoralised opposition could bring little pressure to bear on him. However, in time opposition forces regrouped, and in June 1987 gathering protests against his rule brought demonstrators on to the streets of Seoul in unprecedented, unmanageable numbers. They forced major political concessions including direct popular presidential elections which brought twenty-six years of military-backed authoritarian government to an end. Aided by a divided opposition, Roh Tae Woo then succeeded Chun for a single five-year term under a new, substantially democratic constitution, but while Roh achieved notable gains in the area of foreign policy, he exercised limited political authority by virtue of an opposition-dominated National Assembly. In an attempt to break the resultant legislative stalemate, Roh and two major opposition parties formed a new majority political party, the Democratic Liberal Party (DLP), in January 1991. This marriage of convenience lasted just long enough to deliver the presidency to Kim Young Sam as the DLP candidate in December 1992, and the era of restored civilian presidential rule in the ROK began.

The DPRK greeted Chun with a policy of applying maximum pressure to the ROK, culminating in a failed attempt to assassinate Chun during his state visit to Burma in October 1983. In the aftermath of this operation, DPRK tactics changed, and the period 1984 to 1986 saw the most active phase of inter-Korean negotiation since 1973. However, tentative exchanges in the humanitarian, sporting, cultural, economic and political spheres broke little new ground, and during 1986–90 the talks reached a stalemate once more. Further talks then led to a breakthrough in December 1991 with the signing of a major inter-government agreement, but during 1992 talks again lost momentum and broke down.

In the broader international sphere, in 1981 the ROK secured the 1986 Asian Games and the 1988 Olympiad for Seoul, which immediately boosted its international image at a time when the less savoury aspects of the Chun administration were on prominent display. Chun also benefited from the advent of the Reagan administration in the US and the Nakasone government in Japan. Both these men were conservative, hawkish leaders who offered only muted criticism of ROK domestic policies, while offering strong public commitments to the defence of the ROK. By contrast, although the DPRK remained on good terms with both of its major allies for much of the 1980s, after the Seoul Olympiad it could not withstand the major successes of ROK diplomacy, which led both the Soviet Union and China to establish diplomatic relations with Seoul. Pyongyang was unable to attract similar recognition from either Tokyo or Washington, and so the diplomatic imbalance between the two Koreas grew as the 1990s began.

The Kim Jong Il ascendancy

At the Sixth KWP Congress, convened in Pyongyang in October 1980, Kim Jong Il finally emerged publicly as Kim Il Sung's designated successor when he was named to a series of high-level positions in the party hierarchy. For the first time, the DPRK media referred to him by name, and DPRK officials began to refer openly to him as his father's designated successor in their dealings with foreigners. In 1982 a new ideological work by the younger Kim titled *On the Juche Idea* was hailed as a blueprint for the future of the Korean revolution, and its rapturous reception in the official media confirmed his status as the only approved ideologue in the country other than his father. With his party and ideological credentials established, Kim Jong Il began to take greater responsibility in broad areas of policy, thus consolidating a period of dual father-and-son rule which lasted until the elder Kim's death in 1994.

The significance of the younger Kim's public emergence aroused considerable international speculation. Some observers believed that he heralded the arrival of a younger, reform-minded generation, which in time would emulate the economic reform process which Deng Xiaoping had instituted in China after 1979. However, the content of the major speeches delivered at the Sixth KWP Congress contained no hint of changes to longstanding policies; and, apart from Kim Jong Il himself, no new, younger figures of influence emerged when the Congress announced the new KWP politburo. Instead, Kim Il Sung reappointed old Manchurian guerrilla comrades to eight of the top ten ranking positions in the party – men who in many ways presented him with mirror images of his own background, training and experience. With the exception of General O Kuk-yol, who was himself the son of a deceased Manchurian comrade, Kim excluded the postwar generation of the DPRK military from the Politburo and also marginalised the influence of younger technocrats. Thus, after the 1980 Congress, the Politburo, which was the inner sanctum of party leadership, consisted of nineteen men, only three of whom had had career experience in economic management. This exclusion of technocrat influence at the highest level of the party provides an important insight into the economic decline of the DPRK, for it ensured that no reform agenda even remotely comparable to the Chinese or Vietnamese models emerged in the years that followed. On the contrary, in his published works the younger Kim himself made it clear that his role was to ensure that the party safeguarded the revolutionary tradition of the anti-Japanese guerrillas after the first generation of revolutionaries had passed from the scene. By anointing Kim Jong Il, the Party reaffirmed that traditional policy parameters – high levels of state control and political repression, a centralised command economy, mass social mobilisation, profound militarism, and uncompromising confrontation of the ROK and the US – would continue to guide the state.

The younger Kim completed his rise to power against a background of mounting economic difficulties. Beginning in 1980, the balance of trade worsened significantly as the DPRK's demand for imports of capital goods continued to outstrip the value of its exports of raw and semi-processed materials. It is one of the many ironies of Juche ideology that the DPRK economy never achieved the self-sufficiency of which it talked so proudly. Overriding military priorities ensured that it consistently consumed more than it produced, with the negative balance usually being covered by aid and consignment trade with the Soviet bloc, by remittances from pro-North Koreans in Japan, and by a growing variety of predatory transactions, including debt repudiation, counterfeiting, and widespread smuggling of drugs, alcohol and tobacco under cover of diplomatic immunity. These means enabled the DPRK to support its military build-up during the 1970s, but as the value of DPRK exports continued to decline, and its demand for capital imports grew, chronic trade deficits began to blow out, from an estimated $106 million per year during 1976–79 to $355 million during 1980–83. In 1983 the DPRK recorded a record trade deficit of $551 million, and was forced to take counter-measures.

Kim Jong Il had completed his rise just as the DPRK began to confront a series of adverse regional developments. During the early 1980s Sino-Japanese and Sino-American *entente* continued to strengthen, Chinese domestic policy continued to emphasise economic pragmatism, the United States pressed ahead with the worldwide deployment of sophisticated new weaponry which none of the DPRK's allies, much less the DPRK itself, had any prospect of countering. Moreover, the Non-Aligned Movement faded as an international diplomatic force, and the awarding of the 1988 Olympic Games to Seoul in 1981 symbolised the growing international status of the ROK. The ROK itself remained politically tense, but after 1980 it became increasingly stable under Chun. While we can never be certain how the DPRK leadership actually assessed such adverse developments, rare public acknowledgement by Kim Jong Il in 1982 that the current situation was 'strained and complicated' indicated falling morale and acknowledgement that Korean reunification under the KWP was still a long way off.

During the second half of 1983 the DPRK began to evolve a response to these setbacks. On 9 October 1983, DPRK commandos detonated a bomb at the Martyrs' Mausoleum in Rangoon during an official visit and ceremony by Chun Doo Hwan and his entourage. However, while the blast killed seventeen senior ROK officials, including four cabinet ministers, Chun himself escaped unharmed. After an official investigation, including interrogation of a surviving DPRK commando, the Burmese government declared itself satisfied that the DPRK was responsible. Despite DPRK protestations that the ROK and the US themselves were the guilty parties, the international community found the evidence of DPRK responsibility convincing, not least because such an operation was consistent with the past actions and current outlook of the DPRK leadership. As for its motives, it seems likely that the DPRK leadership saw the operation as a valid means of seeking an advantage over its chief adversaries by creating an atmosphere of fear, confusion and demoralisation in Seoul. In this atmosphere Pyongyang might then have sought to extract concessions from the ROK and its allies.

This event seemed an unlikely prelude to a renewal of active inter-Korean negotiation after a hiatus of more than ten years, but somehow it seemed to serve a strange cathartic purpose, for three months later, in January 1984, a proposal for tripartite talks between the DPRK, the ROK and the US was placed on the table in Washington through Chinese intermediaries. This proposal seemed to many at the time to herald a breakthrough in the negotiating process because the DPRK had always sought direct, or bipartite, negotiations with the US on ending the Korean conflict. Its agenda sought the withdrawal of US forces and the signing of a bilateral DPRK–US peace treaty without reference to the ROK, with whom Pyongyang proposed to negotiate consequently and separately on the political shape of a reunited Korea. Peace negotiations which excluded the ROK were, of course, unacceptable to the US – and, indeed, to all the ROK's allies. A tripartite talks structure, in which the DPRK, the US and the ROK discussed a settlement as three equal partners, would therefore represent a substantial concession from Pyongyang and remove a major impediment to negotiation.

Some of the diplomacy during this period is obscured by cross-purposes and overlapping initiatives, but in essence a US message that it was prepared to negotiate directly with the North if the South participated as an equal party was forwarded to Pyongyang via Chinese intermediaries in September 1983, coincidentally just as the Rangoon operation was about to go ahead. The operation itself seems to have convinced the Chinese of the need actively to seek a settlement to the Korean conflict, and so they urged acceptance of the proposal on all parties. However, clarification of the North's commitment to a tripartite talks process soon established that flexibility was more apparent than real, and that Pyongyang continued to rule out categorically any direct role for the South in negotiating a peace treaty. Under these conditions the impetus for such talks faded, and by March 1984 the tripartite talks proposal was effectively dead.

At this point the inter-Korean dialogue came to life once more. In fact, the period 1984–86 witnessed the most active period of inter-Korean contact and negotiation since 1972–73, as the two Koreas initiated talks in the fields of sport, humanitarian exchanges, economic co-operation and inter-parliamentary dialogue. Negotiations on forming a unified Korean team for the Los Angeles Olympiad took place during March and April 1984, but broke up when the North decided not to attend the Games as part of a Soviet-led boycott. Then, in September 1984, Pyongyang offered relief goods to the ROK after devastating floods in the South. This led to a re-opening of Red Cross talks for the first time in twelve years, and then to talks on inter-Korea trade and economic co-operation.

Negotiations reached a high point during 1985 with an unprecedented exchange of arts performances and family reunion visits in August and September. Simultaneously, secret diplomacy involving high-level officials from both sides culminated in a visit to Pyongyang by Chun's personal envoys in October. The envoys presented Chun's proposal for an inter-Korean summit, but they found the North's counter-proposals, which included a draft non-aggression pact and an ROK undertaking to call off its annual joint ROK–US Team Spirit military exercises, unacceptable. As talk of summitry quickly faded, humanitarian exchanges ceased, and in January 1986 the North unilaterally suspended all talks. The negotiating process entered an extended period of stalemate once more.

The 1984–85 negotiations again underscored the distance between the two Koreas. Progress on humanitarian issues and the staging of media-friendly events such as the arts performances and family reunions created a sense of change and flexibility, but substantive negotiations did not move past the preliminary stage, and only fleetingly involved high-level officials. The South continued to seek confidence-building measures through humanitarian contact, while the North continued to press for immediate negotiation on major military and political issues. As was the case in 1972–73, these stances represented diametrically opposed beliefs: the South believed that the Kimists were sustained chiefly by their isolation and could not withstand the outside contact that multiple people-to-people contacts would provide; while the North believed that the ROK government was an unrepresentative 'puppet' government whose removal would unleash the revolutionary potential of the South Korean masses.

During 1983–84 the DPRK also sought to address its growing economic problems. As noted previously, the fundamental problem was that the DPRK could no longer pay for imports of food, raw materials, advanced capital equipment and military hardware. It therefore sought to stem its growing trade deficit through a number of foreign trade initiatives. Through the enacting of a Joint Venture Law in September 1984 it announced its willingness to trade with Western countries and to import foreign capital, while domestically it sought to raise the profile of light industry, long neglected in the shadow of the heavy industrialisation drive, as the sector most likely to earn export income. To many at the time, it seemed that the DPRK intended to emulate a similar strategy then being carried out in China, but its public pronouncements were not backed up either by significant structural reforms, or by the advancement of new personnel from outside the ageing guerrilla inner circle, or even by public debate on the need for change. No trade-related diplomacy supported the newly announced strategy, while the statistical blackout continued, and the DPRK continued to default on its foreign debts. Under such circumstances, plans to achieve even limited economic reform, let alone engage the international economy, were not realistic.

In fact, Kim Il Sung was already looking to the Soviet Union for solutions to his economic problems. Thus, in May–June 1984, he made a 45-day tour of the Soviet Union and Eastern Europe which effected a major change in the DPRK's relations with the Soviet bloc. This was Kim's first official visit to Moscow since 1961, and was the culmination of Soviet diplomatic efforts to counter a serious deterioration in its strategic position in East Asia. The détente between China, Japan and the US was underpinned by a shared perspective on security issues which was clearly aimed at containing the Soviets, and the DPRK seemed to offer Moscow one of the few options to counter this development. The Soviets therefore offered Kim massive economic assistance in return for important military-strategic assets through renewed access to DPRK naval facilities and airspace.

The revived DPRK–Soviet relationship meant that by the end of 1984 renovation of the existing economic structure under Soviet auspices had become a viable alternative to the option of opening the economy to more contact outside the socialist bloc. No matter how illusory in practice, seeking an economic breakthrough using familiar methods while keeping ideology intact was clearly preferable to substantial reform, which would have directed Kim Il Sung away from his lifetime of commitment to economic centralism and autarky, involving certain risk and uncertain benefit. Accordingly, as Soviet involvement in the DPRK economy intensified during 1985 to 1987, Pyongyang's interest in economic reform declined. When the Third Seven-Year Plan began in early 1987, orthodox command economic methods had again reasserted themselves, and the initiatives of 1983–84 were either marginalised or else effectively reversed.

The Soviet strategy of building a new relationship with the DPRK did not last long, for it was a conservative option which could not withstand the accession of Mikhail Gorbachev to the Soviet leadership in March 1985. Under Gorbachev, Soviet policy began to change radically, retreating from an increasingly unsustainable military and political confrontation with the West in favour of policies of domestic economic reform (*perestroika*) and political liberalisation (*glasnost*). These policies favoured an improved political and economic relationship with the ROK, China and Japan, and undercut the political, strategic and ideological rationale for close ties with Pyongyang. By 1987 it was clear that the DPRK and the Soviet Union had developed sharp policy differences, and as Soviet ties with the ROK strengthened in the wake of the 1988 Seoul Olympiad, Moscow began to disengage from the North. Two-way trade, which accounted for half total DPRK foreign trade, peaked in 1988 at $2.8 billion, and by 1992 had shrunk to less than half this amount. As the DPRK angrily confronted Moscow over its new policy towards the ROK, major weapons shipments and joint military exercises stopped during 1988–89 and the political relationship deteriorated markedly. With the final fall of the Soviet Union in 1991, the DPRK lost a major economic and strategic backer.

Pyongyang's response to the reversals of the late 1980s was characteristically conservative and defensive. Official rhetoric continued to insist that the collapse of the Soviet Union was only a temporary setback on the path to final victory, and was otherwise dismissive of the need to change basic policies. The cult of personality around Kim Jong Il intensified, as did the traditional methods of political and economic mobilisation. Kim Il Sung remained profoundly distrustful of anyone who was not of the guerrilla generation, and continued to exclude younger cadres from the Politburo, whose average age by this time was well over 70. Beyond the short-lived promotion of a Free Trade and Economic Zone in the far north-east in 1991, the leadership advanced no coherent plan to compensate for the collapse of the Soviet economic relationship, and remained attached to the old, failed mass campaigns of the past, such as assorted 'speed battles' aimed at increasing quantitative output. Likewise, although the DPRK's foreign policy had been seriously undercut in the wake of the Seoul Olympiad, Pyongyang's response was rigid and ideological. It met the desertion of former allies with torrents of abuse and evolved no coherent counter-strategy.

It was in this context that the development of nuclear weapons and other weapons of mass destruction offered a viable means of continuing the struggle. Planning for a nuclear reactor capable of producing weapons-grade plutonium began during the 1970s as hopes of achieving victory through conventional military superiority faded, and construction began in 1980. By 1990 the DPRK nuclear programme had come under increasing international scrutiny, mainly as a result of satellite surveillance and continuing misgivings about the DPRK's intentions. In particular, the unwillingness of the DPRK to subject its programme to international inspection by the International Atomic Energy Agency (IAEA), a specialised agency of the United Nations, aroused continuing concern. During the 1990s concern would be replaced by alarm, and the nuclear issue would dominate DPRK foreign policy, leading to serious confrontation.

Meanwhile, the blackout on economic statistics enforced by the DPRK government since the early 1960s ensured that external knowledge of actual social conditions in the DPRK during the 1980s came largely from the accounts of refugees and defectors, or else from inferences drawn from the few statistics made available to international organisations. They gave a consistent picture of a civil society subordinated to the will of the state to a degree unparalleled in other communist states. The state presided over a strict system of reward and punishment, and an internal surveillance apparatus which penetrated deeply into daily life. As the economy began to stagnate in the 1970s, so did social development. Rural–urban migration tailed away as the urban industrial complexes became unable to deploy further labour effectively, and for much of the 1980s an estimated 40 per cent of North Koreans remained on the land. Economic conditions and strict control of internal movement also resulted in very low levels of internal migration. Roughly 5 per cent of the North Korean population changed localities during the 1980s, while the corresponding figure in the South was 20 to 25 per cent. Roughly similar proportions of the population in the two Koreas were engaged directly in agriculture, but the burgeoning white-collar class in the South had no counterpart in the North.

North Koreans continued to live in conditions of considerable poverty, especially outside the major cities, where extreme dependence on a centralised distribution centre, especially in foodstuffs, prevailed. Official policy forbidding such local capitalist activities as farmers' markets remained firm, but over time economic privation led to informal networks for the exchange of goods and influence-peddling. Party officials enjoyed major leverage in such transactions and, as petty corruption flourished, revolutionary zeal diminished to the point at which surveillance to prevent the re-emergence of 'the old way of life' virtually ceased. Lack of mobility meant that local communities had lived together for decades and so there was little inclination towards accusation and denunciation. Instead, as the economy continued to deteriorate, people tended to band together in the face of common adversity. Ironically, times of dire collective need created a more 'liberal' atmosphere.

The ROK Fifth Republic

Meanwhile, in the ROK, the death of Park Chung-hee in October 1979 produced a political vacuum. Park himself had allowed no rival or heir apparent to flourish within his inner circle, and so, while institutions of considerable power and reach such as the KCIA and the President Secretariat existed, they were generally headed by men of limited ability who had little room to manoeuvre towards leadership. Premier Choi Kyu-ha was appointed acting president and confirmed by the Yushin National Electoral College as president in December 1979; but, while Choi presided over government, he had no significant military or civilian power-base. Nor did the ranks of the parliamentary opposition and the dissidents offer a clear alternative. The opposition New Democratic Party (NDP) still suffered from the acrimonious leadership split between Kim Young Sam and Lee Chul-Seung, while the release from detention of former NDP leader Kim Dae Jung further complicated the opposition leadership picture. While it seemed to many at the time that this situation would lead to either the restoration of democracy or the reimposition of military-backed authoritarianism, the actual path ahead was obscure.

When Choi Kyu-ha was confirmed as president in December 1979 he emphasised the transitional nature of his administration and pledged an early revision of the constitution, to be followed by a return to a full democratic order. In the immediate aftermath, portents such as open labour organisation, the return of political exiles, the release of dissidents and the re-emergence of a vigorous political life suggested a trend towards democratisation. Meanwhile, however, countervailing forces within the military worked towards a reimposition of military-backed authoritarianism. Although Park was dead, the Yushin constitution and the machinery of government he had created remained intact. Both the civil bureaucracy and the business sector were characteristically ambivalent about democratisation, and many were still attracted to the Park formula of government as the guarantor of social order and creator of conditions which favoured economic growth, especially through the suppression of labour. Accordingly, parallel with the open civilian political activity in support of democratisation, within the armed forces an equally vigorous process of politicking began behind closed doors with the objective of retaining the essence of the Yushin system.

There was no designated successor to Park, nor was there any formal machinery by which a successor might emerge. It therefore seemed appropriate that the heir began to emerge by means of a violent intra-army putsch. On 12 December 1979, Chun Doo Hwan, a two-star general who headed the Defense Security Command, arrested the martial law commander, Chung Seung-hwa, nominally the senior ROK army figure, and in so doing asserted his control over the ROK armed forces as a whole. Chun did not act alone, but as the designated leader of a fraternity of senior officers from within the 11th graduating class of the Korean Military Academy. This class was widely seen as the spearhead of the younger, post-Korean War generation of military leaders, and included many key figures in the subsequent Chun administration. In addition, many of Chun's colleagues shared a common geographic tie, based on the Taegu area in North Kyongsang Province, which, it will be recalled, was also Park Chung-hee's place of origin. The term 'T–K faction', meaning 'Taegu–Kyongsang faction', became widely adopted to designate this inner circle of power brokers.

Chun further consolidated his control over the military and the internal security apparatus during the early months of 1980, but the trend towards democratisation also continued during this period, most notably through the full restoration of civil rights to Kim Dae Jung and some 600 other dissidents in February. With the reopening of the universities in March 1980, students in particular began to play an increasingly significant role. The issues they highlighted began with government restrictions on campus autonomy, the prolongation of martial law, the retention of the Yushin constitution, and delays in moving towards open, representative government, but they also included broader socio-economic demands which attacked the very basis of the Yushin system. Without the formidable repressive apparatus of the Park régime to contend with, the students swiftly moved off campus, and by May they were converging on downtown Seoul on an almost daily basis for massive, increasingly violent demonstrations.

With the centre of Seoul paralysed for days on end, events moved to a swift climax in mid-May. On 14 May the Army began to deploy troops and armoured vehicles around key buildings; and, on 17 May 1980, Chun Doo Hwan declared martial law. This decree closed the campuses, and reimposed Yushin-era prohibitions on political gatherings, publications and broadcasts – and in effect on all public criticism of the government. More important, Chun used the martial-law provisions to effect a sweeping round-up of all major political figures, ranging from dissidents and opposition figures such as Kim Young Sam and Kim Dae Jung to former key lieutenants of Park Chung-hee, such as Kim Jong Pil and Lee Hu-rak. By this move Chun eliminated former members of Park's inner circle from political life and singled out Kim Dae Jung for severe and exemplary treatment.

Chun's seizure of power was effective throughout the country, but in the south-western city of Kwangju, capital of South Cholla Province and the fourth-largest city in the ROK, it had tragic consequences. On Sunday and Monday, 18–19 May, student demonstrations escalated into violent confrontations between local civilians and martial-law troops. Apart from the arrest of Kim Dae Jung, a native of Cholla from nearby Mokp'o, the particular focus of civilian anger became the reportage of these events, and on Monday evening the local offices of the government-controlled media networks KBS and MBC were set on fire. ROK army paratroopers sent to restore order acted with ill-disciplined ferocity against the civilians, and the protests turned into a fully fledged insurrection the following day as civilians retaliated and seized control of the city, forcing the troops to withdraw. For Chun there could be no turning back if he were to consolidate his *coup*, and after several days of uneasy calm and attempted negotiation, ROK Army troops launched an assault and retook Kwangju in a ruthless display of power.

All told, the Kwangju operation cost the lives of at least several hundred civilians, but the precise number of casualties may never be known. Like no other event before or since, the Kwangju incident created a deep wound in the political fabric of the Republic of Korea. Its immediate effect was to ensure that Chun's name would forever be linked with Kwangju rather than with any other achievement, and its longer-term effect was to serve as a powerful symbol of popular resistance to military-backed authoritarian government, and hence to perpetuate the rift between the civilian and military élites in the ROK. The United States also sustained collateral damage, since the troops used by Chun in the retaking of Kwangju were withdrawn from the United Nations Command for the operation – an action which required the formal assent of the UNC's US commander. Anti-US sentiment in the ROK, especially in student and radical political circles, acquired a powerful focus.

Chun Doo Hwan proceeded to consolidate authoritarian power. In August 1980 he was elected to a single seven-year term as president by the National Conference for Unification – the indirect electoral college system created by Park – and in October a national referendum approved a new constitution which provided the constitutional basis for the reimposition of military-backed authoritarianism. Meanwhile, the government launched a major 'purification' programme. At its lower level, the programme involved the round-up and 're-education' through military-style physical training of thousands of petty criminals and 'decadent' social elements – a broad term which covered almost anyone whose lifestyle deviated from the military's idealised, 'respectable' norm. At a more senior level, the programme involved a combination of dismissal and, at times, con-fiscation of assets from senior people, mainly Park-era hold-overs in the civil service, the media and the banking sector. Thus, Chun pursued the politically astute but cynical objectives of simultaneously dispersing the existing élite, creating job vacancies for the new élite, meeting public expectations of good social order and addressing popular resentment at the excesses of the KCIA and Park-era corruption in general.

The attack on Kim Dae Jung was far more serious. Whereas other major opposition figures were briefly detained, then released and banned from political activity, in July 1980 Kim was sent for trial on the capital offence of sedition, and in September was found guilty and sentenced to death. This process led to a major diplomatic effort, led by Japan and the US, to have the sentence commuted. Eventually, as Chun consolidated his rule, the commuting of Kim's sentence made better political and diplomatic sense, and in December 1982 Kim was released into exile in the United States. By this time Chun Doo Hwan had turned back the forces of democratisation and re-established a régime based firmly on Yushin precedent. He claimed a mandate on the basis of strong national security, political stability, good social order, clean government, and economic recovery and reform. In reality, though, his major achievement had been to usurp power, forestall widespread aspirations towards democratisation, dismantle the remnants of an unpopular régime and replace it with an equally unpopular régime.

South Korean people knew little about their new leader. Comparisons with Park Chung-hee were inevitable, since both had been raised in rural poverty in North Kyongsang Province, and both had opted for a military career as the best means of escaping such poverty. Both graduated from the Korean Military Academy and rose steadily through the ranks, Chun to the major office of head of the Defence Security Command in March 1979 from where he staged his putsch in December 1979. Both also shared the strengths and limitations of the military mind: they were rational, consistent, and knew how to seek and take expert advice in fields outside their direct experience, but Chun's lifetime experience was perhaps more limited than Park's. Park had been more directly involved in tumultuous events, beginning with the Japanese colonial order, and seems to have reflected more profoundly on the fractured times in which he grew up.

On the other hand, assessments of Chun ranged from that of a weak leader who ruled by constant and unscrupulous manipulation, to that of an able, strategically clever army politician who constantly outmanoeuvred and outwitted people of greater intellectual ability. Certainly, in time Chun emerged as a gregarious, somewhat intellectually insecure person whose major talent was as a deployer of personnel. He possessed considerable political acumen, which he used to balance the myriad military and civilian factions which surrounded him, and he also shared authority in a way which would have been inconceivable under Park. To his detriment, however, Chun was unable to harness the strength of mind and will to exercise the same ruthless control over excessive corruption as Park did. This was partly an issue of character, partly an issue of temperament, but it was also an issue of the times in which the two men lived. Park was a nation-builder who ruled over a smaller, more manageable élite which he himself had helped to shape. Chun, on the other hand, presided over a far more complex state and society and sought a role as a reformer and consolidator of the modern ROK industrial state. Meanwhile, greater tolerance of functional corruption was arguably almost mandatory in an opaque, poorly institutionalised system which had become less and less responsive to authoritarian control.

By 1982, Chun had achieved a secure grip on power, with loyalists and long-standing colleagues strategically placed in key positions throughout the government. Labour was quiescent, and economic reforms had drastically reduced inflation, but not at the expense of continuing rapid economic growth, which resumed in 1982 after the prolonged slump of 1979–81. The more collegiate style of Chun had its chief impact in the area of economic policy, for in contrast to the corporatist mentality of Park, Chun gave expanded authority to the technocrats and accepted their basic strategies for stabilising the economy. He quickly grasped the essential truth that he could not maintain Park's highly centralised system of economic management. Accordingly, during 1980–83 economists, who in a ROK setting could be described as economic rationalists, argued long and hard, and by and large successfully, to reduce the command role of the powerful ministries such as the Ministry of Industry and Commerce and the Ministry of Finance. A major reorganisation of sectors such as shipping, heavy industry and the automobile industry was carried out to streamline performance and stimulate competition through forced mergers and closures, and a more liberalised economic model began to emerge as the new engine of rapid economic growth. However, this push was not sustained, and after 1983 liberalisation, which in an ROK context meant rationalising sector competition, reducing red tape and opening markets to international competition, failed to maintain its initial impetus. In many ways, liberalisation had been a response to economic adversity in 1981–82, and so it tended to lose momentum as economic recovery gathered pace. After 1982 the ROK economy resumed its rapid-growth trajectory, and this provided little incentive to pursue more comprehensive reform measures. Consequently, the policies of corporatism were prolonged, and the policies of liberalisation and internationalisation were held back, with substantial later consequences.

However, even as Chun reached the zenith of his power and authority, events began to move against him. In May 1982 the first of a number of damaging financial scandals broke with the arrest of a leading Seoul socialite and private money market speculator over a number of illegal financial transactions. As revelations of stock market manipulation, widespread illegal financial transactions – many involving state-controlled banks – spread, it became clear that Chun's in-laws were deeply involved in influence peddling on a scale that went far beyond the permissible limits of the functional corruption of ROK business life. The demoralised opposition sensed a serious blow to Chun's credibility and took heart. Almost immediately, Kim Young Sam, who was still under house arrest, embarked upon a hunger strike to protest against the Chun administration, and in August 1983, Kim Dae Jung became active again from his place of exile in the United States with a declaration of support for a united opposition to Chun. In June 1984 the two Kims launched a Consultative Committee for the Promotion of Democracy (CCPD), a broad opposition group which could credibly claim to be a dialogue partner in any negotiations towards the restoration of democracy.

Political opposition consolidated further in January 1985, when the pre-1979 mainstream opposition politicians within the CCPD regrouped to form the New Korea Democratic Party (NKDP). The major elements in the party were the personal factions of Kim Dae Jung and Kim Young Sam, and their combined strength produced enough momentum for the NKDP to capture 102 seats in the 299-member National Assembly elections in February 1985. However, there were limits to the effectiveness of the parliamentary opposition, for the NKDP remained a classic umbrella party of rival, antagonistic political factions whose agendas had little overlap except the desire to succeed Chun after he finished his single seven-year term as president in 1988. As such, it did little more than rally the existing opposition vote and could not apply sustained pressure to the government. Meanwhile, the DJP share of the popular vote barely changed, from 35.6 per cent in the 1981 elections to 35.3 per cent in 1985.

As time went by, the commitment to a single seven-year term proved to be a crucial weakness for Chun, because increasingly he assumed lame-duck status just as pressure for a decisive reversion to full democracy continued to build, not only in ROK society but also among the ROK business and technocratic élite. In April 1986 the government began tentative negotiations with the NKDP on the future shape of the ROK constitution, with both sides in agreement on a reversion to democracy but in disagreement on the method of electing a president. The DJP favoured a cabinet-style system with a largely figurehead president, while the NKDP proposed the direct popular election of an executive president. These respective positions reflected perceived strengths, for the DJP, with its extensive powers of patronage and its cohesive organisation, was in a stronger position to control the National Assembly than the fragmented opposition. On the other hand, if the opposition could unite, however temporarily, around a single candidate, its best chance of gaining power would lie in turning a direct presidential election into a referendum against the deeply unpopular military presence in politics. Not surprisingly, then, efforts to identify middle ground foundered.

Finally, the pressure within the NKDP to seek compromise caused the party to split. On 8 April 1987 the two Kims dissociated themselves from NKDP leader Lee Min-woo's attempts to seek compromise on the direct popular election issue and left the NKDP, which proceeded to disintegrate. On 1 May they inaugurated a new political party, the Reunification Democratic Party (RDP), with Kim Young Sam as leader and Kim Dae Jung, still formally banned from political activity, as unofficial co-leader. Meanwhile, on 13 April 1987, Chun broke off the constitutional negotiations and announced that the December 1987 presidential election would be conducted under the Yushin-derived indirect electoral college system, which would, of course, guarantee success to the DJP candidate. Chun's announcement, made with a minimum of consultation, proved to be a major tactical error. While closing the door on further negotiation may have been simple realism in view of the two Kims' stance, Chun succeeded in focusing attention on the government as the party responsible for the breakdown. Moreover, it disappointed widespread expectations that Chun would be the last of his kind. Most important, the timing of the announcement coincided with the beginning of the annual spring ritual of campus demonstrations. By his action Chun placed himself on the defensive and delivered substantial momentum to the opposition.

Student demonstrations grew in strength during May, and the government sustained further major damage to its credibility with revelations of brutal interrogation methods used against student leaders, but few could have predicted that June 1987 would witness the downfall of Chun and the effective end to military-backed authoritarianism. On 10 June the DJP convention ratified the nomination of Roh Tae Woo as its presidential candidate, but when the opposition RDP called a street demonstration to protest at this development it can have held out little hope that the event would be effective as a demonstration, let alone that it would open the path to Chun's downfall. In the event, the demonstration combined with ongoing student protests to produce successive days of street violence unprecedented during Chun's term of office. The opposition had tapped into a rich vein of popular unrest.

Amid signs that normally quiescent white-collar workers were playing a growing role in the swelling, daily, and increasingly violent street demonstrations, Chun was forced into compromise, and on 22 June he announced his willingness to re-open talks on constitutional reform. However, this did not stop the demonstrations, and so the Chun administration entered into its final crisis. Chun could not quell the demonstrations by force without running the risk of major loss of life and perhaps a second Kwangju-style insurrection. This course of action might have preserved his authority, but at unacceptable cost, for it would have cast a cloud over the Seoul Olympiad, placed at risk the diplomatic gains of recent years, and thus undermined the ROK's national security. Chun therefore had little option but to make wholesale concessions, and so on 29 June 1987 Roh Tae Woo announced, with Chun's agreement, that the DJP would accept a new constitution with provision for direct presidential elections. The nation's political parties prepared themselves for a new era in Korean politics.

The events of June 1987 were dramatic and in many ways unforeseen. As late as April 1987, there were no clear signs that the Chun administration was about to enter its last crisis. On the contrary, Chun seemed as secure as ever. The government was engaged in an ongoing dialogue with the NKDP on constitutional reform, the economy was enjoying unprecedented boom conditions, and a strong air of anticipation over the 1988 Seoul Olympiad prevailed. Three months later the Fifth Republic was effectively dead. While short-term tactical errors played a major part in the turnaround during April–June 1987, longer-term factors were also influential. Like Park Chung-hee before him, Chun had received a limited, grudging mandate. However, abuses of power, beginning with Kwangju and including police brutality and major corruption, deprived Chun of even the level of popular acceptance and legitimacy given to Park Chung-hee and made Chun more vulnerable to challenge than Park had ever been. The Fifth Republic was unpopular and undemocratic but it still commanded sufficient acceptance to rule because it fulfilled basic public expectations in the domains of national defence, economic development and social stability, and also because of a lingering public perception that the alternatives were either too uncertain or simply not credible enough. Here it should be restated that most South Koreans maintained a profound belief that domestic political chaos had been a major factor in encouraging the North to invade in 1950.

Chun's administration was also undermined by the increasingly anachronistic nature of its mandate. In 1961 military-backed authoritarianism superimposed itself over a tiny urban élite in an impoverished, overwhelmingly agricultural country, but by the mid-1980s economic prosperity and growing international contact had fuelled the explosive growth of a middle class. In 1960 nearly 70 per cent of the workforce was engaged in agricultural labour, but by 1987 this had fallen to less than 20 per cent. Most had become skilled or semi-skilled industrial workers, but the proportion of white-collar workers had also undergone a significant expansion. For this new emerging class Chun's slogans with their echoes of the Park era provided little inspiration. While such workers did not necessarily identify their political and social aspirations with the opposition parties, they had become increasingly alienated from the Fifth Republic.

Moreover, in 1987 the ruling élite itself was no longer cohesive in defending the existing system against challenge. The military itself had always seemed to acknowledge that a reversion to democracy was inevitable, for while the military command–response model deeply influenced the economic, political and social life of the country, the military made no attempt to set up an alternative, anti-democratic ideology, such as its Japanese avatars did in the 1930s. On the contrary, in its broader thrust, Roh's 29 June statement reflected both the somewhat equivocal predisposition of the Chun administration to move towards a more open political system and the acceptance by the military that their time of political domination had come to an end.

Rapid economic development had also driven a further wedge between the business and government sectors, for as the economy grew larger and more complex, close government oversight of business activities became an increasing burden. Benefits such as a docile labour force and the political exclusion of social protest groups were increasingly offset by liabilities such as corruption and bureaucratic restrictions on *chaebol* expansion into new industries. ROK businessmen became increasingly convinced that they would prosper under civilian government, calculating that such a government would institute a more thoroughgoing liberalisation process and be unable to exercise the strict controls of the Park–Chun era, which had been a source of both benefit and frustration. The sum of these pressures was the swift collapse of military authoritarianism. It had established itself at the centre of ROK political life through the exercise of raw authoritarian power, and had served rough needs during a particular stage of the ROK's growth, but by 1987 it had become anachronistic and counter-productive.

However, although the impact of military-backed authoritarianism *per se* was deep and lasting, so were the continuities which worked throughout its heyday. Although South Korean society had changed radically in a material sense during the twenty years leading up to 1987, the basic elements of Korean social structure continued to provide stability amid rapid, turbulent change. Political allegiances were still strongly based on kinship, place of origin and shared alumnus ties, while the profound acceptance of hierarchy, and preference for consensus decision-making remained widespread. Continuity was also driven by such features as a solid, conservative rural constituency, the general sense of economic well-being felt by a substantial majority of the population, an endemically fragmented opposition which lacked general credibility, the continuing threat from the North, ample funding from the business community for the ruling party, and the ruling party's continuing near-monopoly on leadership and managerial talent. Despite the congratulation and self-congratulation of June 1987, the surest pointer to the future was that, in December 1987, 36 per cent of the population still voted for Roh Tae Woo, the candidate originally nominated by the ruling party to maintain the authoritarian Fifth Republic.

The Roh administration

The ROK government gave rapid effect to the promises made by Roh Tae Woo on 29 June 1987. It immediately restored full political rights to Kim Dae Jung, effected a wide-ranging release of people held for political offences, and set in motion a process of constitutional revision as the country prepared for the first direct presidential election since 1971. However, although opposition forces recognised that they needed to unite behind a single candidate to have any prospect of defeating Roh at the polls, again Kim Young Sam and Kim Dae Jung could not reach agreement on who should step aside. The differences between the two were deep and long-standing, extending back to their different geographical bases and their emergence as rival faction leaders within the New Democratic Party during the 1960s. Moreover, the two had fought against the Yushin system in contrasting ways, Kim Young Sam from within the parliamentary system and Kim Dae Jung from within the dissident movement. Both were subsequently prone to highlight this difference, with Kim Young Sam stressing his credentials as a moderate capable of appealing to a broad cross-section of voters, and Kim Dae Jung offering galvanic leadership as the candidate most committed to full democratisation.

In October 1987, Kim Dae Jung inaugurated his own political party and announced his candidacy for the presidency. With Kim Young Sam already in the race and the ruling DJP united behind Roh, the three-way presidential race began in earnest. Since the new constitution made no provision for a second round of voting between the two largest vote-getters, on 16 December Roh was elected with 36.6 per cent of the vote, Kim Young Sam came second with 28 per cent, and Kim Dae Jung third with 27 per cent. Kim Jong Pil, a former stalwart of the Park régime, attracted most of the remaining votes. Amid somewhat ritual opposition charges of unfair campaigning and electoral fraud, Roh Tae Woo took office to begin a single five-year term. The intended successor to Chun under the old system became the successor to Chun under the new system, and the era of democratisation began.

The Roh presidency (1988–93) is often described as a 'transitional' administration, which implies that it led away from the past towards a substantially different successor administration. In fact, this description conceals more than it illuminates. Roh was a Fifth Republic insider, he was thoroughly at home with Chun's authoritarian order, and he was quite prepared to rule accordingly. However, by the time he acceded to the presidency, the basis of political power in the ROK had changed significantly. The ruling party still commanded the remarkably consistent 35 per cent or so of the vote which it had attracted throughout the 1980s but it was unable to deploy freely the combination of patronage and coercion which made this limited support-base effective under Chun. Roh displayed considerable tactical acumen in coping with these changes, but while significant moves towards dismantling the autocratic Yushin-derived power structure were made, its essential features remained substantially intact. These included: the close, corrupt nexus between the ruling party, the bureaucracy and the major *chaebol*; strict control of the banking and finance system, and hence access to capital; a repressive attitude towards the organisation of labour; and the enforcement of the National Security Law, a law aimed primarily at North Korean subversion but also collaterally at leftist dissidents, who remained subject to internal surveillance practices.

The opposition forces had lost impetus amid mutual recrimination at their failure to defeat Roh in the presidential election, but they regained the initiative in April 1988 when National Assembly elections delivered only 25 per cent of the vote to the DJP, a 10 per cent drop on the 1984 figure and sufficient to deliver only 125 seats in the 299-seat Assembly. The legislature asserted itself in the wake of the April 1988 elections and acquired broader powers of inspection and investigation. In June 1988 the long-quiescent judiciary also reasserted itself with the issuing of a statement by three hundred judges demanding steps be taken to re-establish the judicial independence which had been lost during the Yushin era. This action resulted in the appointment of a new chief justice who had not been closely associated with the Fifth Republic leadership. It also brought about both the removal of internal surveillance agents from judicial and National Assembly precincts and the discontinuation of formal liaison between the judiciary and the Blue House, by which the presidential staff routinely oversaw and influenced court decisions. Such activities were relatively restrained in view of the forthcoming Seoul Olympiad in September 1988, but after the conclusion of the games recriminations began in earnest. Wide-ranging National Assembly hearings in late 1988 presented public evidence of widespread corruption during the Chun administration, and, as a result, some forty-seven of Chun's leading relatives and aides were indicted. In November 1988, Chun himself was forced to hand back to government some $14 million in allegedly ill-gotten assets, and to go into rigorous internal exile at the remote temple of Paekdam-sa in Kangwon Province.

During 1989 these events combined with an economic downturn, and an upsurge of radicalism in student and labour circles, to place Roh's presidency under increasing pressure. The National Assembly stalemate was debilitating, but only coalition politics could overcome it. It was under these circumstances that Roh and Kim Young Sam agreed to pool their forces, and in January 1990 they announced the formation of the Democratic Liberal Party (DLP), a grand coalition comprising the DJP and the regional political machines of Kim Young Sam (Pusan and South Kyongsang) and Kim Jong Pil (Ch'ungch'ong). The last two had no ideological objections to joining with their former oppressors as it offered them substantial power. In particular, for Kim Young Sam the move opened the path to nomination as the new party's presidential candidate at the conclusion of Roh's term in 1992. But, while some drew parallels with Japan's long-established and politically successful ruling Liberal Democratic Party (LDP), this was a coalition from out of the Korean past, in which mutually antagonistic political bosses pooled their weaknesses in the hope of gaining access to power. In particular, the depth of Kim Young Sam's abiding antipathy towards Roh and his colleagues would later become clear.

The new DLP controlled a majority of 219 seats in the 299-seat National Assembly, but it directed most of its energies towards internal rivalry, and so as Roh gradually achieved lame-duck status the DLP proved no more capable of providing energetic reform than its many ruling party predecessors. Moreover, the electorate received the merger with considerable cynicism, and in the March 1992 National Assembly elections the DLP lost seventy seats, with candidates from the Kim Young Sam and Kim Jong Pil factions suffering major losses. Despite this erosion of Kim Young-Sam's support base, however, he was duly endorsed as the DLP candidate in the 1992 presidential election.

Meanwhile, the Roh administration continued to confront mounting economic pressures. The Chun régime left office in the middle of an unprecedented economic boom largely brought about by what commentators often describe as the Three Lows – three international economic factors which were highly favourable to the ROK economy. The first was the falling price of oil, which fell from an average price of $28 a barrel during 1983–85 to an average price of about $16 during 1986–88 owing to overproduction, and this trend substantially reduced the ROK's energy import bill. The second was a fall in interest rates, especially the US prime lending rate. This reduced the cost of borrowing abroad and eased pressure on the ROK's balance of payments. The third factor was a related appreciation of the Japanese yen, which raised the price of Japanese exports and enhanced the ROK's international competitiveness, especially to the US, in areas of competition with Japan such as shipbuilding, automobiles and electronics. As a result, the ROK turned around its endemic trade deficit and achieved an average annual balance of payments surplus of $7.7 billion during 1986–88.

These favourable conditions did not last. The loosening of government controls on labour led to average wage rises of some 15 per cent a year during the Roh administration which, coupled with rising inflation, led to a substantial appreciation of the won and a considerable loss of international competitiveness. In addition, multibillion-dollar trade surpluses with the US were politically unsustainable, and the US pressured the ROK to adopt a code of voluntary restraints, to be accompanied by import liberalisation. Moreover, the in-country wealth fuelled by the surpluses created a bubble economy marked by inflated land and stock market values. This, too, was unsustainable, and after 1990 a prolonged downturn in the stock market affected access to capital and saddled the financial sector with an increasing portfolio of bad loans. The double-digit GDP growth figures of the mid-1980s returned to more modest proportions, and in 1992 fell to 4.5 per cent, the lowest for thirteen years.

While Roh operated under a number of constraints in domestic policy, he could work more freely in the area of foreign policy. Roh's basic policy was to ameliorate the long-standing hostility of China and the Soviet Union towards the ROK and, in the process, bring pressure to bear on the DPRK for a negotiated settlement to the Korean conflict. This policy of improving relations with countries to the north attracted the title of 'Nordpolitik', in emulation of West Germany's 'Ostpolitik', the process by which its relations with communist Eastern Europe improved substantially under Chancellor Willy Brandt during the 1970s. In pursuing his Nordpolitik, Roh brought substantial assets to bear, for he was supported by the ROK's new status as an important regional economic and diplomatic power, by the diplomatic momentum generated by the Seoul Olympiad, and by reformist régimes in China and the Soviet Union willing to depart from their long-standing and increasingly counter-productive policy of refusing to recognise the ROK.

Relations with the Soviet Union began to improve steadily after Mikhail Gorbachev's accession to the Soviet leadership in March 1985. During the 1980s Moscow's continuing non-recognition of the ROK as the dominant state on the Korean Peninsula became more and more anomalous, and so during 1987 the Soviet Union began to expand trade and personal diplomacy with Seoul. This trend accelerated after the Olympics, resulting in the exchange of trade offices in April 1989 and the establishment of full diplomatic relations in September 1990. China moved more cautiously, mainly because of its closer ties with the DPRK, but also because Chinese economic reform was not accompanied by political liberalisation. On the contrary, the unravelling of the Soviet bloc, and in particular the Tiananmen Square incident of June 1989, gave pause to conservative sections of the Chinese leadership which saw the DPRK as a staunch ideological ally at a time when communist régimes seemed to be collapsing everywhere. However, as the immediate sense of danger from these events passed, Beijing again moved towards normalisation of relations with the ROK. During 1990 the tempo of government and commercial exchanges increased rapidly, and in October 1990 the two countries exchanged semi-official trade offices. Full diplomatic relations followed in August 1992.

The main thrust of Nordpolitik was, of course, aimed at the DPRK, for both the ROK and the international community at large shared the perception that the DPRK could not survive without strong support from the Soviet Union and China. Roh's strategy towards the North involved dropping all remaining objections to its allies seeking to expand economic and political contacts with Pyongyang and advancing the concept of reunification via a loose, federated entity to be known as the Korean Commonwealth. However, during 1987–88 the DPRK's major diplomatic efforts were aimed at disrupting the Seoul Olympics. As initial nego-tiations on the staging of some events in Pyongyang faded, the DPRK embarked on a major, though ineffective, campaign to persuade allies and Third World countries to boycott the Seoul Olympiad. More seriously, in November 1987 a DPRK agent planted a bomb on board a Korean Airlines plane, which detonated over the Andaman Sea with the loss of all 115 on board. As with the Rangoon operation, one of the DPRK agents involved failed to avoid capture, was arrested in Dubai and turned over to the ROK authorities. Again, a wide spectrum of international opinion found her subsequent confession detailed and convincing; and again, many governments applied economic and political sanctions to the North. An alarmed South initiated a round of secret negotiations focusing on economic assistance to the DPRK in return for a cessation of further terrorist acts, and eventually the DPRK accepted a billion-dollar package of trade-as-aid as the price of an undisrupted Olympics.

Little substantive contact took place between the two Koreas during 1986–90, but the final collapse of global communism in 1989 again brought the two sides into dialogue. In July 1990, Seoul and Pyongyang agreed to talks at prime-ministerial level, and although the office of prime minister in both Koreas was an administrative rather than a political office, a stop–start process of negotiation over the ensuing eighteen months produced the major Agreement Concerning Reconciliation, Non-Aggression, Exchanges and Co-operation of December 1991. This was a false dawn, however, for during 1992 talks on implementation rapidly reached a stalemate and relations again deteriorated. Like all ROK presidents, Roh was anxious to enter the history books as the reunifier of Korea, but in his last months in office he experienced the chagrin of presiding over a division as rigid as at any time since talks first began in 1972.

Although Roh's Sixth Republic attracted the ironic title of 'Fifth-and-a-Half Republic', and Roh's repeated insistence that he was an 'ordinary person' (*pot'ong saram*) dedicated to the interests of the ordinary citizen met with similar derision, the achievements of his administration were significant. There was no reversion to authoritarianism, and the investigation of past abuses of power, while incomplete, was nevertheless open and wide-ranging, and eventually resulted in the public humiliation and imprisonment of both Chun and Roh. Moreover, Roh oversaw a significant increase in the independence of the judiciary and also reined in the military–security apparatus, which essentially ceased to function as a state within a state. This meant that while the presidential secretariat remained a powerful force in government, it devolved significant power to other branches of government. Not the least of these was the re-establishment of elected local government, which had been discontinued under Park Chung-hee in the 1960s. Roh also presided over significant developments in ROK civil society, ranging from a media able to function with a degree of freedom unknown since the 1960s, to the lifting of almost all remaining restrictions on foreign travel, to the gradual emergence of special-interest citizen lobbying groups, such as in environmental protection. Finally, Roh acted forcefully, albeit realistically, to warn off both the military and his own family from involvement in presidential politicking. As a result, he presided over the first peaceful transfer of substantial power to a civilian president in the history of the ROK.

Assessment of the Roh administration must, of course, take into account the limited nature of its mandate. Roh began his term in office with the twin liabilities of a minority vote and close identification with the preceding régime. He was always an unlikely steward of the democratisation process, which axiomatically included an accounting for abuses of power committed while he was a member of Chun's inner circle, and he remained under constant domestic political pressure throughout his régime. As the opposition concentrated chief, though rather unfocused, attention on the squaring of past accounts, and as Roh proved unable to exercise sufficient control over an increasingly corrupt government–business nexus, he became increasingly unable to direct and give shape to domestic policy. This set of political circumstances gave rise to a constant policy ambivalence in Roh and a tendency to follow rather than lead public opinion, which in turn gave the impression of weakness.

This situation had a major effect on economic policy. Here Roh proved unable to counter the many forces which were rapidly eating away at the base of ROK economic success. By the late 1980s most ROK industrial workers attracted high wages, and former export staples such as textiles, garments and footwear had become sunset industries, to be closed down and moved offshore to low-wage countries, mainly in South-East Asia, where the ROK now became a major foreign investor. This change was rapid, but the corresponding movement of the workforce into more capital- and knowledge-intensive industries was not as rapid. This process therefore narrowed the base of ROK manufacturing industry and made it highly dependent on a number of key products which were subject to increasingly rigorous international competition. Moreover, high interest rates, high consumption, and continuing substantial wage rises became established features of an ROK economy which was also losing competitiveness owing to an inefficient finance and banking system, inadequate transport and communication infrastructure, increasing reliance on foreign technology, and over-reliance on *chaebol* performance. These were all well-entrenched, tightly interlocking legacies of the corporatist era, and they tended to undermine the periodic attempts at piecemeal reform.

ROK society in the 1980s

By the late 1980s the cumulative forces of modernisation and especially the enormous wealth generated during the 1980s had begun to transform South Korean culture and attitudes. Pressures for change continued to arise from such phenomena as industrialisation, urbanisation, the changing family structure, the decline of patriarchal and generational authority, and growing awareness of international norms. As society grew more complex, so the reconciliation of these opposing values itself became more problematical. Traditional appeals to frugality and collective sacrifice became increasingly unconvincing as Koreans began to enjoy the fruits of individual achievement, and as the new middle class became less and less restrained by the collectivist values of their parents' generation. Consequently, ROK society continued to stretch in two somewhat contradictory ways – vertically in accordance with a deeply ingrained sense of hierarchy, but also horizontally, as a mass society which insisted that authority, whether political or managerial, ensure a fair distribution of fruits of economic success.

Affluence became deep and widespread during the 1980s, and for the first time people found themselves living in a society no longer dominated by economic debates and economic imperatives. Meanwhile, the under-achievers in the education system entered the blue-collar workforce and became fringe participants in ROK society, discriminated against in terms of social prestige and material benefit. Workers were subject to numerous laws which prohibited organisation and political participation, and were generally ignored as a political force by government and opposition parties alike. The union movement could not organise any political parties, nor could it make direct contributions to support existing political parties. This, of course, contrasted strongly with the almost unlimited flood of contributions from employers to the major parties. In addition to government control, internal weaknesses also contributed to this marginal position. Although union membership expanded rapidly after June 1987, by the end of the Roh administration it still only covered some 2 per cent of the ROK workforce, 8 per cent of whom were under the government-sanctioned Federation of Korean Trade Unions (FKTU). This repression of labour led to the rise of a number of dissident trade unions such as the radical Chonnohyup, which an estimated 3 per cent of the workforce supported, and whose members pursued strategies of direct, often violent strike action, especially in companies with a history of poor workplace relations such as the Hyundai Group.

As the 1980s progressed, the habitual tendency to view social problems through the prism of economic policy faded, and awareness of social problems and issues grew in ways that were unthinkable to the previous generation. The Korean division and the intensely materialistic, anti-communist culture which grew up in the South after 1953 had channelled intellectual life down narrow paths. By the late 1980s, however, radical student groups and dissident intellectuals had grown familiar with many strands of Western radical thought, including Marxism, liberation theology and dependency theory. No great Korean thinkers emerged to synthesise and indigenise such thought, but *minjung sasang* ideology continued to underpin a culture of dissent which increasingly drew its symbols and idioms from the imagined Korean past of resistance and rebellion on the part of the masses and of the folk arts such as dramatic recitation (*p'ansori*), masked dance (*t'alch'um*), puppet theatre (*kkoktu gaksi*) and shaman chants (*muga*), which were held to embody this culture of resistance.

Meanwhile, growing wealth and leisure led middle-class Koreans outward, towards adaptation, and emulation of emerging global cultural norms in popular culture, as refracted to them through the foreign, and especially the US, media. But simultaneously another path led inward to a revival, re-emphasis and redefinition of Korean tradition as a means of expressing new-found national pride and identity. The manifestations of this revival of tradition were diverse, and included a renewed interest in traditional Korean performing arts and crafts. Performances of traditional Korean dance and music became more and more common, and people began to show increased interest in their family genealogical registers. The Korean antique trade flourished, as did the wearing of traditional Korean clothes on special occasions, the revival of traditional dishes in restaurants, and the holding of traditional weddings.

The international attention focused on the ROK as a result of the Seoul Olympiad further encouraged a simultaneous flowering of national pride and introspection. The sense that the ROK's achievements represented the triumph of Korean values became palpable, and the theory that Confucianism and Asian cultural values in general had played a major part in the ROK's economic transformation received enthusiastic endorsement. Such trends were a predictable and perhaps necessary declaration of independence after decades of strong Western and especially American intellectual and ideological influence, but they also announced a partial closing of the Korean mind, marked by growing stress on what were purported to be unique, ineffable qualities of Korean culture and society, which many public figures insisted exempted the country from various key problems and conflicts in less ethnically unitary states. Close analysis of the nature of labour–management relations, of regional differences and even of the division of Korea itself became obscured by the constant refrain that all problems were solvable on the basis that 'We are all Koreans together'. Such rhetoric formed a dubious basis for penetrating debate on social reform.

Women continued to face strong barriers in personal and professional life in obedience to the Confucian dictum that women took care of household affairs while men dealt with the outside world. As is so often the case in developing societies, the higher one's social status, the less rigorous this dictum tended to be in application, but while the forces of modernisation were, on the whole, liberating to Korean women, they were liberating in an uneven fashion. For example, Korean women joined the workforce in unprecedented numbers, but their participation was concentrated strongly at the lower end of the pay and skill scale. Rates of college graduate participation in the workforce remained stable during the 1980s, reflecting a continuing acceptance of marriage as the 'sensible' option for an educated woman. Education choices reflected this career path, and during the 1980s well over 40 per cent of women undergraduates chose humanities and social science majors, while less than 5 per cent majored in engineering. This meant that those who sought to break with the general pattern of education as preparation for marriage had to plan well in advance and have supportive families in order to gain qualifications which were strongly sought after in the job market. Outside traditional areas of employment, this job market remained a hostile place, with criteria for promotion determined by male-dominated hierarchies, and with appeals procedures likewise channelled through male-dominated trade unions and employer organisations.

Conclusion

The inability of the DPRK to evolve some sort of counter-strategy to deal with the multiple political, economic and diplomatic crises which developed and became acute during the late 1980s is both striking and puzzling. In fact, throughout its life the DPRK has displayed the contradictory traits of a revolutionary Leninist party state pursuing increasingly conservative and anti-modern strategies. In its early stages it overthrew the existing traditional social structure, enacted a wide range of socially progressive laws, and embarked upon a process of rapid economic development. However, conservative, anti-modern features were embedded in such modernism, a number of which eventually proved more significant in deter-mining the destiny of the DPRK than the avowed revolutionary objectives of state ideology. Chief among these was a political structure which monopolised almost all meaningful forms of political power and isolated the leadership from the consequences of increasingly irrational decision-making. More generally, such control demanded a government monopoly on the circulation of information, and over time freedom of information ceased to exist except for the privileged party few. Lack of such freedom became an enormously stultifying influence on DPRK society, stunting curiosity and initiative and bringing about galloping technological obsolescence.

The policy initiatives of the period 1984–85 encouraged an external perception, especially in the ROK, that the DPRK was adjusting to the changed international environment of the 1980s. However, such assessments tended to overestimate the degree of change which actually took place. The Rangoon bombing indicated a continuing attachment to the leadership's roots in irregular warfare, and the course of the resumed South–North talks likewise did not reveal any new policy framework, while the rejection of Chinese-style economic reform and the retention of the command-economy structure under heavy Soviet subsidy demonstrated a severe consistency with past policies. Had the main points of mooted policy changes actually taken effect, in the 1990s Pyongyang might well have found itself proceeding uncertainly down the thorny road of modernisation, dealing with the types of adjustment problems encountered by China and Vietnam, instead of facing a seemingly never-ending series of intractable, state-threatening crises.

The outstanding political development in the ROK during this period was of course the successful reversion to democracy. Many factors combined to force democratisation in the ROK – so many as to beg the question why it didn't occur before 1987. These factors include Chun's flawed legitimacy, the growth of ROK civil society, the feeling that the Olympics could not be held under authoritarian auspices, and Chun's own political miscalculations. Less perceptible but no less significant was the feeling even among the very enforcers of authoritarian rule that theirs was a transitional role and that democratisation should and must eventually prevail. The observation at the time that Koreans sought and respected strong leadership was widespread and was even backed up by public-opinion polls within the ROK, but this was easy to misinterpret. The daunting array of domestic and foreign challenges called for resolute leadership, and delivered a constituency to any group which could pose credibly as the guarantor of strong security and domestic social order. However, such leaders were not to be embraced with enthusiasm, but rather tolerated as a painful necessity.

Perhaps the chief revelation of the 1987 democratisation was the extent to which the largely passive political role played by ordinary people derived not only from repression but also from causes which had deep roots in Korean culture and society. Until 1987 it was possible to argue that the political opposition could not effectively represent grass-roots sentiments because there was no prospect of gaining power through peaceful means. However, as opposition figures gained power, little discernible change occurred in either public policy or the actual process of politics, which remained remote, élitist and heavily Seoul-based. The opposition parties habitually based their attacks against the government on liberal principles, but in power these parties themselves remained conservative and authoritarian in structure and temperament. In truth, such liberal rhetoric ran counter to basic conservative and authoritarian forces within their own constituencies and in civil society more generally. Although a democracy, the ROK remained short of democrats.

Selected reading

Amsden, Alice 1989, *Asia's Next Giant: South Korea and Late Industrialization*, New York: Oxford University Press.

Bernard, Mitchell and Ravenhill, John 1995, 'Beyond Product Cycles and Flying Geese: Regionalisation, Hierarchy, and the Industrialization of East Asia,' *World Politics*, vol. 47, pp. 171–209.

Brandt, Vincent S. R. 1985, 'Aspirations and Constraints: Social Development in South Korea by the Year 2000', in Sung-joo Han (ed.), *Korea in the Year 2000: Prospects for Development and Change*, Seoul: Asiatic Research Centre, Korea University.

Cotton, James (ed.) 1993, *Korea under Roh Tae-woo*, Sydney: Allen & Unwin.

Eckert, Carter J. 1990–91, 'The South Korean Bourgeoisie: A Class in Search of Hegemony,' *Journal of Korean Studies*, vol. 7, pp. 115–48.

Foster-Carter, Aidan 1992, 'Explaining Korean Development: Some Issues of Ideology and Method', *Papers of the British Association for Korean Studies*, vol. 3, pp. 19–35.

Kim, Kwang-ok 1993, 'The Religious Life of the Urban Middle Class,' *Korea Journal*, vol. 33, no. 4, pp. 5–33.

Koo, Hagen (ed.) 1993, *State and Society in Contemporary Korea*, Ithaca, NY: Cornell University Press.

Oh, Kongdan and Hassig, Ralph C. 1994, 'North Korea's Nuclear Program', in Young-Whan Kihl (ed.), *Korea and the World: Beyond the Cold War*, Boulder, CO: Westview Press.

8 Hallowed by the price, 1992–2006

As the 1990s began, the regional and international environment which had shaped both Koreas underwent profound change. The most visible political signs were the end of the Cold War and the collapse of global communism in 1989, but the outright collapse of the Soviet Union and the ongoing major economic reformation of China in turn highlighted major structural changes in the international economy. The substance of these changes was an unrelenting drive towards globalisation, economic liberalisation and the competitive pursuit of investment capital. This resulted in significant economic restructuring in many protectionist states, aimed at lowering barriers to foreign competition in their domestic markets. This environment brought a new set of challenges to bear on the two Koreas, and profoundly affected both states, though in contrasting ways.

The end of the Cold War heightened Pyongyang's sense of threat and hardened its resolve to resist growing international pressure for economic reform and political liberalisation. Consequently, the DPRK economy entered into a period of sustained contraction, which in ten years almost halved its estimated gross domestic production, and in the process took the lives of an estimated 2 million people, roughly 10 per cent of the population, as the country endured prolonged famine. Concurrently, the DPRK became the centre of a major and continuing international crisis through its pursuit of nuclear weapons and missile development programmes. Such trends underlined the extent to which international political and economic forces had marginalised the North, while they also caused many to question whether the DPRK state itself would survive or suffer collapse and incorporation into the South. Amid such state-threatening crises, in July 1994, Kim Il Sung died of a heart attack at the age of 82. However, as his son assumed leadership of the country it became clear that the younger Kim had no intention of changing his father's hallmark policies. The increasingly quixotic quest to 'live in our own way' as the world's last unreconstructed Stalinist state continued.

The pressures on the ROK generated by the end of the Cold War were less direct, but were none the less substantial. The 1988 Seoul Olympiad symbolised the emergence of the ROK as a major East Asian state which pulled substantial diplomatic weight and which contributed significantly to the ongoing economic dynamism of the Asia–Pacific region. However, as international money markets and credit-rating agencies steadily acquired major influence in determining global investment flows, longstanding weaknesses in the ROK economy, especially in its banking and financial services sector, received closer scrutiny. Following financial crises in Thailand and Indonesia during 1997, the Korean won came under heavy pressure in November 1997, causing the ROK government to seek massive and unprecedented intervention by the International Monetary Fund (IMF) to stave off the threat of total economic collapse. Immediate recovery was rapid, but the goal of fundamental reform to the financial sector, to the *chaebol*, and even to basic practices of governance remained elusive.

These economic-policy challenges coincided with successive weak presidencies. Kim Young Sam (1993–98), Kim Dae Jung (1998–2003) and Roh Moo-hyun (2003–08) all entered office with high expectations, initially enjoyed high popularity ratings on the basis of their populist programmes, but all soon declined into impotence and even ignominy as the perennial twin curses of money politics and legislative intransigence took their toll. This was not really surprising in the case of the two Kims, both older-generation politicians to whom money politics was a fact of political life, but the failure of Roh, a political outsider with strong reformist credentials, again drew attention to the tight institutional constraints imposed on political leadership in the ROK.

Meanwhile, an unprecedented summit between Kim Dae Jung and Kim Jong Il in June 2000 led many observers to believe that the two Koreas had turned an important corner in their relationship. However, although inter-Korean trade, aid and aid-as-trade continued to grow exponentially, once again the two Koreas were unable to achieve basic progress on the many contentious political and military issues that divided them. Pyongyang's traditional policy parameters of militarism, isolationism, central economic control, and pervasive internal security remained largely intact, as did its international profile as a rogue state dedicated to the acquisition of nuclear weapons and delivery systems.

The North in trouble

Kim Il Sung and his son continued to function smoothly as a duumvirate up to Kim's death in 1994. Together they dominated a seriously ageing, loyalist Politburo in which non-guerrilla cadres held only marginal positions. There was no hint of decline in Kim Il Sung's faculties before he died of a sudden heart attack on 8 July 1994, aged 82. In fact, barely two weeks previously he had held lengthy and detailed talks with former US president Jimmy Carter on his country's nuclear standoff with the United Nations Security Council.

Judgements of Kim Il Sung will almost certainly vary considerably for generations to come. Like Lenin, Stalin and Mao before him, he profoundly shaped the destiny of his country and the consciousness of his fellow countrymen, but assessments currently suffer from a lack of the type of first-hand, detailed information which permits balanced assessment. Among many other points of speculation, we cannot really know of the alternatives available to him, or of his thought processes in making major decisions. Assessments will probably continue to fall between the polarities of Korean nationalist genius-leader and reckless tyrant. The positives may be swiftly stated: as a guerrilla he was physically brave and persevering, he possessed a positivist view of politics and life which contrasted with many of his generation, and showed great tenacity of purpose throughout his life. Sufficient space has already been devoted to his shortcomings, and they need not be reiterated here. Kim's legacy was an exhausted, malnourished population living in a desperately poor, widely reviled state which faced an invidious future under the ideology which bore his name.

As the country entered a three-year period of mourning, a smooth transfer of full power to Kim Jong Il took place. No purges or dismissals of senior cadres occurred, nor were any major new policies or personnel appointments made, and as time passed it became clear that the younger Kim intended to rule in a manner virtually indistinguishable from that of his father. Almost every major publication in the DPRK continued to sing the praises of the younger Kim in characteristically extravagant terms, hailing him as 'Supreme Leader of the Party, State and Army', and stressing his co-responsibility with Kim Il Sung for the Korean revolution as 'a great leader who has steered the revolution and national construction to victory together with the great leader Comrade Kim Il Sung'. Initial speculation focused on whether Kim Jong Il could command the support of the nation's military leaders – a task at which he appears to have succeeded. The role of the military appears to have become pronounced, partly because of increased threat perceptions in Pyongyang, but also because the younger Kim's personality involves a deep identification with his father's anti-Japanese guerrilla comrades. He clearly shared with the survivors of this era a belief in the efficacy of toughness and force in confronting the country's internal and external challenges.

After an official three-year period of mourning from 1994 to 1997, Kim Jong Il assumed the position of general secretary of the KWP, a largely symbolic move since he had clearly exercised absolute authority over the country since his father's death. The first session of the Tenth Supreme People's Assembly on 5 September 1998 then restored to public prominence the basic governmental infrastructure of the state. In a series of amendments to the 1972 state constitution, the SPA abolished the state presidency and made the National Defence Committee chairman, a post held by Kim Jong Il since 1993, head of state. These moves seemed designed to confirm Kim Jong Il's status within the governmental structure and pay homage to Kim Il Sung by leaving him as the first and only president of the DPRK, but otherwise they left the thrust of the 1972 constitution virtually intact. While Kim Jong Il did not in any way rely on this constitution to reinforce his standing, the amendments institutionalised his personal power.

Meanwhile, the economic decline of the DPRK became steep and sustained during the 1990s. This was basically due to both the cumulative effect of past economic policies and the sudden impact of the political and economic collapse of the Soviet Union, which undermined the basis for much of the DPRK's existing economic policies. During 1990–95 foreign trade contracted by half, the economy as a whole shrank by an estimated 20 per cent, food shortages became endemic, and the economic planning system itself fell into chaos. Counter-measures were based on the priority of defending the system established so definitively by Kim Il Sung in the early 1960s, and endorsed with equal enthusiasm by Kim Jong Il.

Essentially, tactical compromise defended strategic intransigence, and so while the government allowed expanded cross-border trade with China, established a Free Economic and Trade Zone at Rajin-Sunbong in the far north east, and allowed trade with the ROK to expand considerably, both Kims regularly and publicly affirmed that there was no need for a China-style economic reform programme in the DPRK, and that therefore they would retain policies of rigid economic autarky and political centralisation.

The food situation deteriorated rapidly under these circumstances. Despite official claims over the years that the Kims' leadership had led to major break-throughs in agricultural production, the food supply in the North had always been precarious, with only a small margin separating chronic shortage from outright famine. By the early 1990s food self-sufficiency had fallen to about 60 per cent, and malnutrition was widespread. Catastrophe followed in the mid-1990s, when the country could not withstand the simultaneous and cumulative effect of adverse weather patterns, unsound agricultural and environmental management policies, lack of foreign exchange to make up for shortfalls in grain and fertiliser, and in fuel to operate farm equipment, and severe disruption to the centrally controlled distribution system.

The immediate cause of the North's food crisis was widespread flooding in August 1995, which affected as much as 30 per cent of the country. Lack of resources to maintain and repair deteriorated flood control and irrigation works had a devastating effect, almost destroying the year's rice crop. In contrast to its usual procedure of not reporting crimes or disasters, the DPRK media referred openly to the floods and, for the first time ever, sought disaster relief from inter-national agencies. An estimated 500,000 people died of hunger in 1995, by the end of 1996 the toll had passed 1 million, and by the time the situation stabilised somewhat in 1998 a further million, mainly comprising infants, young children and elderly people, had perished.

This calamity reflected the decline of a highly centralised distribution system through which all citizens outside the party received their allotments of such necessities as food, housing, clothing, jobs and medical care. Most people had little independent access to such goods and services, and so, as domestic food pro-duction continued to decline, and as alternatives such as food aid or commercial purchase ran out, and as the party and military continued to cannibalise the economy, the government could not provide its people with enough food to eat, or supply the medicine to deal with resultant health problems. The crisis was further exacerbated by lack of leadership from either government or party. The leader-ship's attitude was summed up by Kim Jong Il in a speech to cadres at Kim Il Sung University in December 1996, in which he made clear his view that dealing with the country's food situation was a matter for economic administrators and that they, not he nor indeed the party leadership, should accept responsibility for the famine. In fact, many argued that the term 'famine' was itself a misnomer since it was within the power of the government to release grain from its defence stockpile and purchase more on the international market – actions which Pyongyang refused to take since such moves would have required unacceptable ideological compromises.

Such policies exacted an enormous toll. Foreign aid doctors and workers in the DPRK reported the collapse of the country's public health, medical and pharmaceutical systems. Malaria, thought to have been eradicated in the 1970s, reappeared, while a nutritional survey by United Nations experts in 1998 estimated that 63 per cent of all North Korean children exhibited signs of long-term under-nourishment such as lassitude, susceptibility to minor illness and infection, increased mortality and morbidity, stunted growth and impaired cognitive functions. In the absence of effective government action, international agencies bore the brunt of the relief effort, which included outright food aid, support for the collapsed pharmaceutical industry, agricultural restoration work, medicine, and health and education programmes. Altogether, these programmes soon totalled several hundred million dollars per year and involved a variety of UN agencies, including the World Food Program (WFP), the Food and Agricultural Organisation (FAO), the United Nations International Children's Emergency Fund (UNICEF) and the World Health Organisation (WHO). By the year 2000 international aid provided an estimated 40 per cent of the DPRK's food needs; that is, it fed an estimated 8 million in a population of 20 million. The mass deaths of the mid-1990s no longer occurred, but chronic undernourishment continued to extract a more insidious toll, reducing the productivity of the economically active population, making even minor illnesses potentially life-threatening, and increasing mortality and morbidity owing to chronic degenerative diseases in later life.

On 1 July 2002 the DPRK announced a series of economic reform measures which were widely seen abroad as turning the country away from its extreme centralism. The role of the state rationing system was de-emphasised, and in an effort to soak up the flood of US dollars circulating on the black market, the foreign exchange rate was placed at a more realistic level, causing the fixed rate of 2.2 won to the dollar to push out to 150 won to the dollar in 2002 and 900 in 2003. External assessments of the impact of these measures ranged from euphoric talk of the DPRK opening up to the global economy, to dismissal of the reforms as temporary expedients as a means of defending the fundamental command economy structure. But, whatever the intended effect, it was clear that the leadership intended to carry out these measures without ideological or political compromise. No changes to either government structure or key personnel accompanied the new measures, and no discernible public debate emerged to rally people behind the measures. This suggested that the government was essentially extending its economic control by legitimising and extending the major practices which had grown up piecemeal over the previous decade – especially the spread of open domestic produce markets as a means of mitigating famine. Thus, the impact of these measures on economic life, not to mention on North Korean society as a whole, remained marginal, with most foreign estimates of economic growth for the period 2000–06 in the range of 1–2 per cent per annum, well below the growth rates of the DPRK's neighbours.

These events took place against the background of an ongoing crisis over the North's drive to acquire nuclear weapons. Since the 1950s both Koreas had conducted small-scale nuclear research programmes, and the climate of strategic uncertainty in the 1970s led both Pyongyang and Seoul to seriously consider the option of developing nuclear weapons. The ROK soon abandoned its programme of nuclear weapons research, but, as the regional military and strategic balance tipped firmly against the DPRK in the late 1970s, Pyongyang's interest in nuclear weapons grew. During the 1980s the DPRK developed a major facility at Yongbyon, north of Pyongyang, and by 1990 the US concluded from satellite surveillance that this programme had a significant military purpose.

Despite the conclusion of major accords on improving relations and removing nuclear weapons from the peninsula, signed between the two Koreas in December 1991, the early 1990s were marked by tension and brinkmanship over the North's nuclear programme. This was eventually, though only partially, resolved by the conclusion of a compromise agreement, known as the Geneva Framework Agreement (GFA), between the DPRK and the US – the first such bilateral co-operation agreement – in October 1994 which essentially capped the DPRK nuclear programme, though it left unresolved the matter of how much weapons-grade plutonium the DPRK had already extracted at Yongbyon. Under the GFA the DPRK agreed to suspend its nuclear programme and the US agreed to compensate the DPRK for the alleged lost energy-generation potential. The key components here were the building of two light-water nuclear reactors in the North to generate electricity and the supply of major amounts of heavy fuel oil.

The GFA became the cornerstone for negotiation between the DPRK and its adversaries after 1994. For the DPRK the advantages of the agreement were considerable. Not only did it gain an economic subsidy amounting to several billion dollars, but it also did not have to account for existing stores of weapons-grade plutonium. For its adversaries the advantages were perhaps less clear, but Pyongyang had forced their hand. The immediate gain was the defusing of a potentially serious military confrontation, while more generally the ROK and its allies believed that they had bought time, arguing that time was on their side in dealing with the DPRK. They also believed that they had provided sufficient inducement to Pyongyang for the eventual return of the North's programme to the safeguards régime. A new, tense phase of diplomacy with the DPRK began, marked by the provision of alternative energy supplies, by attempts to ensure inspection transparency, and by a multitude of confidence-building proposals.

The DPRK's nuclear programme also included missile delivery systems, which increasingly became an issue of contention in foreign relations. In August 1998, Pyongyang's relations with the US and Japan deteriorated sharply with the test-firing of a DPRK rocket which overflew northern Japan and landed in the Pacific Ocean some 1,500 kilometres away. After initial confusion, the US publicly assessed the firing as a failed satellite launching, but the military implications remained clear: the DPRK had acquired the capacity to fire payloads over increasingly longer distances. Japan reacted strongly to Pyongyang's action by freezing its 20 per cent contribution to the $4 billion light-water nuclear reactor programme, while such evidence of continuing intransigence also prompted the US to undertake a comprehensive review of policy towards the North, known as the Perry Report. Released in September 1999, this complex document offered the North a substantial array of tightly interlinked inducements, including food aid, economic relations and eventually full diplomatic recognition, if Pyongyang would agree to discontinue the development of weapons of mass destruction, including nuclear weapons and missiles. However, despite continuing intensive diplomacy during the final months of the Clinton administration, the US and the DPRK remained locked in familiar antagonistic stances, amid signs that the incoming Bush administration would adopt a harder attitude towards Pyongyang. Meanwhile, despite economic setbacks, and notwithstanding the ongoing inter-Korean dialogue, DPRK military assets remained formidable and growing.

The concentration on bilateral negotiations with the US and the North's endemic economic crisis produced a prolonged stalemate in negotiations with the South, marked by lack of DPRK interest in pursuing official contacts with the ROK, and by occasional armed incursions and military incidents on the DMZ. Kim Il Sung's unexpected agreement to a summit meeting with ROK President Kim Young Sam during talks with former president Jimmy Carter on 16–17 June 1994 seemed to open up new possibilities, but whether such talks would have achieved anything or, in fact, taken place at all became moot when Kim's death soon after brought about the temporary suspension of all inter-Korean negotiations. During 1994–98 the North maintained a number of unofficial points of contact with the South, involving businessmen, religious figures, people-to-people and humanitarian organisations, but no substantive negotiations took place.

Relations with the South began to improve after the election of Kim Dae Jung as ROK president and the announcement of a new policy of engagement with the North, known as the 'Sunshine Policy'. In April 1998 the two Koreas resumed official talks in Beijing. The North's main agenda item was a request for 200,000 tonnes of fertiliser, but it would not accede to the South's standing condition that further official food aid be linked to an exchange of home visits for divided families. The talks ended inconclusively, but not before a stinging Pyongyang attack on Seoul for not sending a condolence mission to Kim Il Sung's 1994 funeral, for politicising the rice deliveries in 1995, and for obstructing the DPRK's efforts to improve relations with the US and Japan. Similar efforts to restart dialogue foundered in June 1999 over agenda disagreements. Relations further deteriorated after a serious naval clash off the western coast on 15 June, in which one DPRK torpedo boat was sunk and at least five others were seriously damaged.

A dramatic turnaround in inter-Korean relations occurred in April 2000, when both sides agreed to exchange leadership visits. In June, Kim Dae Jung travelled to Pyongyang and concluded a five-point agreement, covering the easing of military tension, measures of reconciliation and peace, reunion visits of separated families, and the expediting of economic, social and cultural exchanges. Follow-up talks on implementation proceeded more slowly, but by the year's end the two Koreas had achieved some success on humanitarian and security issues. These included agreement on the reopening of rail links severed during the Korean War, the reopening of liaison offices in the border truce village of Panmunjom for the first time since 1996, an exchange of family reunion groups in August for the first time since 1985, and the promise of a reciprocal visit to Seoul by Kim Jong Il in 2001.

However, despite expanded senior-level talks in a number of policy areas, the North's moves on humanitarian exchanges fell well short of Seoul's expectations, its military deployments remained highly offensive, and substantive talks on security matters again became subject to a familiar pattern of delay. There was little practical follow-up to the various agreements, and during 2001 the talks lost momentum once more. Kim Jong Il's promised reciprocal visit to Seoul did not take place, while the ministerial talks made little headway, and after a fruitless session devoted to family reunion visits and economic co-operation in November 2001, momentum from the June 2000 summit seemed effectively exhausted. Efforts to revive the North–South dialogue seemed to bear fruit in the second half of 2002 with a reconvening of the ministerial conference and detailed discussion of joint economic projects. However, almost simultaneously, revelations from Pyongyang about its ongoing nuclear weapons programme stalled further progress. Nevertheless, despite this political and diplomatic uncertainty, the tempo of economic exchanges with the ROK continued to grow substantially, reportedly increasing some sixfold in the five-year period after the 2000 Joint Agreement. This process was led by construction of a major new industrial processing zone at Kaesong, just north of the DMZ, and the conclusion in 2003 of a series of economic co-operation agreements, first announced in 2000 but then stalled.

The issue of the North's nuclear weapons programme soon overshadowed progress in the inter-Korean sphere. In November 2002, Pyongyang openly acknowledged that, despite the Geneva Framework Agreement, it had been running a secret uranium-enrichment programme for use in nuclear weapons. While most analysts had more or less assessed that the GFA did not signal the end to the DPRK's nuclear ambitions, the political pressure generated by this public revelation hardened the US attitude and effectively destroyed the remnants of the GFA, especially its light-water reactor construction, annual 500,000-ton crude oil supply and IAEA inspection provisions, all three of which had provided some manoeuvring space for both parties. The North's response was again to offer to renounce its nuclear weapons plan in return for the signing of a non-aggression treaty with the US, which at present could only be achieved at severe cost to the US–ROK relationship. In December 2002 the DPRK reactivated its Yongbyon nuclear facility, disabling IAEA monitoring devices and ordering the IAEA monitors to leave the country. In January 2003 it announced its withdrawal from the IAEA.

Efforts to head off confrontation arising from these moves focused on the creation of a multilateral six-party talks structure, involving the two Koreas, the US, China, Russia and Japan. Both the inaugural meeting in Beijing in August 2003 and subsequent meetings in February and June 2004 were inconclusive as the US sought the effective dismantling of the North's nuclear programme, while Pyongyang offered only a highly conditional freeze on further development. At the fourth six-party talks, in September 2005, the two parties' positions were somehow reconciled within a joint agreement on principles to guide further negotiation. Such a procedure did not promise early breakthroughs, and in fact no further substantive discussions had taken place when the North first test-fired a number of missiles into the Sea of Japan in July 2006 and then conducted what appeared to be a low-yield underground nuclear test in October 2006. A fifth round of talks in December 2006 was inconclusive, the North Korean actions having ended prospects for progress on the basis of the September 2005 agreement for the time being.

The Kim Young Sam administration

On 19 May 1992 the power-brokers of the Chun–Roh political machine kept their promise, and the DLP endorsed Kim Young Sam as its candidate in the December 1992 presidential election. Two other major candidates formally entered the race in the months that followed: Kim Dae Jung and Chung Ju Yong, the founder and patriarch of the Hyundai *chaebol*. In the absence of major scandals or crises, strong financial and regional political bases were essential for electoral success, and here Kim Young Sam had the formidable advantage of the well-entrenched system of political patronage and corruption which radiated outward from the Taegu–Kyongbuk (T–K) regional subgroup of the DLP to embrace a significant proportion of the country's élite. He himself contributed the strength of his long-established base in Pusan and South Kyongsang Province, though he had forfeited much of his appeal to the liberal electorate through his opportunistic 1990 merger with the DLP. Kim Dae Jung could not match Kim Young Sam on either count. His regional base of the Cholla provinces was less populous and less favoured by economic policies than the Kyongsang provinces. Moreover, while he was lionised by many for his courage in confronting the Park and Chun régimes, Kim Dae Jung was regarded with suspicion by many more as a potentially divisive figure with little to offer in the 1990s. Chung Ju-Yong had an enormous personal fortune and the resources of a huge conglomerate at his disposal, but had no significant regional base and was all too transparently a spoiler candidate, pursuing Hyundai's battles with the government on the national political stage. The actual election took place in a low-key atmosphere free of violence – though free of passion as well, since no candidate seemed to point very reliably to the shape of things to come. Kim Young Sam's moderate reformist image, the general public respect for his character, and a lack of public confidence in the other candidates gained him 42 per cent of the vote, while Kim Dae Jung gained 34 per cent and Chung Ju Yong 16 per cent.

At his inauguration in February 1993, Kim Young Sam emphasised the two major themes of anti-corruption and financial restructuring. His first cabinet appointments installed ministers with reformist and liberal credentials in a number of key areas, especially in foreign affairs and national security portfolios. In a series of presidential decrees he also dismissed a number of high-ranking military officers with strong links to the T–K faction of the DLP, and enforced full disclosure of economic assets held by himself, his cabinet, senior DLP figures and public servants. Highlighting corruption as an issue in this way enabled him to tap into a rich vein of public discontent, and also to enlist popular support for a major attack on the Fifth Republic insiders within his own party, whom he seemed to regard with far greater antipathy than he did the politicians of rival political parties. Given the pervasive nature of corruption within the ROK government, both in its functional and dysfunctional forms, it was not surprising that within a few weeks of Kim's inauguration he found grounds to dismiss a number of prominent figures, including three ministers, the mayor of Seoul and the speaker of the National Assembly, after public allegations of past corruption.

The liberalising tendency also swept through the military and security apparatus. In March 1992, Kim replaced both the Army Chief of Staff and the Commander of the Defence Security Command. Their successors had no links to the quasi-secret military fraternities which had monopolised senior military appointments during the Fifth Republic. Kim also placed the Agency for National Security Planning, the successor organisation to the notorious KCIA, under liberal administration, resulting in a drastic curtailment of its domestic surveillance activities. Agents operating inside domestic organisations were recalled, while the practices of mail censorship and electronic surveillance were curtailed. Alert to the symbolic dimension in policy, Kim also opened the streets around the Blue House to public traffic and lifted a long-standing ban on the ownership of shortwave radios. Accordingly, in the first few months of his presidency, his popular-approval rating achieved heights previously unheard of in ROK political history.

Such activities showed Kim at his best, operating in an area defined by personal conviction, populist instinct, political self-interest, and lack of opposition pressure. However, in the greater political challenge of structural reform to the financial system Kim moved beyond this familiar terrain. The nation had inherited a governmental structure which reflected Fifth Republic values in its lack of accountability, transparency, flexibility and responsiveness. Wide-ranging purges of individuals and moral exhortations constituted one means of effecting change, but action on the mantra-like objectives of liberalisation and internationalisation also required political leadership and profound institutional responses, ranging from a more liberal, transparent judicial process and financial regulatory environment to major political reforms encompassing party and election funding and management. Kim proved unable to provide such leadership, and by mid-1994 clear signs of drift began to emerge in his administration. In dealing with dissent within the ruling party and also with the re-emergence of widespread labour and student unrest, he became increasingly authoritarian, reacting harshly to major strikes at Hyundai and the Korean National Railroads. An inveterate poll-watcher, he reacted to a poor showing by his party in the June 1995 local elections by renewing judicial attacks on Chun Doo Hwan and Roh Tae Woo on charges of corruption, mutiny and treason. As a result, in August 1996, Chun was sentenced to death and Roh received a lengthy prison sentence for their roles in the Kwangju uprising. Both sentences were later commuted.

This ongoing trial seemed to restore Kim Young Sam's political fortunes, and contributed to a significant victory by Kim's party in the Fifteenth National Assembly elections in April 1996, in which it secured 139 of 299 seats. However, this constituted the last upswing in Kim Young Sam's popularity. By early 1997 he and his inner circle were embroiled in what became known as the Hanbo Affair.

In this scandal, the Hanbo Iron and Steel Company, burdened with debts estimated at over $5 billion, used its political influence to stave off liquidation, and in the process revealed a close and corrupt financial relationship with Kim's immediate entourage. The Kim administration's economic management also came under increasing scrutiny as the Asian financial crisis began to take hold in Thailand and Indonesia at mid-year, and his ineffectiveness in dealing with the crisis as it spread to Korea in October 1997 seemed to crystallise the reservations many Koreans had always held about their leader's competence in managing the economy. Kim Young Sam left office amid crisis and scandal, with an embarrassingly low public opinion rating and with few clear, enduring achievements to his credit.

The failure of Kim Young Sam was a compound of personal and systemic shortcomings. From the beginning, expectations of his performance were unreasonable. Kim was widely seen as an honest and decent man of limited intellect. In truth, he may have been devoid of vice, but he was also devoid of many qualities required for leadership. At heart, he was a shrewd, opportunistic old-time Korean political boss, and thus a skilful manipulator of the myriad interest groups and political networks which formed the basis of ROK political life. However, while he articulated visions of 'globalising' the ROK economy, he lacked the broader intellectual horizons required to translate such visions into public policy. He had few political compass points other than an almost obsessive reliance on public-opinion surveys, and the role of ideas and public debate in setting public policy and rallying public opinion were all but unknown to him. A profoundly conservative man, Kim headed an increasingly conservative administration in which he was strongly reliant on a circle of key advisers, many of whom were themselves highly vulnerable to pressures within the system, and who proved to be corrupt. Kim himself often seemed oblivious to the practical necessities faced by such men, and his purposeful avoidance of involvement in the seamier side of money politics increasingly smacked of wilful ignorance at best, and hypocrisy at worst.

Meanwhile, the 1997 presidential election took shape as a contest between the ruling-party candidate, Lee Hoi Chang, and a rejuvenated Kim Dae Jung. The electorate seemed little attracted to either candidate in a long, lurching campaign which featured the exchange of high levels of personal abuse between the candidates, a corresponding lack of policy debate, and frequent appeals to regional sentiment. However, as the ROK economy came close to collapse in November/December, the desire of the electorate to reject the ruling party outweighed the reservations it held of Kim Dae Jung, and on 18 December 1997, Kim Dae Jung was elected president by a narrow margin. Kim, defeated three times in previous campaigns, and unable to gain more than 35 per cent of the vote in his two previous campaigns, gained 40.2 per cent of the vote, against 39.7 per cent for Lee.

The election was held in the midst of a grave local and regional economic crisis. After decades of sustained economic growth, during the summer of 1997 the Asia–Pacific region was hit by a sudden and severe economic and financial crisis. The crisis affected different economies in different ways and with different levels of severity, though common denominators were also present. The three worst-hit economies were Thailand, Indonesia and the ROK, though no country in the region escaped collateral damage. Throughout the region, stock market prices and the value of currencies declined sharply, business failures multiplied, banks became insolvent, inter-regional and international trade declined sharply, and overextended financial systems became deeply dysfunctional under the resultant mountain of bad debt. The sometimes hubristic rhetoric about an impending 'Pacific Century' ceased as the region contemplated an economic downturn more severe in its effects than any since the Great Depression.

The immediate crisis began in early 1997 as an exchange rate crisis in Thailand, when investors began to doubt the ability of the Thai government to maintain the dollar value of their baht investments. A rapid run on the baht depleted Thailand's foreign-exchange reserves, forcing the government to seek IMF intervention. This in turn focused attention on other economies with similar profiles of high rates of private foreign debt, volatile financial sectors, dubious regulatory/supervisory practices, and overvalued fixed foreign exchange rates. Consequently, Indonesia, Malaysia, the Philippines and the ROK all experienced abrupt flights of foreign capital, which severely undermined their finance and business sectors.

Initially the ROK economy seemed to be an anomaly among the countries most affected by the 1997 crisis. Along with Japan, it was one of only two Asian members of the Organisation for Economic Co-operation and Development (OECD), and compared with the other crisis economies was an infinitely larger, more sophisticated economy which had enjoyed massive support of international banking and lending institutions throughout its extended period of economic development. However, in the prevailing climate of scrutiny, underlying strengths were ignored in search of current weaknesses. Such weaknesses were easy to identify, and in fact the argument that the economic success of the ROK concealed many potentially serious structural weaknesses and deficiencies had been a long-standing subject of public debate in Seoul among academics and other commentators across a broad ideological and intellectual spectrum.

Kim Young Sam's preoccupation with corruption and populist politics had distracted attention from the declining terms of Korean trade. The economy was founded on export growth, and its institutions and major companies were tooled to achieve economies of scale as exports moved from reliance on the staples of textiles, garments, footwear and other light industrial goods to a reliance on greater value-added products such as domestic electrical appliances, pharmaceutical products, chemicals, automobiles, ships, precision machinery and semiconductors. In the early 1990s, however, China was cutting into major markets that Korea had previously dominated, especially in the US and Japan. Moreover, despite favourable international conditions such as a strong Japanese yen, low international interest rates and a buoyant global economy, Korean exports did not keep pace with the rapidly expanding imports of consumer goods and capital equipment. As a result, the ROK current account deficit increased sharply. In 1996 external debt rose to the unprecedentedly high proportion of 22 per cent of GDP, much of which had been rolled over into short-term debt as debtors waited for trading conditions to improve. A succession of corporate collapses during early 1997, including the Hanbo, Sammi and Jinro conglomerates, underlined the precarious position of the debt-ridden *chaebol*.

In late October 1997 major falls on the Hong Kong stock market, an ongoing series of corporate insolvencies, and cumulative investor concern about the ROK government's ability to deal with *chaebol* indebtedness produced a major acceleration in foreign capital flight from the ROK. As credit rating agencies such as Moody's and Standard & Poor downgraded the credit rating of major ROK banks, lending institutions refused to roll over short-term debts, while foreign reserves dwindled rapidly as the government sought to defend the fixed exchange rate of the won. Finally, on 21 November, the ROK gave up the unequal struggle and sought IMF assistance, securing a total of $57 billion in loans and back-up loans. During December the immediate crisis began to be contained by the strong level of support from the major world economies, by effective negotiations led by an international consortium of major banks to roll over much of the Korean banks' short-term debt, and by the election of a new president who gave a strong public undertaking to begin an immediate, radical economic reform process.

The Kim Dae Jung administration

Kim Dae Jung's victory in the 1997 ROK presidential election constituted an extraordinary personal triumph, achieved after literally decades of struggle. On the other hand, however, few democratically elected heads of state in modern times can have taken office in a greater atmosphere of peacetime crisis than Kim. At the time of his election, Korea's major banks still faced the real prospect of a massive default on their short-term debt to a range of international lenders, while the longer-term implications of the crisis were far from clear. The Korean won had depreciated against the US dollar by 67.7 per cent in the previous twelve months, the stock market had lost 37 per cent of its capitalisation value in three years, and seven of the nation's top thirty *chaebol* were either technically or actually insolvent. Moreover, economic policy was effectively controlled by the International Monetary Fund as the condition of an immediate guarantee of $35 billion to support the won, which had lost more than 50 per cent of its value during 1997. Accordingly, the incoming administration undertook to carry out a wide range of financial counter-measures under IMF supervision, including the restructuring of the corporate and financial sectors, the removal of a range of restrictions on foreign investment, implementation of tight monetary and fiscal policies, and a substantial freeing up of the labour market. As a result, unemployment rose from 2 per cent pre-crisis to 8.5 per cent by September 1998, and the economy contracted by 5.8 per cent during 1998 as domestic demand shrank drastically.

Under these circumstances, it was not surprising that a substantial roll-back occurred in the government's reform agenda, for while immediate reform measures achieved impressive results, attempts to address more deep-seated problems encountered a powerful array of vested interests. In the banking and financial sector, the government closed or merged twenty-five of the country's fifty-six leading commercial and merchant banks, but despite efforts at recapitalisation and restructuring this sector remained clogged by a high level of non-performing loans. Similarly, legislation to impose tight supervisory control over the entire financial system was rapidly enacted in December 1997, but it soon encountered an entrenched banking culture in which credit-risk analysis and loan monitoring remained perfunctory tasks, since credit allocation was essentially determined by ruling-party politics, and not by the banks themselves. The government also quickly enacted legislation which gave firms wide latitude in restructuring their workforce. These initial moves were made with the active consent of the major trade unions, but as the unemployment rate rose sharply the leading unions began to distance themselves from the government. Militant strike action, such as at Hyundai Motors in August 1998, successfully challenged the February accord and secured substantial backdowns on plans for mass lay-offs.

The major *chaebol* were successful in mounting a campaign of resistance to the government's efforts to stimulate competition and reduce their role in the economy. In December 1998, Kim Dae Jung engineered a major agreement with the top five *chaebol* in which the companies agreed to rationalise their operations by a process of wholesale closure, swap and merger of unproductive subsidiaries. The heavily indebted *chaebol* also agreed to reduce their debt-to-equity ratios, at the time estimated at 500 per cent or more, to below 200 per cent by December 1999. However, despite public rhetoric that the era of the *chaebol* had ended, progress towards *chaebol* restructuring and reform slowed as reform fatigue set in.

Unlike Kim Young Sam, Kim Dae Jung did not enjoy a long political honeymoon. His opponent, Lee Hoi Chang, had lost by a small margin in a bitter campaign, while Lee's Grand National Party (GNP), which was essentially the successor party to the grand coalition DLP, held a majority in the National Assembly. The ruling and opposition parties quickly squared off, as Lee used his numbers to press his own reform agenda, and as Kim used presidential power to cajole and coerce independent and wavering National Assemblymen. By late 1998, ROK politics had assumed a familiar pattern, with practically the entire opposition leadership under investigation on alleged corruption charges, and the government party itself coming under increasing attack for cronyism, regionalism and corruption in office.

Kim Dae Jung's economic and foreign policies issued from a domestic political coalition which comprised three main elements. The first was the core group of political professionals who had been associated with him since the 1970s. On the whole, they were themselves former dissidents who had developed strong ties of personal loyalty to Kim through years of dissidence, adversity, physical intimidation and repression. Many were from Cholla Province and shared Kim's outsider status in the world of Seoul politics. The second element rallied to Kim in the mid-1990s when he became a major contender for the presidency once more. They did not share a common geographical tie, but rather comprised members of the Seoul-based government-academic élite whose loyalty to Kim was contingent on the prospect of exercising power, rather than on commitment to Kim's political values *per se*.

The third element, formally described as the United Liberal Democrat Party (ULDP), comprised members of former prime minister Kim Jong Pil's personal political machine. It emerged as a result of an improbable alliance struck during the election campaign, in which Kim Dae Jung gained the estimated 7–8 per cent of the popular vote anticipated by the ULDP in return for ULDP participation in the Kim administration, beginning with the awarding of the prime ministership to Kim Jong Pil himself. Ironies abounded within this marriage of convenience between a reformist liberal party and a conservative rump party. Not the least of these ironies was that Kim Jong Pil had been prime minister in 1974 when Kim Dae Jung had been kidnapped and almost murdered by the Korean Central Intelligence Agency – which Kim Jong Pil himself had established in the early 1960s. Kim Dae Jung thus found himself in the unusual situation of being a centrist, having to curb the enthusiasm of his ex-dissident colleagues and at the same time honour promises of power-sharing to the conservative ULDP. In such circumstances, the economic crisis presented a heaven-sent opportunity, for it mandated a series of economic reforms which gave purpose and direction to the new administration. Instead of having three-way debates within the ruling party on economic policy, as would have been the case in calmer times, Kim was able to cite IMF exigencies for a range of stringent economic measures.

However, the gulf between expectation, rhetoric and performance exacted an inevitable toll on Kim's presidency during 1999, and his public approval rating declined significantly. The major issue was not economic policy, on which the public seemed to hold realistic expectations of the government's limited power to influence events, but rather a succession of corruption cases, which claimed the public reputation of a number of Kim's closest allies. The effect of these cases was compounded by revelations that domestic surveillance through wire-tapping and mail censorship had actually increased under Kim, and by perceptions that the administration was using tax evasion charges to settle old political scores. In fact, although such methods had become standard in Korean politics, they seemed stark, given Kim's self-image as a crusader for open government, and so gave rise to considerable cynicism. Nevertheless, such scandals in themselves did not debilitate the Kim administration, and in National Assembly elections in April 2000 his party gained 140 seats, against 133 for the GNP.

Kim's subsequent success in bringing about a summit meeting with Kim Jong Il in June 2000, and the international prestige which he subsequently gained as Nobel Peace Prize laureate, temporarily restored the fortunes of a presidency which at times seemed likely to end in a similar fashion to that of Kim Young Sam, but as the dialogue with the North stalled, and as the will to sustain domestic reform wilted, Kim increasingly assumed lame-duck status against a background of progressively lower public-approval ratings. Accumulated disappointment with the Kim administration led to major electoral reverses in three October 2001 by-elections, and accumulating pressure from within the ruling party led Kim to resign as Millennium Democratic Party leader in November, ostensibly to ensure that the 2002 presidential election campaign could proceed without partisan conflict.

By this stage Kim's Sunshine Policy for dealing with the North had generated major controversy. In August 2001 the members of a non-partisan South Korean delegation to Liberation Day celebrations in Pyongyang breached established protocol and caused a major political controversy in the South by visiting the birthplace of Kim Il Sung at Mangyongdae, outside Pyongyang. In September 2001 this action, coupled with general disillusionment in the South at the returns from the Sunshine Policy, led to the National Assembly impeachment of Unification Minister Lim Dongwon, one of its chief architects under Kim Dae Jung. Consequently, in 2003 a special prosecutor revealed details of an illegal transfer of $500 million to the DPRK just before the 2000 summit, evidently at the North's demand. The Sunshine Policy had long been seen as the policy plaything of successive ROK leaders who sought a secure a place in history as unifiers of the Korean Peninsula, and was usually subject to polite debate in Seoul. This now became harsher as the media and government critics accused Sunshine Policy proponents of lacking principles and consistency in dealing with the North.

The Kim Dae Jung presidency was a limited success at best. Kim came to office amid a crisis which tied his hands in many areas of economic policy, and with a limited mandate. His uneasy strategic alliance with Kim Jong Pil, his age (73 years old when elected) and health problems imposed further constraints. On the credit side he adjusted smoothly from dissident opposition leader to head of state, and proceeded to act swiftly and purposefully to counter a grave economic crisis. In foreign policy, like Roh Tae-Woo he enjoyed a much higher and more positive profile abroad than at home, largely due to his Sunshine Policy. However, despite the many plaudits garnered by this policy, and despite the June 2000 Pyongyang summit, under his leadership the inter-Korean dialogue made little progress beyond that which was achieved by the agreements of 1972 and 1991. Meanwhile, in the domestic sphere, despite Kim's record as a lifelong ardent campaigner for democracy, his administration was not noticeably more open or less corrupt than that of his immediate predecessor, nor was it noticeably more effective in carrying out the fundamental economic reforms which broad sections of public opinion seemed to agree were necessary if the ROK were to avoid the type of prolonged economic stagnation which overtook Japan during the 1990s. In noting this, one is perhaps saying little more than that Kim failed to rise above the many institutional constraints on the ROK presidency, but this came after literally decades in which Kim based his credentials for power on strident criticism of the practices of government in the ROK, and on promises that, if elected, he would make a fundamental difference.

The Roh Moo-hyun administration

The December 2002 presidential election campaign began as a contest between the government MDP candidate Roh Moo-hyun, a former activist and human rights lawyer, and the major opposition Grand National Party candidate Lee Hoi-chang, whose platform was seen as more conservative in a Korean context, emphasising the role of business and promising a harder line on relations with the North. Like its recent predecessors, the actual campaign was extended and heated. The MDP did not benefit from continuing revelations of influence-peddling by a number of Kim Dae Jung's intimates, which led to the imprisonment of his two sons, Kim Hong-yup and Kim Hong-gul, and this enabled Lee Hoi-chang to maintain a strong lead in the polls. Doubts over Roh's ability to win led to the emergence of a third candidate, Chung Mong-jun, whose father Chung Ju-yong had run in 1992 on what some called the Hyundai ticket. However, in a rare moment of peaceful compromise, Chung, whose poll standing rivalled that of Roh, withdrew and declared his support for Roh after both had concluded that Lee would inevitably win a three-horse race. Chung then earned the deep enmity of Roh and the ruling party by subsequently withdrawing his endorsement of Roh, but his original compromise was none the less decisive in helping Roh to prevail over Lee by a close margin of 2.3 per cent. As in 1992 and 1997, South Koreans greeted a new president with strong reformist credentials elected by about 40 per cent of the electorate. The major question for immediate debate was whether Roh could succeed where his predecessors had failed.

In many ways, Roh Moo-hyun presented yet another attempt at a decisive break with the past. He came from a poor background, his formal education had ended after high school, he had no firm political base in his home town of Pusan, which gave Lee 67 per cent of the presidential vote, and he was an outsider with few contacts within the ROK establishment. In policy terms, too, he entered office with an agenda of change, though one guided more by campaign slogans and principles than by clear policies. His main reform agenda was familiar: end the close, usually corrupt nexus between business money and politics; reform the business sector, particularly the *chaebol*; minimise labour unrest; achieve reunification through the Sunshine Policy; and redefine the US alliance. However, the strengths that the electorate, especially younger voters, perceived in Roh the candidate were also liabilities for Roh the incumbent, for they underscored his narrow constituency and his lack of experience at dealing with conflicting public policy positions.

Unused to the restrictions of elected office, Roh struggled to broaden his constituency without alienating his activist base. His main tactic was to bypass the bureaucracy, the business world, the media and the National Assembly, where the MDP had in any case lost its majority, and appeal directly to social groups in the name of 'participatory government'. Perhaps predictably, this led to frequent and controversial off-the-cuff remarks which distracted attention from policy issues. In domestic policy, financial scandals relating to illegal campaign dona-tions rapidly engulfed Roh's inner circle, and in 2004 these led to controversial impeachment proceedings against him which ultimately failed on constitutional grounds. However, Roh was not able to rebound from this episode, and his uneven handling of economic policy, along with controversial decisions on matters ranging from key personnel appointments to supporting the US with ground troops in Iraq, left him with approval ratings in the 20–30 per cent range and with little influence on the course of events. As Roh neared the end of his time in office, his presidency increasingly resembled that of his two predecessors, Kim Dae Jung and Kim Young Sam. Like the two Kims, initial euphoria and expectation of significant economic and political reform were lost amid allegations of corruption, scandal and an inability to use the office of the president effectively.

ROK society in the 1990s

By the year 2000, ROK society combined within itself a number of contradictions drawn from the close juxtaposition of its rural past and its industrial present. It retained a strongly hierarchical society adapted over centuries from Chinese Confucianism, but its cultural outlook had changed considerably. A dynamic view of the purpose of life, emphasising progress and improvement, had displaced the traditional cyclical, passive outlook. Similarly, self-advancement and social mobility constituted key concepts alongside the more restrictive horizons of family and community loyalty. Notwithstanding images of spiritual yearning, materialism was rampant, and the here-and-now had become the most significant dimension of time to most Koreans. A problem-solving mentality which took pride in efficiency, technological achievement and manufacturing success was nurtured by the new industrialised society, as was adaptability to broadening social horizons. These changes induced widening spheres of interest and activity, and a growing awareness of other people and situations, all of which transcended the small-group, personalistic social frame of previous generations.

ROK society was also increasingly evincing characteristics generally associated with mature industrial societies. Economic development no longer dominated public policy debates as people became increasingly aware of quality-of-life issues, involving both their working life and their living environment. Reserves of tolerance for authoritarianism, always thin, practically disappeared, banishing the military from any significant role in political life, and ensuring a constant public sensitivity to the potential of the defence and security apparatus for interference in civilian politics.

The new business and professional class became a powerful symbol of the aspiration and achievement in post-industrial ROK society. Its members comprised a younger generation raised in a level of comfort and security unknown to their parents, amid a new urban environment. They lived in a 'new' Korea, though they were still governed by the rhetoric of the old. Although 'Westernised' in some ways, they established their chief behavioural models and precedents through a curious blending of old gentry emphasis on 'good ancestry' and proper behaviour with the avid pursuit of material possessions – a pursuit which was in many ways the antithesis of the old gentry ethos. The new middle class had come into being at an extraordinarily rapid rate – most had parents and grandparents who had been agricultural workers – and they were therefore still close to their roots, keenly aware of, and bound by, family ritual and obligation.

During the 1990s public opinion polls consistently showed a continuing high level of concern about social inequality. In the earlier stages of economic development, issues of income and wealth distribution were less relevant in a society where most people lived in extreme poverty. However, with the passage of time the benefits of economic development became more and more unevenly distributed. The industrialisation process itself brought with it many divisions between haves and have-nots, including those between large companies and small or medium-sized companies, the primary production sector and the manufacturing sector, urban and rural communities, junior and senior workers, blue-collar workers and management, non-college graduates and college graduates, urban landowners and renters, as well as regional divisions such as between Cholla and Kyongsang, where a broad range of statistics supported the widespread Cholla sense of grievance that it had been systematically discriminated against in the development process.

But, while such disparities of wealth and opportunity sat uncomfortably in the Korean mind, comparative statistics suggested that ROK income distribution was one of the most level in the world among countries undergoing economic development. Relevant factors here included the 1950 land reform, the socially levelling effect of the Korean War, the meritocratic and relatively egalitarian education system, equality-oriented policies such as the Saemaul farm-price support policy and price controls on necessities in urban daily life, and constant government pressure on the wealthy to avoid displays of conspicuous wealth. This concern with equality was perhaps more rhetorical than actual, but it demonstrated the egalitarian, rather than the hierarchical, Korean ethos at work – an ethos which supported the general conviction that, as people who only a generation ago had almost all been poor, they should observe the principle of equal benefit from subsequent prosperity.

Quality-of-life issues remained salient, for the ROK still continued to bear the traces of its rapid-growth trajectory in the form of many social indices which remained low by international standards. Most Koreans now lived in overcrowded, highly polluted urban environments, where standards in housing, transport and leisure facilities fell considerably short of standards in comparable industrialised societies. Similarly, ROK pride in its economic achievements was tempered by growing awareness that it lagged considerably behind other comparable economies in quality-of-life issues. Life-expectancy rates compared unfavourably with those of other Asian Tigers, the health and social welfare systems remained primitive, and as the ROK celebrated its entry into the OECD group of advanced industrialised countries it might well have paused to note that its life expectancy was well below the OECD average and its infant mortality rate well above. One set of statistics released by the United Nations Development Program in 1997 placed the ROK thirtieth out of 174 nations on its overall human development index, a ranking derived from statistics on education, social welfare, life expectancy and income levels. By 2005 it had risen to only twenty-eighth position, underlining the continuing challenges of social policy-making.

Concluding remarks

More than a century has passed since the kingdom of Choson took its first tentative steps towards joining the modern world of independent nation-states, and more than fifty-five years have passed since the division of Korea. At the point of division in 1945 all Koreans faced the future with the shared experience of an intricate and profound traditional political and social culture, a compromised sovereignty, the destruction of dynastic rule, the experience of Japanese colonial rule, dependent economic development, the persistence of traditional authority and hierarchy patterns at the village level, the political weakness of Korean commercial interests, and the rising potential for mass political action. Today, however, while many, if not most, Koreans, especially in the South, continue to insist that a common sense of 'Koreanness' will ultimately transcend 'foreign' ideologies and form the basis for reunification, shared Koreanness, whether in Seoul or in Pyongyang, presently seems to linger chiefly as a common style and a common social etiquette. This facilitates and gives warmth to personal contacts, but on an official level the respective political, economic and social systems remain profoundly different, to the point where they often seem to lack even a common vocabulary.

The circumstances under which the two Koreas may again reunite remain far from clear, and the impasse which currently exists remains as unyielding as at any time since the opening of dialogue in 1972. It is an impasse reinforced by the conflicting interests of two very different Korean states, such that the Korean division will remain the defining characteristic of modern Korea for the foreseeable future. Even if the two Koreas were to begin a substantive process of reunification immediately, many years would pass before they could in any sense call their nation reunified, for the economic, social and cultural gulfs that have opened up between them in the last fifty years are now almost unimaginably wide. Nevertheless, the pull towards some sort of unification formula persists. It derives from deeper sources than political expedience, ideological education, economic and geo-political logic, or desire to end the painful division of families. It is unlikely ever to go away because the unity of the Korean state constitutes an article of faith which occupies a profound and emotive place in the Korean mind as a potent expression of cultural and historical identity. Division is therefore a culturally unnatural and unsatisfying state to be endured, but never accepted.

A recurring theme in the history of the DPRK state has been the powerful twin influences on Kim Il Sung of his guerrilla years and of his exposure to Stalinism, both during his sojourn in the Soviet Union from 1941 to 1945 and afterwards during the Soviet occupation of North Korea. From these he developed a durable, resilient political and institutional framework for rapid industrialisation, modern-isation and military strength, characterised by mass mobilisation, economic commandism, overt appeals to nationalism, high levels of political repression, personal dictatorship, and a cult of personality. The initial achievements of this framework were substantial, but from the mid-1960s onward stagnation and decline have been continuous processes.

It was not Kim Il Sung's intention to produce such political, economic and social stagnation – on the contrary, his outlook was a dynamic one, focused in the first place upon reunification and beyond that upon world revolution, as he understood the concept – but Kim's chosen methods were dictated by his models, and beyond a certain level of development these models themselves were agents of stagnation.

As we trace the history of the DPRK, it emerges that commitment to revolution concealed anti-modern features which ultimately were more influential than revolutionary zeal in determining outcomes: pervasive internal security and surveillance, a dogmatic, xenophobic rejection of international political and economic structures and institutions, denial of freedom of information, the rise of a new class system based on nepotism, the absolute primacy accorded to party loyalty, rigid ideological criteria, and high levels of militarism. The North's window on the outside world extended little further than the closed society of the Soviet Union, and while this brought substantial benefits in the short run, in the long run the massive ideological, political and economic borrowings from that quarter proved disastrous.

As a result, after nearly fifty years of independence, the Kimist legacy is a DPRK which remains weak in all indices of power except military, yet which also remains dedicated to the pursuit of radical ideological goals. These goals cannot envisage economic development under market economy principles, nor can they accept peaceful coexistence with the ROK and its allies, which include major regional and global powers, and they therefore oblige the DPRK to operate largely outside international economic and political frameworks. Accordingly, the DPRK enjoys the only form of national security which its chosen form of isolationism allows: raw military threat, which gives it very little influence on broader events beyond its borders, and which can only be achieved at high human cost within its borders. Kimist ideology, especially its militant stance on reunification, has ensured strong reciprocal military pressure on the part of its adversaries, and at the same time has prevented the DPRK from developing its economy. North Korea now confronts a situation in which it cannot remain viable without reform, but cannot reform without threatening its ideological base and hence its very existence. This, broadly speaking, has been the dilemma that has become increasingly apparent since the 1970s.

The years since the 1994 Geneva Framework Accord have witnessed a rapid increase in the quantity and quality of the DPRK's points of foreign contact: ROK *chaebol* have established substantial light-industrial and electronics plants; ROK technicians are supervising the building of the two light-water nuclear reactors; Western officials, politicians and prominent private citizens visit Pyongyang on a regular basis; the United States government is engaged in a number of bilateral negotiation processes; the DPRK has established diplomatic relations with a broad range of major industrialised countries; and a number of United Nations and private aid agencies operate substantial relief programmes, often in areas not previously accessible to foreigners. However, while this process will have a continuing impact on what might loosely be termed popular attitudes in the North, it has not produced any observable changes to basic policies. Minimal tactical adjustments have occurred, but the leadership itself remains untouched by these developments, and basic state policies and practices remain firmly in place, as does the son of the leader who so assiduously installed them.

The immediate problem is economic. Pyongyang's economic relations with the outside world are still largely confined to predatory or outright illegal transactions, or else to the exploitation of its own low-wage workforce – largely as an end in itself rather than as a concerted means of building a national skill and technology base. The country cannot pay its way, nor can it meet even the most basic needs of its people. However, meaningful economic reform would need to proceed from a process of political and ideological change, and this is not currently in prospect. Kim Jong Il bases his claim to legitimacy not on his ability to improve living standards but on the notion that only he can effectively maintain Kimilsungism. Thus, he continues to reject the concept of any economic reform which is incompatible with Kimist ideology.

The scenarios for significant change to the DPRK system are therefore limited to either inherently unpredictable forms of convulsive change through popular unrest, military mutiny or palace revolt, or intra-party change or evolution which does not involve ideological compromise. This latter scenario is difficult to imagine in the setting of a monolithic ideology which lays such inordinate stress on loyalty to the leader. Yet, even if this impediment were substantially removed, the option of substantial reform, which may be defined as applying many of the economic practices that have become prevalent in China since the early 1980s, would have a limited impact. The underlying logic of the DPRK economic system, where more than half the resources of the economy are believed to be consumed by the military sector, is incompatible with that of a market economy, and so reform entails nothing less than the wholesale modification of an existing economic system – the only one the DPRK has ever known – in co-ordination with the construction of a new one. The experience of the Soviet Union since 1989 indicates that economic problems of this nature and magnitude are not susceptible to a piecemeal approach. This is a job not for economic reformers but for economic revolutionaries.

Currently the DPRK appears to be succeeding in maintaining a credible military threat. In the end, this threat may prove to have been largely illusory, given the many dysfunctional aspects of the North Korean system, but at present its neighbours have little option other than to take the threat seriously. Under the Geneva Framework Agreement, Pyongyang gained significant new energy assets, retained a small, useful quantity of weapons-grade plutonium, and was free to work in other areas of its nuclear weapons programme, including triggering-device technology and missile delivery systems. It has now triggered a low-yield nuclear device and test-fired a number of short- and medium-range missiles which will eventually be capable of carrying a nuclear payload. It has achieved all this while also enduring a food crisis, mainly because it was been willing to allow the almost 80 per cent of the population which lives outside the privileged party and armed forces distribution networks either to live in continuing, chronic undernourishment, or to be fed by the international community. Such a high level of callused determination indicates the extent to which Pyongyang associates maintenance of rigid ideological parameters with régime survival.

Predicting the future of the DPRK has long been a hazardous occupation. Those observers who emphasise continuity with past practice and those who foresee significant change both routinely refer to a small common pool of general knowledge about the North, but they place very different interpretations on the known facts. Both also address the paradox whereby the régime is both hardening and weakening – hardening because it is weakening and weakening because it is hardening. However, in the absence of formal, sanctioned public debate in the North, it is not possible to read the signs with any clarity, and a clear prediction on the DPRK's future is not warranted on the basis of either theory or data. Current indications are that under Kim Jong Il the DPRK is unlikely to embrace China-style economic reforms as the way of the future, though some selective system-defending measures may be adopted. Otherwise, although policies aimed at further opening up the DPRK to outside engagement may have some effect in the longer term, in the mean time external forces have little prospect of influencing the DPRK leadership to deviate from its current path, either by promises or by threats – 'carrots' and 'sticks' in common diplomatic parlance. We are left with a régime in decline and decay, though seemingly with an almost infinite capacity to continue this trend.

When we consider the future of the Republic of Korea, it is worth recalling that in 1945 many foreign observers in Korea contrasted the purposeful, efficient administration in the northern half of the peninsula with the political violence and economic chaos of the southern half, and doubted the South's ability to withstand the northern challenge. However, in the longer time-frame of decades, it has transpired that the South's bleak prospects in 1945 obscured features that were highly relevant to the building and sustenance of a powerful modern economy and a pluralist society. The grass roots of South Korean society were spared the ravages of ideology-driven class warfare, while the strong incentive for overseas study and reliance on Western powers and the United Nations for basic security kept open a broad international window. This window facilitated the broad dissemination of information, ideas and basic skills and technologies necessary to the building of a modern economy, while also acting as a check on excessive political repression and tempering the xenophobic tendency of Korean nationalism.

The above perspective underlines how profoundly the security factor has influenced the timing, pace and direction of ROK industrialisation. After a brutal war which had significant civil components, the two Koreas have remained in a state of war. The various forms of suffering this has inflicted on the North Korean population have been well documented, but the implications for the South have also been significant. The implications for internal security are simply expressed: for over fifty years South Koreans have pursued rapid economic growth while at war with a people indistinguishable from them in terms of culture, language and physical appearance. No less severe has been the drain of the military on economic resources, for not only has the ROK laboured under the enormous economic burden of maintaining a huge standing army, but also virtually every major economic decision, whether relating to infrastructure such as expressways, or to the timing and scale of entry into important industries, has been viewed through the distorting prism of its military implications.

The modern economic transformation of the ROK is a well-documented, often-told story. Most observers accord a central role to Park Chung-hee who, upon coming to power in 1961, presided over the creation of many of the key economic institutions of change, and extended close government control over virtually every area of economic and political life, including the banks, the *chaebol*, local government, the media, the labour unions, and a wide range of non-government professional bodies and associations. However, as we have seen, the ROK already possessed significant assets. The members of the entrepreneurial élite who built up the major *chaebol* had already begun to take shape under the Japanese, while much of the basic economic management training and planning infrastructure was created in the late 1950s. Park was not so much a creator as a leader who ruthlessly and effectively deployed pre-existing and substantial human resources.

Factors other than leadership are complex and still warmly debated. Some scholars have pointed to timing as a key factor, arguing that the ROK adopted a rapid economic development culture later than other industrialising nations, and so learned a great deal from such prior experience. Others highlight factors intrinsic to Korean society and politics, such as strategic, judicious government intervention in the economy, cohesive business–government relationships, a strong work ethic and positive attitudes to education. Others, again, point to extrinsic factors, for the ROK's chosen strategy required a relatively open international economic system, and an expanding global and regional economy to be successful. Only such an open system could enable efficient access to the massive, continuing stream of investment capital and technology which the development of an export economy required.

The 1997–98 economic crisis constituted a major watershed for the ROK. It mandated a shift in policy from GNP maximisation to consolidation and institution-building, but it left the basic growth philosophy in place. Long after the basic threats to ROK security had eased, an entire generation of the ROK élite had been raised on the mantra of high growth led by export-oriented large firms. Economic interests have therefore maintained their entrenched position. Some leading *chaebol* have suffered dramatic declines, but this has not been due to any loss of their privileged status in the ROK economic hierarchy, where they continue to benefit from strong government linkages, distribution networks largely closed to outsiders, and from the reduced effectiveness of political oversight. Rather, they have faced growing economic challenges of a different, largely self-inflicted kind, ranging from declining competitiveness and the lack of obvious new technologies with which to restore competitive advantage, and the burden of their bad debts. The task of *chaebol* reform is daunting, for the *chaebol* is simultaneously an exploiter and sustainer in many sectors of the ROK economy, most notably the small and medium industry sector.

International political and economic pressures have transformed many *chaebol* strengths into liabilities. The *chaebol* are geared for mass production and economies of scale, and cannot easily adjust to the growing importance of niche markets. Moreover, the innovative capacity of ROK industry is becoming a looming issue for the future. By and large, the ROK has lost many elements of its competitive advantage and is not yet competitive with the advanced international economies in leading-edge industries. It is a manufacturer of software, rather than hardware, and its royalty payments for the use of foreign technology have continued to rise over the years. It remains committed to developing specific leading-edge technologies, rather than developing a basic culture of innovation.

The political system remains the major obstacle. Its polity is still democratising, partisan conflict remains rife, and consensus upon informal, unwritten rules and conventions is shallow. Politics still tends to function as a myriad of overlapping personal networks, involving distinct regional, organisational and educational underpinnings, and like most élite communities it is also ridden with intense, labyrinthine rivalries which have the propensity to induce paralysis in decision-making as these separate interest groups trade off. Thus, political institutions such as the National Assembly remain centrist, personality-dominated, and characterised by weak ideological and party allegiances. Its review functions remain weak, passive and largely ineffective in interposing a legislative interest between the bureaucracy and the executive. At the executive level, the co-opting of Kim Young Sam into the ruling party in 1990 marked a process of policy convergence between government and main opposition groups, and since then personality-based partisan rhetoric has dominated national policy debate. Meanwhile, ongoing revelations of endemic corruption encompassing the bureaucracy as well as politicians have debilitated successive administrations and contributed to a widespread sense of public cynicism.

Legislative incoherence reflects a broader incoherence in the reform debate, where the ROK remains painfully torn between memories of past abuses of authoritarianism and awareness of current limitations of democratisation. Some ROK commentators argue that this devolves from a fundamental division in the country between those who identify reform with extension of the political process of democratisation, and those who adopt a more narrow, economic definition of reform, identifying it with the achievement of greater economic transparency and efficiency through market-economy principles. This in turn reflects the schism which first emerged during the Second Republic between those who placed primary stress on democracy and social policy, and those who placed primary stress on economic development. Since the early 1960s they have formed two separate, largely non-communicating groups who remain at cross-purposes with each other, in both intellectual and policy terms.

This points to a future ROK economy moving slowly towards reform through a mixture of new and old policies. Currently, the ROK faces a number of major challenges – internationally from declining competitiveness in many sectors, and domestically from a broad perception of growing social and economic inequity, which in turn empowers a strong, militant trade-union movement. The intellectual framework through which these policy issues are debated remains dominated by the habits of the past thirty years, which include important residues of the command–response military model. Many such habits have become counter-productive, but they cannot easily be modified. Moreover, despite the scale of the ROK's international dealings, internationalism still has shallow roots in Korean society, while chauvinistic nationalism – a modern phenomenon as much as a reflection of the so-called Hermit Kingdom syndrome – still has deep roots, which are still often nurtured and encouraged in the nation's education system. The prognosis, then, remains for a halting process of reform and an economy increasingly marked by a mixture of well-performing and underperforming sectors, presided over by a set of political and regulatory institutions which will struggle to provide clear direction and leadership.

Selected reading

Bertini, Catherine 1997, 'North Korea: Famine in Slow Motion', *The Economics of Korean Reunification*, vol. 2, no. 2, pp. 20–25.

Bracken, Paul 1998, 'How to Think about Korean Reunification', *Orbis*, vol. 42, no. 3, pp. 409–22.

Chang, Yun-Shik and Lee, Steven Hugh, 2006, Transformations in Twentieth Century Korea, Abingdon/New York: Routledge.

Eder, Norman 1996, *Poisoned Prosperity: Development, Modernization, and the Environment in South Korea.* Armonk, NY: M. E. Sharpe.

Kang, Myung-Hun 1996, *The Korean Business Conglomerate: Chaebol Then and Now*, Berkeley, CA: Center for Korean Studies, Institute of East Asian Studies, University of California.

Kendall, Laurel 1994, 'A Rite of Modernization and Its Postmodern Discontents: Of Weddings, Bureaucrats, and Morality in the Republic of Korea,' in Keyes, Kendall and Hardacre (eds), *Asian Visions of Authority: Religion and the Modern States of East and Southeast Asia,* Honolulu: University of Hawaii Press.

Lett, Denise Potrzeba 1998, *In Pursuit of Status: The Making of South Korea's 'New' Urban Middle Class*, Cambridge, MA: Harvard University Asia Center.

Namkoong, Young 1996, 'Trends and Prospects of the North Korean Economy', *Korea and World Affairs*, vol. 20, no. 2, pp. 219–35.

Noland, Marcus, 2004, *Korea after Kim Jong Il*, Policy Analyses in International Economics 71, Washington, DC: Peter G. Peterson Institute for International Economics.

Son, Key-young, 2006, *South Korean Engagement Policies and North Korea: Identities, Norms, and the Sunshine Policy*, Abingdon: Routledge.

Major events, 1910–2006

22 August 1910	Korea becomes a colony of Japan when Prime Minister Yi Wan-yong signs the Treaty of Annexation, which is proclaimed by Emperor Sunjong on 29 August 1910.
12 October 1910	105 Koreans, including many prominent Christians, educators and intellectuals, arrested on grounds of conspiracy to assassinate Choson Governor-General Terauchi.
1 November 1911	Rail bridge over the Yalu River completed, joining the Korean rail system with Manchuria.
15 April 1912	Kim Il Sung born at Mangyongdae, near Pyongyang.
13 August 1912	Major land survey begins, continues until 1918, helps brings about stable tax base.
28 July 1914	First World War begins.
18 January 1915	Japan seeks expansion in China by presenting list of Twenty-One Demands to the Chinese government, but is forced to withdraw them by the European powers. If acceded to, the demands would have given Japan effective control of the Chinese financial and banking system.
16 October 1916	Hasegawa Yoshimichi succeeds Terauchi Masatake as Governor-General.
7 November 1917	The Great October Socialist Revolution brings the Bolsheviks to power in Russia.
August 1918	After riots in major Japanese cities over the high price of rice, the Japanese government decides to increase grain production rapidly in Japan and Korea.
11 November 1918	First World War ends.

8 January 1919	US President Woodrow Wilson enunciates his Fourteen Points.
22 January 1919	Death of former Choson king/emperor Kojong.
1 March 1919	March First Movement begins. The demonstrations, often accompanied by strikes and business shutdowns, spread throughout the peninsula, increasing in frequency throughout March and reaching their peak in early April.
9 April 1919	Korean Provisional Government formed in Shanghai.
4 May 1919	May Fourth student movement in China leads to anti-Japanese, Chinese nationalist movement.
12 August 1919	Japanese prime minister Hara Kei reorganises Japanese rule in Korea under the slogan *Nissen yuwa* ('Harmony between Japan and Korea'). Admiral Saito Makoto appointed as Governor-General, implements 'Cultural Policy'.
5 March 1920	*Choson Ilbo* founded in Seoul.
1 April 1920	*Donga Ilbo* founded in Seoul.
February 1922	The Washington Naval Conference establishes new postwar order in the Pacific, embracing capital ship tonnages and *status quo* on construction of naval bases. Japanese participation symbolises a new internationalist era in Japanese foreign policy during the 1920s.
1 September 1923	In the wake of the Kanto earthquake in Japan, between 6,661 (Japanese official figure) and 20,000 (Korean estimate at the time) Koreans massacred.
June 1925	Proclamation of the Peace Preservation Law signals a new cycle of repression within Japan, which soon spreads to Korea.
10 June 1926	Attempts to launch nationwide protests on the day of former emperor Sunjong's funeral unsuccessful.
February 1927	The Singanhoe, major united-front organisation for Korean activists becomes active.
April 1927	General Tanaka Giichi becomes prime minister, initiates aggressive foreign policy towards China and systematic suppression of communism in Japan.
4 June 1928	The assassination of Manchurian warlord Chang Tso-lin shows the Japanese Kwantung Army to be operating outside political control.

14 May 1929	Kim Il Sung arrested in Kirin, Manchuria, for participating in a communist youth group meeting. First evidence of Kim's communist youth activities.
24 October 1929	The Wall Street Crash leads to the worldwide Great Depression.
November 1930	Prime Minister Hamaguchi shot by an ultra-nationalist would-be assassin in the wake of ratification of the London Naval Treaty. The incident effectively ends civilian control of government in Japan.
15 May 1931	The Korean nationalist movement within Korea is permanently split when the communists adopt a hostile stance against moderate nationalists at the first national conference of the Singanhoe. The communists proceed to concentrate efforts on organising labour and peasant unions.
June 1931	Saito Makoto replaced by Ugaki Kazushige as Governor-General, the Cultural Policy is abandoned and is gradually replaced by policies of mobilisation in support of Japanese expansionism in China.
September 1931	The Manchurian Incident precipitates the Japanese military takeover of Manchuria, which becomes the Japanese-controlled state of Manchukuo.
15 May 1932	Assassination of the last of the civilian party-political prime ministers, Inukai Tsuyoshi, who is succeeded by a 'national unity cabinet' under heavy army and navy influence.
April 1933	First large-scale Japanese military operations against Korean communist guerrillas in Manchuria. By 1935 the principal Korean partisan units are forced to abandon permanent partisan bases and become mobile forces.
5 August 1936	The appointment of General Minami Jiro, a key figure in the Mukden Incident, as Governor-General marks an intensification of mobilisation policies.
16 March 1937	The Government-General orders the exclusive use of Japanese language in official government documents and transactions.
April 1937	Raid on border village of Pochonbo gives Kim Il Sung a strong profile in the Manchurian communist guerrilla movement. However, it also provokes sustained a Japanese offensive which drives Kim back deeply into Manchuria.

June 1937	Gradual escalation of Japanese military activity in China culminates in all-out war against China following the Marco Polo Bridge incident outside Beijing.
March 1938	The Korean language removed from the middle-school curriculum.
August 1939	Promulgation of Labour Mobilisation Law, under which hundreds of thousands of Korean labourers are brought to Japan, first as volunteers and then as conscripts.
3 September 1939	Second World War begins.
10 November 1939	Promulgation of the Name Order, under which 84 per cent of Koreans eventually adopt Japanese names.
10 August 1940	All non-official Korean-language newspapers closed.
September 1940	Kim Il Sung abandons guerrilla campaign and retreats into the Soviet Union, where he and his group eventually join the Red Army.
7 December 1941	The Pacific War begins with the Japanese bombing of Pearl Harbor.
1 December 1943	At the Cairo Conference the US, Britain and China resolve to place postwar Korea under trusteeship, preparatory to independence 'in due course'.
8 August 1945	The Soviets enter the Pacific War.
10 August 1945	The first Soviet troops land in north-east Korea.
15 August 1945	The Japanese surrender to the Allies, Choson Governor-General Abe Nobuyuki hands over power to the local committees of the Provisional Committee for Korean Independence (PCKI) under the chairmanship of Lyuh Woon-hyong.
24 August 1945	The Soviets arrive in Pyongyang and transfer power to the local PCKI committee, which they reorganise into 32 members, including 16 communists.
6 September 1945	The PCKI summons a congress of local People's Committees to press claims as legitimate national government. The congress elects a central committee, which establishes a quasi-governmental structure called the People's Republic of Korea (PRK).
8 September 1945	US Lieutenant-General John R. Hodge arrives in Seoul, receives formal surrender from the Japanese commanders, and inaugurates the United States Military

	Government in Korea (USMGIK). The USMGIK withholds recognition from all indigenous Korean political groups, including the PRK.
19 September 1945	Kim Il Sung and 66 other Korean officers arrive in Wonsan from Siberia and are demobilised.
28 September 1945	Assassination of local communist leader Hyon Chun-hyok in Pyongyang.
8 October 1945	The Soviets gather together a Five Provinces Temporary People's Committee (50 per cent communist, 50 per cent nationalist) under nationalist Cho Man-sik. This leads to the establishment of the Five Provinces Administrative Bureau, an embryonic North Korean government.
14 October 1945	Kim Il Sung's first major public appearance at a Pyongyang rally.
16 October 1945	Syngman Rhee returns to Seoul. He quickly establishes a strong public political profile, and soon falls out with the USMGIK.
12 December 1945	The USMGIK outlaws the PRK.
18 December 1945	Kim Il Sung becomes chairman of the newly formed North Korean Communist Party.
27 December 1945	The Moscow Conference re-imposes trusteeship on the Koreans.
3 January 1946	The Korean Communist Party announces support for trusteeship.
4 January 1946	Cho Man sik publicly opposes trusteeship, and disappears into house arrest, while his fellow nationalists are rapidly eliminated from power in the North.
20 March 1946	The Joint American–Soviet Commission, an outcome of the Moscow Conference, meets. Moscow demands that only those who accept the principle of trusteeship be consulted on the issue. The US disagrees, and the Commission reaches a stalemate.
23 March 1946	Kim Il Sung announces his Twenty-Point Programme – a programme which establishes the main economic and political structure for the new North Korean state.
8 May 1946	The Joint American–Soviet Commission adjourns *sine die*, unable to reach any decision on procedures for Korean independence.

10 June 1946	All remaining North Korean industry previously owned by the Japanese nationalised.
July 1946	The US State Department issues policy directive for the USMGIK to encourage a coalition of 'moderates' as a first step towards a unified interim Korean government.
24 September 1946	Widespread campaign of violent strikes begins in the South, reaching a peak in early October.
12 October 1946	Establishment of a half-elected, half-appointed Korean Interim Legislative Assembly announced. The elected half is largely rightist in the wake of the suppression of communist and leftist riots by rightist national police.
March 1947	The US enunciates the Truman Doctrine, signalling a hardened attitude towards Moscow.
July 1947	Breakdown of Marshall Plan negotiations, start of the Cold War in Europe.
19 July 1947	US attempts to seek unification through coalitions of Korean political groups effectively end with assassination of leading leftist Lyuh Woon-hyung.
23 August 1947	The US places the Korean question before the United Nations.
24 November 1947	The UN agrees to US resolution establishing a UN commission, UNTCOK, to expedite moves towards Korean independence.
8 February 1948	Official creation of the Korean People's Army; 60,000 recruited by the end of 1948.
27–30 March 1948	The Second Korean Workers' Party Congress results in major purge of the Northern domestic communists.
1 April 1948	The Cold War worsens with the start of the Soviet blockade of Berlin. The blockade is eventually lifted in May 1949.
3 April 1948	Communist-led uprising on Cheju Island breaks out. It is repressed with estimated 30,000 casualties.
10 May 1948	After National Assembly elections in South Korea, Syngman Rhee emerges as president-designate of the Republic of Korea (ROK).
17 July 1948	New ROK constitution promulgated.
20 July 1948	Syngman Rhee appointed president of the ROK.

15 August 1948	Proclamation of the Republic of Korea.
3 September 1948	Promulgation of the constitution of the Democratic People's Republic of Korea (DPRK).
9 September 1948	Proclamation of the DPRK.
20 October 1948	The Yosu military rebellion breaks out. It is repressed with estimated 2,000 casualties.
26 June 1949	Assassination of right-wing nationalist leader Kim Ku in Seoul.
October 1949	US Congress passes the Mutual Defense Assistance Act. It provides funds for a 65,000-man ROK Army to cover a US withdrawal.
1 October 1949	Proclamation of the People's Republic of China.
5 January 1950	US President Truman announces the termination of US military assistance to the Nationalist Chinese.
12 January 1950	US Secretary of State Acheson delivers policy speech in which he excludes the Asian mainland from the US's defensive perimeter in Asia.
April 1950	After meetings with Kim Il Sung in early April, Stalin finally sanctions a DPRK military offensive in general terms, subject to Mao's approval.
6 April 1950	ROK government implements Agricultural Land Reform Law.
13 April 1950	Kim Il Sung visits Beijing. He obtains Mao's general approval for a military offensive against the ROK.
30 May 1950	Second ROK National Assembly election. Most sitting members replaced by neutral or anti-Rhee independents.
10 June 1950	A final meeting in Moscow approves Pyongyang's battle-plan, with the exact timing of the invasion left up to Kim.
25 June 1950	Korean War starts on the Ongjin peninsula. Within hours a large-scale invasion is under way.
27 June 1950	US President Truman orders the US 7th Fleet to prevent all military action in the Taiwan Strait.
28 June 1950	Korean People's Army (KPA) captures Seoul.
30 June 1950	US forces enter the war.
5 July 1950	First US troops engage KPA at Osan.

7 July 1950	Establishment of the United Nations Command (UNC), a unified military command under the US with the purpose of restoring the *status quo ante* on the Korean Peninsula.
August 1950	KPA advance reaches its maximum point.
15 September 1950	UNC landing at Inch'on cuts off and destroys three-fourths of the KPA.
30 September 1950	As UN forces pursue the KPA remnants northward, China issues public warning to the US not to cross the 38th parallel.
1 October 1950	ROK army units under the UNC cross the 38th parallel.
2 October 1950	The Chinese government resolves to send troops to Korea.
7 October 1950	After diplomatic efforts to achieve a ceasefire fail, UN resolution allows UNC troops to cross the 38th parallel.
8 October 1950	China informs the DPRK it is entering the war.
25 October 1950	China crosses the Yalu.
24 November 1950	The UNC launches its 'home by Christmas' offensive to counter the Chinese advance.
28 November 1950	UNC in full retreat following Chinese counter-attack.
5 December 1950	China recaptures Pyongyang. Mao's goals unclear, but orders troops south of the 38th parallel.
16 December 1950	President Truman declares a national state of emergency, calls up 3.5 million men, imposes price controls, and effects rapid increase in US defence spending.
21–23 December 1950	Mu Chong and other military leaders from the Yan'an group purged at the Third Plenum of the 2nd KWP Congress.
31 December 1950	Chinese offensive south of the 38th parallel begins. Seoul is again taken, and the offensive is not stopped until late January.
10 February 1951	Seoul retaken by UNC troops.
1 March 1951	With CPV 'human wave' attacks proving increasingly ineffective, Mao tells Stalin he is changing to tactics of attrition, acknowledging that military victory is out of reach.

20 March 1951	UNC commander MacArthur dissents from US war aims by writing his 'no substitute for victory' letter to House minority leader Joseph Martin.
11 April 1951	MacArthur dismissed.
22 April 1951	The final CPV offensive is launched, but reaches a stalemate by 20 May amid signs of collapsing CPV morale. The CPV sustains an estimated 70,000 casualties, ten times reported UNC casualties.
13 May 1951	Mao submits for Stalin's approval armistice terms based on a restoration of the prewar *status quo* along the 38th parallel.
June 1951	The UNC publicly abandons pursuit and destruction of enemy forces, and the US declares its readiness to accept an armistice at or near the 38th parallel.
10 July 1951	Formal armistice negotiations begin.
27 November 1951	Substantive agreement on an armistice line. The POW issue remains the major issue of dispute.
23 December 1951	Syngman Rhee organises personal support-base into the Liberal Party.
18 January 1952	ROK National Assembly rejects constitutional amendment for direct popular presidential elections.
April 1952	Steady progress in armistice negotiations, but the low number of voluntary CPV and KPA returnees produces deadlock.
June 1952	The US resumes massive bombing of the North to break negotiation deadlock.
4 July 1952	Under duress, the ROK National Assembly passes constitutional amendment for direct popular presidential elections.
5 August 1952	Syngman Rhee elected president with 74 per cent of the vote.
November 1952	Dwight D. Eisenhower elected US president; threat of expanded UNC operations begins to grow.
7 February 1953	Last public appearance of DPRK foreign minister and South Korean communist leader Pak Hon-yong. He and his colleagues are publicly accused of factionalism.
April 1953	Suicide of KWP Soviet-Korean faction leader Ho Ka-i.
5 March 1953	Upon the death of Stalin, a settlement in Korea becomes a high priority for his successors.

4 June 1953	The POW issue is substantially resolved when the communists accept an ambiguously worded clause which leaves the nonrepatriate POWs in the South for the time being.
3 August 1953	Major show trials of Southern communists in the North begin. The major defendants are sentenced to death.
15 August 1953	The ROK government returns to Seoul from Pusan.
1 October 1953	Signing of ROK–US Mutual Security Pact. The pact constitutes the cornerstone of ROK defence.
27 July 1953	Military Armistice Agreement signed.
January 1954	DPRK begins major agricultural collectivisation drive.
20 May 1954	Third ROK National Assembly elections strengthen Syngman Rhee's control over the legislature.
29 November 1954	ROK National Assembly carries amendment allowing Syngman Rhee to seek a third presidential term.
December 1954	Leading Yan'an group members within KWP purged for factionalism and 'weak class consciousness'.
28 December 1955	Juche ideology begins to take shape as Kim Il Sung delivers landmark speech titled 'On Eliminating Dogmatism'.
4 January 1956	Pak Chang Ok removed as chairman of the Economic Planning Commission – end of pro-Soviet influence over economic planning.
February 1956	CPSU general secretary Nikita Khrushchev denounces Stalin at secret session of the 20th Congress of the Communist Party of the Soviet Union. The speech triggers similar moves towards de-Stalinisation in other Soviet-bloc countries, including the DPRK.
23–29 April 1956	The Third Congress of Korean Workers' Party convenes.
15 May 1956	Syngman Rhee re-elected ROK president.
30 August 1956	Emergency plenary session of the KWP politburo attacks Kim Il Sung's personality-cult leadership. However, attempts to replace him fail, and the leading dissenters are arrested.
September 1956	Party purification drive to eliminate anti-Kimists begins, continues throughout 1957.

3–6 March 1958	The first KWP Conference purges remaining anti-Kimist politburo members.
2 May 1958	Fourth ROK National Assembly elections. Liberal Party vote declines to 38.7 per cent.
5 May 1958	The Great Leap Forward proclaimed in China.
August 1958	The DPRK announces completion of the collectivisation of agriculture.
September 1958	Chollima Campaign launched to accelerate economic output.
26 December 1958	The ROK government secures passage of amendments to the National Security Law which impose wide-ranging restrictions on political activity.
June 1959	The Sino-Soviet split begins in earnest when Soviets renege on military agreement with China by withholding nuclear technology.
14 December 1959	Large-scale programme of repatriation of Korean residents of Japan to the DPRK begins.
15 March 1960	Syngman Rhee re-elected ROK president, but widespread fraud and vote-rigging initiates nationwide protest demonstrations.
19 April 1960	Police firing kills an estimated 400 demonstrators, mainly students, throughout South Korea. This causes major escalation of demonstrations, and the Rhee administration rapidly unravels.
26 April 1960	Syngman Rhee resigns. He goes into exile in Hawaii on 29 May.
16 June 1960	The new constitution of the Second ROK Republic promulgated.
29 July 1960	National Assembly elections give the new Democratic Party a majority of 175 of 233 seats. Chang Myon becomes prime minister.
22 September 1960	Democratic Party splits when 86 legislators form the New Democratic Party. By the end of October, Chang controls 118 seats, but credibility is seriously undermined.
12 December 1960	38 per cent voter turnout in provincial elections reveals strong level of public disenchantment with government.

16 May 1961	The Chang Myon government overthrown in military *coup* led by Park Chung-hee. The following day Park announces junta of 30 colonels and brigadier-generals, dissolves the National Assembly, and prohibits political activity.
19 May 1961	Junta renamed Supreme Council for National Reconstruction.
6 June 1961	The junta promulgates a Law for National Reconstruction which gives it effective control over all branches of government.
July 1961	Kim Il Sung visits the USSR and China, and signs mutual-defence treaties.
11 September 1961	The 4th Korean Workers' Party Congress, known as the 'Congress of Victors', opens in Pyongyang.
November 1961	DPRK sends congratulatory message to the Albanian communist party on its 20th anniversary, marking a public split with Moscow on the issue of equality between all communist parties. DPRK–Soviet relations quickly deteriorate.
22 October 1962	Cuban missile crisis begins when US President Kennedy reveals existence of Soviet missile sites in Cuba. The crisis ends on 2 November when Soviet leader Khrushchev announces the dismantling of the sites. The DPRK is openly critical of the Soviet move.
10 December 1962	The Fifth Plenum of the Fourth KWP Congress enunciates the Equal Emphasis policy for strengthening the national defence forces. This policy radically transforms broad areas of DPRK state policy.
17 December 1962	National referendum approves new ROK constitution featuring a strong presidency and weak unicameral legislature with a proportional-representation component.
January 1963	After publicly attacking the DPRK as pro-Chinese, the Soviet Union abruptly cuts off military and economic aid.
26 February 1963	Park Chung-hee institutionalises his power through the formation of the Democratic Republican Party. The party remains the ruling party until 1980.
15 October 1963	Park Chung-hee elected president of the Third ROK Republic.

October 1964	Khrushchev ousted; DPRK sends congratulatory message to the new Soviet leadership.
February 1965	Relations with the Soviet Union restored with visit to Pyongyang of Soviet premier Alexei Kosygin.
22 June 1965	Normalisation of ROK–Japan relations effected with the signing of the Korea–Japan Basic Treaty.
13 August 1965	The ROK government resolves to send troops to Vietnam.
November 1965	Mao launches the first attacks of the Cultural Revolution.
5–12 October 1966	Second KWP Party Conference. An estimated 20 per cent of KWP central committee members, including five politburo members, purged.
March 1967	Purge of leading cadres Pak Kum Chol and Yi Hyo Sun.
3 May 1967	Park Chung-hee re-elected president.
21 January 1968	DPRK commandos attack ROK presidential compound.
23 January 1968	DPRK seizes US navy surveillance ship *Pueblo*.
31 January 1968	Viet Cong and North Vietnamese Army launch Tet offensive.
4 November 1968	KPA guerrillas land on the east coast of the ROK.
17 October 1969	National referendum approves constitutional amendment allowing Park Chung-hee to run for a third term.
26 March 1970	The US advises the ROK of intention to withdraw 20,000 troops, one-third of its total force in Korea.
5–7 April 1970	Trend towards better relations with China sealed with Zhou Enlai's visit to Pyongyang – the first high-level contact since 1964.
7 July 1970	Opening of the Seoul–Pusan Expressway.
2–13 November 1970	The 5th KWP Congress held in Pyongyang.
27 April 1971	Park Chung-hee re-elected president for third term.
16 July 1971	US President Nixon announces trip to Peking.
20 August 1971	First session of Red Cross talks between North and South takes place.
20 November 1971	North–South dialogue broadens with beginning of secret political talks.

4 July 1972	South–North Joint Communiqué signed between the two Koreas, establishing principles for Korean reunification.
17 October 1972	Park Chung-hee declares martial law, enacts the October Revitalising Reforms, including the authoritarian Yushin Constitution amendments.
December 1972	The DPRK announces enactment of new state constitution.
13 February 1973	Organisation of the Three Revolutions Teams Movement, a key base for Kim Jong Il's authority within the KWP.
8 August 1973	Kim Dae Jung kidnapped from Tokyo hotel room by KCIA operatives. After aborted assassination attempt, he is released into house arrest in Seoul on 13 August.
2 October 1973	Public dissidence against the Yushin Constitution intensifies with campus demonstrations. By late November most campuses are closed.
1 December 1973	Lee Hu Rak removed as KCIA director, and the agency is brought under stricter government control.
8 January 1974	Park Chung-hee issues emergency decrees banning criticism of the Yushin constitution. They are the first of a series aimed at curtailing political dissidence.
April 1974	Regular references to Kim Jong Il begin in KWP journals using the codewords 'Party Centre'.
15 August 1974	Attempted assassination of Park Chung-hee results in death of his wife, Yuk Yong-su.
15 November 1974	Discovery of major infiltration tunnel, running north to south under the DMZ.
April 1975	Fall of South Vietnam and Cambodia. Kim Il Sung visits Beijing 18–26 April, his first official visit abroad for eleven years, and unsuccessfully seeks Chinese support for military push against the ROK.
June 1975	The DPRK makes first public acknowledgement of growing foreign-debt problem.
August 1975	The DPRK is admitted to the Non-Aligned Movement.
December 1975	The Three Revolutions Teams Movement begins under Kim Jong Il's direction.
18 August 1976	Axe killings at Panmunjom bring US–DPRK

	confrontation to flashpoint. Kim Il Sung expresses regret after major US show of force.
9 March 1977	US President Jimmy Carter declares intention to withdraw US ground forces from the ROK within four to five years.
September 1978	Signing of the Sino-Japanese peace treaty.
December 1978	Deng Xiaoping asserts control over the Chinese Communist Party, launches economic modernisation policies.
1 January 1979	Sino-American diplomatic normalisation takes effect.
18 October 1979	Martial law declared in Pusan after major student riots.
26 October 1979	Assassination of Park Chung-hee; martial law declared.
12 December 1979	Chun Doo Hwan arrests Martial Law Commander Chung Seung-hwa and effectively seizes control of the ROK military.
29 February 1980	Civil rights of leading dissidents restored, including Kim Dae Jung and Yun Posun.
17 May 1980	Chun Doo Hwan declares nationwide martial law and effects full takeover of the ROK government.
18 May 1980	Violent confrontations between troops and demonstrators in Kwangju; government forces withdraw on 20 May, and retake the city on 27 May. The military action causes heavy loss of civilian life.
27 August 1980	Chun elected president by the National Conference for Unification.
17 September 1980	Kim Dae Jung sentenced to death on charges of sedition.
10–14 October 1980	Sixth KWP Congress convenes in Pyongyang; Kim Jong Il assumes public profile as designated successor to his father.
22 October 1980	Chun consolidates rule when ROK constitutional amendments, including indirect election of the president, approved in national referendum.
30 September 1981	Seoul chosen as site for 1986 Asian Games and 1988 Olympic Games.
15 February 1982	Kim Jong Il turns 40, publishes major theoretical treatise *On the Juche Idea*, a major exegesis of Juche thought.

1 September 1983	Korean Airlines Flight 007 shot down by a Soviet fighter jet with loss of 269 lives after entering Soviet airspace over Sakhalin Island.
8 October 1983	The Chinese tell the US that the DPRK is willing to participate in tripartite talks involving the ROK.
9 October 1983	DPRK commandos detonate bomb at the Martyrs Tomb in Rangoon, killing seventeen senior ROK officials but failing to assassinate Chun Doo Hwan.
10 January 1984	Tripartite-talks proposal involving the DPRK, the US and the ROK made public.
16 May 1984	Kim Il Sung begins forty-five-day tour of the Soviet Union and Eastern Europe. The visit inaugurates major new phase of DPRK–Soviet economic and strategic co-operation.
14 September 1984	ROK accepts DPRK offer of flood-relief goods, beginning new phase of inter-Korean contact and negotiation.
20 December 1984	ROK opposition forces unite to form the New Korean Democratic Party (NKDP).
12 February 1985	The NKDP's strong performance in the 12th National Assembly government gives impetus to opposition forces.
6 March 1985	President Chun Doo Hwan lifts bans on political activity by major opposition figures, including Kim Dae Jung, Kim Young Sam and Kim Jong Pil.
10 March 1985	Death of Soviet leader Konstantin Chernenko. The last of his generation, Chernenko is succeeded by Mikhail Gorbachev, who initiates a wide-ranging programme of economic and political change.
4–6 September 1985	DPRK politburo member Ho Dam pays secret visit to Seoul in unsuccessful attempt to arrange a Chun–Kim summit.
20 September 1985	First-ever exchange of hometown visiting groups between the two Koreas.
July 1986	Soviet leader Mikhail Gorbachev's Vladivostok speech presages major changes to Soviet foreign policy, especially in East Asia.

13 April 1987	After prolonged negotiations, Chun Doo Hwan breaks off further talks with opposition parties on constitutional reform.
10 June 1987	DJP convention nominates Roh Tae Woo as Chun Doo Hwan's successor. This move sparks widespread street demonstrations against the Chun administration.
29 June 1987	After major street demonstrations, Roh Tae Woo announces an eight-point declaration, including acceptance of direct popular presidential elections.
July 1987	A turning-point in China's Korean policy comes in the summer of 1987, when Chinese leader Deng Xiaoping states for the first time that China would not support DPRK military action. A phase of secret ROK–China diplomacy begins.
27 October 1987	National referendum approves constitutional amendments, thus clearing the way for direct ROK presidential elections.
29 November 1987	Bomb planted by DPRK agents downs KAL airliner over Bay of Bengal.
16 December 1987	Roh Tae Woo wins ROK presidential election.
26 April 1988	The ruling DJP party gains only 25.5 per cent of the vote in the 13th National Assembly election. This sets the scene for prolonged legislative deadlock.
7 July 1988	Roh Tae Woo's Nordpolitik statement opens the path for Japan and other ROK allies to seek rapprochement with the DPRK.
16 September 1988	Gorbachev's Krasnoyarsk declaration presages Soviet economic exchanges with Seoul.
17 September– 2 October 1988	Seoul Olympic Games held.
31 October 1988	The US opens non-official talks with DPRK.
21 November 1988	ROK announces that it will permit trade between private ROK companies, foreign companies in the ROK and the DPRK. Inter-Korean trade begins to grow sharply.
3 April 1989	The Soviet Union opens a trade mission in Seoul.
May 1989	First US public statements expressing concern about the DPRK's nuclear programme.

4 June 1989	The Tiananmen Square massacre.
10 November 1989	The dismantling of the Berlin Wall begins in earnest. The event symbolises the final collapse of the Soviet bloc.
9 February 1990	Roh Tae Woo, Kim Young Sam and Kim Jong Pil amalgamate their parties to form the Democratic Liberal Party.
4 June 1990	Roh–Gorbachev summit meeting in San Francisco. Gorbachev agrees to establish full diplomatic relations between Moscow and Seoul.
3 July 1990	The ROK and the DPRK break a prolonged stalemate in inter-Korean dialogue by agreeing to hold talks at prime minister level.
4 September 1990	First talks at prime-minister level between the ROK and the DPRK begin.
25 September 1990	Japanese political kingmaker Kanemaru Shin begins negotiations on normalisation of Japan–DPRK relations in Pyongyang. He concludes an agreement, but this is subsequently repudiated by Tokyo.
30 September 1990	Soviet Union establishes diplomatic relations with Seoul.
17 January 1991	Operation Desert Storm begins, results in withdrawal of Iraqi troops from Kuwait.
30 January 1991	ROK opens trade office in Beijing.
3 August 1991	ROK announces intention to enter the UN after China announces it will not oppose entry.
17 September 1991	The ROK and the DPRK become full members of the United Nations.
December 1991	Dissolution of the Soviet Union.
13 December 1991	Agreement on Reconciliation, Non-Aggression, and Exchanges and Co-operation Between the South and the North signed between the two Koreas.
30 December 1991	DPRK announces plans to establish a Free Economic and Trade Zone at Rajin-Sunbong.
22 January 1992	First US–DPRK high-level meeting held in New York between KWP International Bureau Chairman Kim Young Sun and US Under-Secretary of State for Political Affairs Arnold Kanter.

31 January 1992	DPRK signs IAEA safeguards accord.
24 August 1992	China and ROK formally establish diplomatic relations.
November 1992	The IAEA requests inspection of two sites at the Yonbyon nuclear facility. The DPRK refuses, causing the IAEA to implement special inspections under the DPRK's safeguard agreement.
18 December 1992	Kim Yong Sam elected president to succeed Roh Tae Woo. Kim gains 42 per cent of the vote.
12 March 1993	The DPRK announces withdrawal from NPT. South–North dialogue again ceases at this point.
12 August 1993	Kim Young Sam decrees implementation of real-name financial transaction system.
May 1994	Contrary to NPT obligations, the DPRK downloads spent fuel from its 5-megawatt reactor without full inspection by the IAEA. This move precipitates a major confrontation between the US and the DPRK.
16–17 June 1994	During talks with former US president Jimmy Carter, Kim Il Sung agrees to negotiate settlement on nuclear issues with the US, and to meet with Kim Young Sam.
8 July 1994	Kim Il Sung dies of heart attack, aged 82. The DPRK enters unofficial three-year period of mourning.
October 1994	Signing of the Geneva Framework Agreement with the US, aimed at capping the DPRK nuclear programme.
27 June 1995	Local elections held in the ROK for the first time in thirty-four years.
August 1995	Floods cause an estimated 2 million tonne shortfall in the DPRK rice harvest, inducing famine.
October 1995	Roh Tae Woo publicly confesses to accumulating massive wealth while in office. The confession initiates an extensive round of investigations, and in August 1996 he is sentenced to a lengthy prison term.
August 1996	Chun Doo Hwan sentenced to death on charges relating to events surrounding the establishing of the Fifth Republic, and in particular the Kwangju uprising.
12 February 1997	Senior KWP official Hwang Jang Yop defects to Seoul.
26 July 1997	Construction begins in the DPRK on two 1,000-megawatt light-water nuclear-power reactors under the Geneva Framework Agreement.

October 1997	Kim Jong Il adopts title of KWP general secretary.
23 November 1997	In the face of a major financial crisis the ROK requests IMF intervention to support the Korean won.
18 December 1997	Kim Dae Jung elected president.
April 1998	Inter-Korean talks resume in Beijing after four-year hiatus but do not achieve substantial outcome.
15 July 1998	The US confirms it still lacks solid information on DPRK plutonium stocks after four years of talks under the Geneva Framework Agreement.
26 July 1998	Elections for the 10th DPRK Supreme People's Assembly. Held three years late, they result in a noticeably higher military representation.
31 August 1998	DPRK test-fires an intermediate-range missile which overflies Japan and lands in the Pacific 1,380 kilometres from the North Korean coast. The test damages relations with Japan and the US.
5 September 1998	The 10th Supreme People's Assembly amends the DPRK constitution to make the National Defence Committee chairman – a post held by Kim Jong Il since 1993 – head of state.
7 December 1998	Korea's five largest *chaebol* business groups agree on a package of sweeping reforms by which they will reduce the number of their subsidiaries from 264 to about 130 through mergers, sales and swaps.
15 June 1999	Major ROK–DPRK naval confrontation in the Western Sea. The ROK navy sinks one 40-ton torpedo-boat and severely damages five others.
23 June 1999	Inter-Korean vice-ministerial talks stall after the two sides fail to agree on agenda and preconditions for further meeting.
19 July 1999	President Kim Dae Jung states that the proposed revision of the National Security Law would take more time because of opposition from conservatives. It marks the first time that Kim has indicated that he would stall action on the law. Such action had been a major platform in his presidency.
15 September 1999	William Perry, US policy co-ordinator on DPRK affairs, submits his report of policy recommendations to President Clinton and to the US Congress. Major

recommendation is for US easing of economic sanctions in return for DPRK suspension of missile test-firing.

9 March 2000 ROK President Kim Dae Jung's Berlin Declaration proposes inter-Korean government-level economic co-operation and promises extensive investment in North Korea's social infrastructure.

13 June 2000 President Kim Dae Jung travels to Pyongyang and holds first-ever inter-Korean summit with North Korean leader Kim Jong Il.

15 June 2000 ROK president Kim Dae Jung and DPRK leader Kim Jong Il sign five-point South–North Joint Declaration.

9 October 2000 KPA vice-marshal Jo Myong Rok visits Washington, DC, the first such visit by a senior KWP figure.

6 June 2001 The US announces review of US policy towards the DPRK. The new policy offers economic and political incentives for the DPRK to return to the GFA and to accept surveillance of missile-technology exports.

29 January 2002 US president George W. Bush identifies the DPRK, Iran and Iraq as an 'axis of evil' in the world.

29 June 2002 ROK–DPRK naval clash kills nineteen ROK sailors. In the political fallout, ongoing talks between the US and the DPRK are halted and the Sunshine Policy comes under sharp domestic attack.

1 July 2002 The DPRK announces wide-ranging changes to its traditional economic system. The changes have allowed greater influence of market factors in the economy and have further devolved planning and management functions.

16 October 2002 Public revelations that the DPRK had been conducting a secret nuclear weapons programme again halt US–DPRK officials talks. Deliveries of fuel oil under the GFA are suspended soon after.

19 December 2002 Roh Moo-hyun elected ROK president, inaugurated on 25 February 2003.

27 December 2002 DPRK expels IAEA inspectors, subsequently withdraws from the NPT in April 2003.

14 February 2003 Kim Dae Jung offers public apology for $500 million secret Hyundai payment to the DPRK on the eve of the June 2000 summit.

19 March 2003	US-led forces invade Iraq.
23–26 April 2003	US–China–DPRK talks on nuclear issues mark resumption of dialogue but are inconclusive.
27–29 August 2003	First round of six-party talks held in Beijing, largely consisting of a statement of positions. Subsequent meeting 25–28 February 2004 likewise fails to produce joint statement.
12 March 2004	President Roh impeached by ROK National Assembly; is cleared by constitutional court on 14 May 2004.
15 April 2004	ROK National Assembly elections result in pro-Roh majority.
12 December 2004	Japan threatens economic sanctions after DNA testing reveals human remains of Japanese returned by Pyongyang after earlier abduction are false.
10 February 2005	The DPRK makes official announcement that it has developed nuclear weapons.
18 April 2005	DPRK announces shutdown of Yonbyon reactor and removal of fuel for weapon manufacture.
14 September 2005	Fourth session of six-party talks produces no progress.
4 July 2006	DPRK test-fires a number of missiles into the Sea of Japan.
9 October 2006	DPRK conducts low-yield underground nuclear test.
18 December 2006	Fifth round of six-party talks inconclusive.

Index